AFTER SORROW COMES JOY

*One Woman's Struggle to
Bring Hope to Thousands of
Children in Vietnam
and India*

CHERIE CLARK

Lawrence & Thomas Publishing House
Westminster, Colorado

Published by
Lawrence and Thomas Publishing House
4772 West 103rd Circle
Westminster, Colorado 80031
Email: LTPubl@aol.com

Visit Cherie's Web site at www.cherieclark.com

Front Cover and text design by Mayapriya Long—www.bookwrights.com

Typesetting by Sarah Hinman—Stornetta Publications

Editing by Loma Huh—Fit to Print

Printing by Michael Amrhein, Publication Printers—Denver, Colorado

Cover photo of Cherie Clark © Jim Jones and used courtesy of
the Kuan Yin Foundation

Cover and title page photos © Paul J. Miller

ISBN 0-615-11562-4

This book is for my children

Ron, Dan, Nam, Joanna, Beth, Jenny, Brian, Thanh, Shauna, and Preya

And my grandchildren

Kai, Maya, Shawn, Mia, Sunil, Jason, Katria, Sunita, and Khazana

And for those who have joined our family circle

Brad, Thai, Andrew, Kamala and Huong

It is dedicated to the memory of my mother

Mary Jean Cover

Acknowledgments

My heartfelt gratitude to all those who made this work possible:

Paul Miller, Dan Clark, Cheryl Markson, Sue Walter, Susan Moir, Ngo Thanh Tung, Richard Wisner, Sister Theresa Le Blanc, and the IMH-VN Board. Thanks to all who countless times brought my spirits up to continue when the task seemed daunting and the memories too painful. I am grateful to all of you who gave of your time. I wanted to tell this story and with your help, I finally have.

Much of what is written was taken from an old manuscript that I had kept of a book I started in 1975. That text was priceless as it enabled me to remember events, names, and incidents that had long been forgotten. I have also used letters that I wrote to Tom Clark from Vietnam and relied heavily on letters sent to me from Vietnam by Steven Johnson.

In an effort to be as factual as possible, I searched for and located many of those people who were present during the last days of the war. Through the Internet and by using search services, as well as advertising in newspapers, I was able to locate all of the Americans who were involved on the last flight and some of the Vietnamese. It was my greatest desire to write this story as truthfully and accurately as possible. In the process long-lost friendships have been rekindled, and I welcome the people who shared such an important part of my life back into my circle of friends.

I take full responsibility for any errors in this book. It is true to my memory and as accurate as possible. The story was not written to dramatize an event. It is a story that has been written as authentically as possible to serve as a small piece of history for those children that we worked with in Vietnam who are now adults and have many questions about their lives prior to their adoption in America. I have not taken this responsibility lightly and hope that this book will answer at least some of their questions. We were living in a period of time that preceded the modern communication tools that we now take for granted. Several Vietnamese names have been changed but none of the events surrounding that period.

The title of this book comes from a writing of Ho Chi Minh where he expressed: "What could be more natural, after sorrow comes joy."

Introduction

By Paul J. Miller — Pulitzer Prize-winning photojournalist

*C*herie Clark, a woman of outstanding character and fortitude.

I've known Cherie and her ten children for more than a decade, and have traveled with her up and down Vietnam, watching her at work with sick, dying and unwanted babies and children.

As a photographer, I've lived a great part of my life capturing images through a camera lens, and over the years, I've developed a habit of observing life and situations as a series of photographs.

Whenever I see Cherie, a series of images passes through my mind's eye. I think back to all the experiences we shared over the years, and I see her in her own element: holding a starving baby, talking animatedly with some local official, playing with a group of kids in one of the centers, or, too often, looking tired and drained at the end of another eighteen-hour day.

Cherie is a caring and giving woman; she gives of herself deeply, never asking for reward, but receiving pleasure from watching as a life is saved or another baby lifted from the black pit of despair and loved back to health and happiness in one of the centers or hospitals she built and supports.

Like many strong-willed people, Cherie can be daunting at times as she burns with passion for her calling—an energy that often leaves strong men tiring in her wake. Walking through a small village, or marching down the halls of a government building, her long stride and determined manner personify the strength of the woman.

Never accepting a denial or refusal, she moves with an almost reckless ease from a normal situation to a bizarre, to beyond daring. I clearly remember how Cherie dealt with one such bizarre and dangerous situation. We were traveling late at night on the road from Saigon to Phnom Penh in an aged van, packed with supplies urgently needed in Cambodia. Rounding a bend on a roughly surfaced country road, we suddenly came face to face with a makeshift roadblock barring our way. As we pulled to a halt, Cherie jumped straight out of our van to face the young Cambodian soldiers, dressed in dirty fatigues and carrying the ubiquitous AK-47's, who were guarding the roadblock.

Lacking a common language, she tried to explain our mission and our need to pass through. The situation became tense as the soldiers sullenly shook their heads. Her frustration mounted and reached critical mass. I felt the tension inch higher as Cherie quietly walked past the lead soldier and moved toward the barrier—I saw a carbine raised and aimed. In the pregnant silence, as Cherie raised the barrier, the only sounds were insects buzzing in the nearby jungle and our engine coughing on the cheap fuel.

The barrier was up, and the soldiers just stared at Cherie, nonplussed. They were the infamous soldiers of Cambodia, known throughout the world. How could this middle-aged Western woman just pass them by? The soldiers exchanged looks of consternation. Suddenly the gun was lowered, and the soldiers muttered to each other in desperation. What could they do?

Cherie climbed aboard, and amid much waving and smiling thanks, we slowly drove through the roadblock. It was five minutes and a few miles before we dared to speak. The bowel-wrenching fear finally left me, and the tension eased in the van. Cherie had done it again, risking her life to help some poor children she hadn't even met.

Such is the strength of Cherie Clark. When all the trite words have been put aside, there remains, at the core, a humanitarian of indomitable spirit who will walk into harm's way without pause, confident of her role in this world to help the needy.

I have read *After Sorrow Comes Joy* from cover to cover. Much of the story I knew before the book was written, but now I find myself reading about Cherie and her work with an interest that makes me keep turning the pages to share her life-changing experiences with her.

There is a message for everyone in this book—for the babies, children and adults who were saved by Cherie's efforts; for government bureaucrats who initially shunned her directness; for you, the reader. Look at Cherie Clark, and hope that you have the fortitude to give so deeply of yourself for a cause you believe in.

Paul J. Miller
May 23, 2000

Prologue

November, 1971
Qui Nhon, Vietnam

*I*n the predawn most of the inhabitants of the small South Vietnamese coastal city are asleep, undisturbed by the distant sounds of war being fought in the mountains that surround their homes. Rockets and bombs provide a backdrop that has become all too familiar, so familiar that the sounds have blended into their dreams.

Life goes on, despite the war, in much the same way as it has for hundreds of years. To the local inhabitants, who work by day in the nearby fields or eke out a living fishing in the shallow coastal waters, the war is an annoyance. They see the convoys of troop-laden trucks raising dust as they career through the city. They see and hear the jets wheeling overhead, and often the air beats with a resonating thump as helicopters fly by their homes at low altitude. For a moment, they look up from their labor and peer calmly at the disturbance. Momentarily they ponder the big picture, but soon return to the task at hand, knowing the futility of trying to influence events outside their control.

❧

In the early morning hours a light shines from one tiny dwelling. Inside, a scene as old as time itself plays out. A young woman lies on a cot, exhausted with the effort of childbirth. Despite the chill in the room, sweat beads on her brow as she gathers her strength to bear down one last time. An old woman wipes her hands on her shirt and reaches down to help the infant who is just leaving the warmth of the young woman's body. The infant's first cry echoes through the night, voicing anger and fear at the harshness of the new, alien world; forever lost is the comfort and security of the womb.

With each wail, the young woman feels her pain and tension decrease. Her body, which has labored for so long, now quivers with the sudden emptiness. She takes a deep breath and turns to look at the child she has just borne. It is a girl. She touches the tiny face and remembers the black American soldier who came to her one night and briefly set aside the horror of war to conceive this child.

The first day of the baby's life passes slowly for the exhausted woman. A cool wind blows, filled with rain off the nearby South China Sea. She is saddened at what she knows must come later.

As dusk falls, the new mother gathers her strength, rises from the cot, and snugly wraps the baby in a newspaper. She slips on her own threadbare jacket and then, carrying her daughter, she steals out into the night chill.

Finally the mother and daughter reach their destination, unseen by all but God. Quietly she takes a long, last look at her newborn daughter, not yet a day old. She gently places the infant on a darkened doorstep, reaches up and pulls the bell at the door, once, twice and then a third time. In a world without hope, the mother has made the best choice she can for her child; she turns and steals away into the darkness of the night.

The baby, suddenly missing the warmth and smell of her mother, begins to cry—small, questioning sobs that quickly rise in volume to become a full-throated cry as she lies abandoned on a cold stone doorstep.

Inside, behind the worn door, tiny Sister Theresa of St. Paul's Orphanage pads tiredly to answer the ring of the doorbell. In the passageway, she hears the cries of the newborn. Sister Theresa sighs and offers up a quick prayer. Opening the door she is not surprised to find yet another child on the doorstep. She stoops and lifts the newspaper-clad bundle. She peers at the baby in the dim light. Before closing the door behind her, she looks into the darkness for the mother, knowing in her heart it is a wasted gesture. The mother is gone, back to her previous life. The newly born baby has been left to fend for herself in the harsh world beyond the doorstep.

The nun closes the door and treads the stairs to the first-floor room that now serves as a nursery for the orphanage within. Continual crying of sick, lonely, abandoned babies and children assails the ears in the small room.

Sister Theresa awakens the elderly woman who keeps watch over the nursery throughout the long night hours, another worker overcome with the exhaustion of coping for too many with too few resources. Wordlessly, she discards the newspapers and ties a piece of rough cloth around the infant's bottom to serve as a makeshift diaper. She is slipped into a tattered, stained shirt, and then laid in a crib with another baby.

In the morning, the orphanage director, Sister Marie de la Passion, finds the newcomer in her nursery. She looks at the child, sleeping now, exhausted after hours of crying for a mother who will never return. She can only shake her head at the dark face and curly hair; another child of war, another child who does not belong.

Sister Marie and her fellow Catholic nuns attached to St. Paul's Cathedral are a religious minority in Vietnam, a country where nine-tenths of the population are Buddhist. Displaced by a raging civil war, they moved south away from the carnage, seeking sanctuary in Qui Nhon, a coastal city about five hundred miles north of Saigon. Now the city is isolated, surrounded by the enemy. They never intended to run an orphanage; they simply followed the dictates of their calling.

The nuns are overwhelmed as more and more babies are abandoned to their care. Their homespun and underfunded charity is stretched to the breaking point. What passes for a nursery are simply rooms, converted to house hundreds of unwanted babies.

The feeding of the children is allotted to helpers from the townsfolk women. They prepare the watered-down milk that will be fed systematically to the infants crowded in the nursery. As the waking babies cry, demanding food, they are fed by rows to accommodate those who feed them. Next door, the nuns pray in St. Paul's Cathedral. They ask God to bless the new arrival and they choose a name for her, Thu Loan.

There is never enough formula, staff or clothing to satisfy the ever-increasing demand. There is no time for any human niceties, no time to hug a crying baby, no time to calm the fears of the elder roommates. There are too many mouths, too many needs and not enough helpers to cope.

Thu Loan is just one of hundreds of orphans and abandoned infants who can be found at St. Paul's. In one way or another, each has arrived in a similar manner, the youngest casualties in a seemingly endless war. Thrown together by an unkind fate, they now form a vast family, welded together by the circumstances of their birth and subsequent abandonment.

The babies in the orphanage have been born into a country torn by war, a country whose fate has been decided for more than a hundred years by politicians in far-off lands. The constant tides of war have broken and uprooted families, usurping centuries of tradition. Political strategies have forced the young men of Vietnam to stay constantly on the move, and brought hundreds of thousands of foreign soldiers into this small country. Too often relationships have been ended by death, a military movement or displacement by the encroaching enemy.

So it was that in the fall of 1971, the mother took her child to the Catholic orphanage in Qui Nhon, located within walking distance of the South China Sea. The tiny girl's placement in the orphanage was not a guarantee of survival. Eight out of every ten children in South Vietnamese orphanages did not survive their first year.

Care in St. Paul's was the best the compassionate, overworked and underfunded staff could provide, but there was no time for love. Many of the newborns, like fragile blossoms, withered and died without the softness and strength gained from a mother's breast, died without knowing that there was more than pain and suffering involved in being alive.

They easily succumbed to the epidemics of pneumonia, measles, and chicken pox. Some babies literally drowned in their formula because harried staff cut large holes in the bottle nipples to make the milk flow more freely, for faster feeding. Babies who lacked the strength to turn their heads away from the sudden onrush of milk suffocated. At least one child a day died at St. Paul's, sometimes two or three.

Against these odds, Thu Loan survived. Deep within her was the will to live.

A year passed, as Thu Loan existed in the confines of the crib where she was first laid. She rarely heard a spoken word and those she did came from Sister Theresa, who was drawn to that one child, from the many scores in her care. It was so little, but it meant so much.

Sister Marie wrote to Rosemary Taylor in Saigon to tell her of Thu Loan's abandonment. Rosemary, an Australian social worker, had been working in Vietnam since 1967. In the letter, she asked if Thu Loan could be moved to one of the clean, well-equipped nurseries that Rosemary operated in Saigon. Perhaps nothing would come of it, but there was at least the chance that the child would be sent to a loving home in America, her father's country.

Sister Marie explained that Thu Loan had been in the nursery for a year, and no one had inquired about her well being—she was truly an abandoned baby. She asked if the volunteers who flew from Rosemary's center into Qui Nhon several times a month, bringing money and precious supplies, could take the child with them to Saigon on their next trip.

When the nurse from Saigon arrived, she brought supplies for the orphanage and the news that Rosemary would accept Thu Loan. She was one of a handful of children from St. Paul's chosen to make the arduous journey south. For the first time in her short life, her African ancestry worked to her advantage, for that was why Rosemary made her decision so quickly. She knew that even if the child survived in the orphanage, she would never be accepted in Vietnam, because of her mixed-race heritage.

Once in Saigon, the little girl was taken to an orphanage that Rosemary called "To Am," an Australian Aborigine word meaning "warm nest." There she was greeted with joy and excitement. The rough cloth was replaced with a real diaper and her tattered shirt by a soft sleeper. Baby clothes were donated by concerned people around the world, people unable to stop the war, but determined to do whatever they could to help its most fragile victims.

Thu Loan was given the vitamins she so desperately needed; her boils were lanced and treated. For the first time, she was fed undiluted formula. She was bathed and taken outside to bask in the warm sunshine. Most importantly, she was cuddled and loved.

Once Thu Loan's medical needs were met, the staff began the search for a family for the child. The search narrowed down quickly. Prejudice was not limited to Thu Loan's homeland. Prospective adoptive parents often asked for an Amerasian child, but nearly all of the families were white, and few felt comfortable adopting a child with African-American ancestry.

There was a sense of urgency. The volunteers in Rosemary's homes were carrying on their work as best they could, but the numbers of abandoned children grew continuously.

Finally, a potential family was selected. A small black-and-white photograph of Thu Loan was placed in an envelope, along with a brief letter. Rosemary gave the letter to friends who could send mail through American government channels and allowed her use of their APO boxes. For the families thousands of miles away, who paced the floor waiting for word from Vietnam, that mail was the focal point of their existence.

❦

The envelope carrying Thu Loan's picture was routed to rural Illinois. The mailman who delivered along the route had no idea that he was bringing such special news; the letter was no different to him than any other he sorted that day. But for me there was always a fresh surge of hope when the mailman appeared, the familiar blue mail car winding slowly down the lane to our home.

I breathed a fervent prayer as I approached the mailbox, "Please God, let there be a letter from Vietnam."

I was jolted to find the familiar self-addressed envelope that I had sent along with our hopes and dreams across the ocean to Vietnam.

My hands shook as I pulled the envelope apart. Out dropped a grainy black-and-white picture of a little child, held by a nun. Tears ran down my cheeks as I read the accompanying letter.

"I have a little girl for you," it began. "Her name is Thu Loan."

The letter and photograph were the starting point of my daughter's journey to be reborn in a new land. And although I did not then realize it, it was also the beginning of mine.

Chapter One

I was born Sherry Louise Velkovich in a small town in Indiana in 1945. I was the second of two children from my mother's first marriage.

My parents, Jack and Mary Velkovich, were separated when I was born, and in fact had been separated for months before I was conceived. Much later, I discovered that in a way I owe my existence to my paternal grandmother. She attempted a reconciliation between my estranged parents that lasted the length of a New Year's Eve party—and nine months later, on the eighth of October, I was born.

Being born into a single-parent family was a rarity in small-town Indiana in those days. My mother was not bitter about my father's abandonment; rather, she accepted that they had married too young and that they were both too immature to raise a family together.

My brother Larry was two years older than I was, and we were fortunate that our mother's parents, Lawrence and Louise Cover, were willing to help take care of us while my mother worked and played.

We lived with them in a big house outside of Peru, a small town in northeast Indiana. We called them "Mom" and "Pop." My grandparents adored my brother Larry and treated him more like a son than a grandchild.

My grandfather was a devoted union man, a staunch Democrat, and a caring grandfather. It was not until years later that I would come to realize that, in addition to all of his wonderful qualities, my Pop was an alcoholic.

My father's parents accepted Larry and me, perhaps with a degree of guilt on behalf of my missing father, and each year we were dispatched by train for a two-week summer holiday with them in Cincinnati. My grandfather, a Serbian immigrant, would amaze us with stories of his village life in Yugoslavia, where his large family slept on straw mats and cows shared the same room as the family. We listened intently as he told us of coming to America on his own when he was just sixteen years old. His tales were fascinating and stirred my imagination.

My mother remarried shortly after her divorce from my father, and my brother Larry went to live with her parents. I was shuttled between wherever she was staying, my grandparents' house and that of other relatives. That marriage was brief too, and she remarried yet again when I was five years old.

My mother was pregnant with my brother Ken when she remarried this time, and just ten months after his birth came my sister Sue. We called my stepfather by his first name, and I have very few memories of anything but stress and arguments.

But I never thought of Ken and Sue as anything other than my darling baby brother and sister. They were dear to Larry and me, and we soon became their caretakers, for we were often left alone with them when they were only infants and we were still so young.

My mother's parents were upset at my mother's third marriage and the resultant birth of two more grandchildren, especially as my mother was reluctant at times to even care for Larry and me. Family gatherings grew tense. My mother was the only one in the family to have ever divorced, and no one else in the family, save my grandfather, drank alcohol.

When I was about nine, perhaps in a last-ditch effort to save their marriage, my mother and stepfather bought a farm near my grandparents' home. The farm bordered on the small town of Denver, Indiana, which had a population of about four hundred and was twelve miles outside of Peru. My mother's older sister, Joan, and my Uncle Bob, who was the town sheriff, lived there as well.

I looked forward to moving to the farm because my cousins Ellen, Nancy and Sid lived nearby. I had always envied their family life and envisioned us becoming a similarly happy unit.

The farm was a great place to live. We enjoyed endless summer days of running through the fields and playing in the barn. We had a horse that I named Sugar. In many ways, it seemed as if our life as a family was finally coming together.

During the summer, my extended family would rent a cottage at a lake where we would gather to fish and swim. I can still hear the waves lapping on the pebble shore, see the glow of the lightning bugs, hear the laughter of the adults playing cards, and smell the fish frying in thick iron skillets.

The memories of those childhood summer idylls are precious to me. But for all the attention and regard I was shown, I still felt distant from my family, as if I was a waif, left at the doorstep, that had become an obligation to care for. Yet I can look back at the pictures of my youth and realize that, for all the uncertainties of my earliest years, someone always loved me. Life was to show me the blank and hollow faces of too many children in the years to come for me to deny that someone had cared. Perhaps it was the difference of being loved, but never having been wanted, that seemed to leave me with such emptiness.

Ironically, given my mother's apparent lack of interest in religion, she was determined that Larry and I would go to the same conservative Christian two-room schoolhouse in Peru that she and her siblings and even her mother had attended. Our move to Denver did not change that. We were still sent to school in Peru. I attended the first eight years of school with the same children. My class had eight students, and as far as I can remember, Larry and I were the only ones at the school with divorced parents. In the early 1950s in that conservative environment, we were left open to teasing and ridicule.

Our education was predominantly religious, with a single teacher for the first through third grades and another for the fourth through eighth grades. I remember them only as stern and strict and without compassion—at least for me. A great deal of the school day was spent in prayer and in memorizing passages from the Bible. To this day, I can still recite the books of the Bible.

Other subjects simply passed me by. We were seated in alphabetical order, and with the last name of Velkovich, I was guaranteed a seat in the back, where I was free to daydream. Although I was moved up each year from grade to grade, I learned little except how to read, and how to read well. As the teacher drilled multiplication tables, I would stare out the long, high windows and look forward to going home, where I could lose myself in a good book. We were near the Wabash River, which flooded frequently in the spring, forcing the school to close. I spent my morning prayer sessions praying for floods, no matter what time of the year it was. I learned only one real lesson in that school, one that was to haunt me all of my life: I did not belong.

Every day Pop took me to school on his way to work and collected me in time for a ride home each evening. After school closed, I made my way to the city library, where I waited for him to finish work. Visiting the library was the high point of my day. I would sit at the polished oak tables, lost in romantic tales of faraway places. I devoured all the classics and imagined myself living in distant lands.

After an unhappy eight years in elementary school, I attended a consolidated high school for children who lived on farms and in several small towns. We were taken by bus each day to the high school in Mexico, Indiana, where my cousins Anita and Sonny, the children of my mother's older brother, lived. I quickly realized how little I knew about normal school subjects. Being able to recite Bible verses was of scant value in math and biology classes. The only bright spot in my freshman year was when I was elected queen of my class.

At the age of fifty-two, Pop fulfilled his doctor's diagnosis that if he didn't stop drinking, it would kill him. His death devastated me, shattering my teenage sense of immortality.

My mother was brokenhearted to have lost the only person in the family who understood her. By that time, she was drinking heavily as her third marriage fell apart.

In an attempt to rescue me from the conflict in our house, my Uncle Jack, my mother's younger brother, and my Aunt Barbara invited me to Lawton, Oklahoma, where he was stationed while serving in the Army. I grabbed at the invitation as if it were a lifeline. However, I spent a miserable year in a huge high school, worried about my family so far away. When I finally returned to Indiana, I had barely enough credits to be considered a sophomore.

During my sojourn in Oklahoma, my mother had divorced again and moved back to Peru, leaving the farm I had loved. Larry stayed with my grandparents to continue his education. Ken and Sue were living with my mother, moving every few months from rental to rental as she dodged angry landlords demanding their money. Sometimes my mother would keep the kids at the Eagles Lodge where she worked, letting them sleep on chairs pushed together, using their coats as blankets.

Nearly every cent my mother made as a waitress was poured into the adjoining bar. There were countless days when our refrigerator held only half-empty jars of mayonnaise and mustard, alongside the remainders of a six-pack of beer. Too often, we hid silently, crouched behind walls and furniture as landlords pounded on the door, demanding overdue rent.

Most nights, I was left home watching over Ken and Sue while my mother went out to a bar. When she returned, she would keep me up for hours, talking of her pain and loneliness. Later I called those rambling, interminable conversations her "drunkalogues."

Despite my discomfort with her drinking, I learned much from my mother as she recounted tales of her life. She told me that during the Depression, she and Pop had gone to Detroit to work in the factories. Working in a large city, she was exposed for the first time in her life to a multiracial society, and she made friends with both black and white people; she never forgot those times and the friendships she made.

Though only fifteen, I realized that my mother was very tired and lonely, but I had no way to fix her problems. I never felt angry at her inability to hold down a job or to provide properly for us. She was a gentle, compassionate woman, a woman who had lost her way. My mother did give me a sense of the world as a larger place, and the knowledge that prejudice was wrong.

We had many things in common. I shared her passion for reading. I read Pearl Buck's novels about Asia and dreamed of going there and experiencing the exotic world I had read about. Once I read my mother a newspaper article about India. The reporter said that there was "no hope" for the people of India because of the enormous overpopulation. We wondered what "no hope" meant.

What wonderful kids Ken and Sue were. With virtually no parenting and sometimes barely enough food or warm clothing, they never had a brush with the law, were good students, and stayed loyal to a broken mother and a tired sister.

I was sixteen when I finally gave up on my education and quit high school; my mother never said a word. At about the same time, Larry graduated from high school and immediately joined the Navy.

My mother was working part-time at best, so to help with things at home, I got a full-time job at a local sewing factory, which was located in a huge, unheated, barn-like building. Paid a trainee's salary of a dollar an hour, I worked long hours and watched as my hands became red, sore and callused from the hard piecework, sewing canvas coveralls in the constant, numbing cold.

During those years, my mother was having an affair with a married man, which no doubt intensified her loneliness. I was none too happy with the relationship, which I felt exposed my younger brother and sister to far more than they needed to know.

I had my own sadness to cope with. I had fallen in love with an airman from Maryland and dreamed of running away with him, a dream that fell apart when he was transferred overseas.

On my way to and from work, I passed Saint Charles Catholic Church, just a few blocks away from the school where I had suffered my childhood away. One day, I had an impulse to peek inside through the enticing doorway. The ornate statues and the rich, heady smells of incense and candle wax were exotic to me. I wandered around the church like a child in a fairytale land. Before long, I was stopping by at the church almost every day on my way home from work. I would sit in one of the polished wooden pews and stare at a beautiful statue of Mary, thinking of my own mother, also named Mary, lost at home in her depression.

A young priest soon took notice of me and asked if I needed to talk. As my confidence grew, I gradually spilled out everything about my life. I was alone. I was tired. I was trapped. I told him I felt as if I belonged to no one and to nowhere. He gave me a prayer card inscribed with the words of Cardinal John Henry Newman, a nineteenth-century cleric. Titled "I Have My Mission," it read in part:

> *God has created me*
> *to do Him some definite service:*
> *He has committed some work to me*
> *which He has not committed*
> *to another.*
> *I have my mission . . .*
> *I am a link in a chain,*
> *a bond of connection*
> *between persons.*
> *He has not created me for naught.*
> *I shall do good. I shall do His work.*

The words struck a chord deep within me. The prayer card became one of my most treasured possessions, and I carried it with me for years. The priest never encouraged me to convert, but always patiently answered my questions about the church and Catholicism. Our conversation touched on many different subjects. I asked him about Mother Teresa, the nun who was working with the "poorest of the poor" in India, whom I read about in articles he had at the church. I longed to do something meaningful with my life and was deeply impressed at what one person could accomplish.

As the weeks went by, I became more convinced that I wanted a life within the church. One day I told the kindly priest that I wanted to become a nun and live a life of purity and service. I don't remember the name of the priest who gave my poor soul so much faith in that long, cold winter of my sixteenth year, but I will never forget him.

When I surprised my mother with the news that I was going to convert to the Catholic faith, she did not object. Other family members were shocked at the news and complained to my mother that I would be allowed to "worship idols." I bought a lovely black lace veil to cover my hair and went to Mass each Sunday. I always sat alone. I knew no one in the congregation but the priest, yet I felt that I had found my spiritual home.

In an attempt to further escape my depressing home and work life, I changed the spelling of my name from Sherry to Cherie. Years later I would have it legally changed. I was lost in those teenage years and desperate to leave my home and the poverty and sadness it represented.

For months, I vacillated between wanting to be a nun and committing myself to a life with Christ—or joining the Navy and committing myself to a life serving America. For some time I was also drawn to the idea of being a nurse, but I soon dismissed that dream, for I knew I didn't have the education.

I joked with my family that maybe all I really wanted was to join some organization that would let me wear a uniform, so that I would feel that I truly belonged. The friendships that our family made with the airmen from the nearby Bunker Hill Air Force Base further convinced me that I wanted to travel and see the world.

In desperation, I wrote to my brother Larry, who by then was stationed at a submarine base in Portland, Maine. I asked if he would let me come visit him. I cried when he told me he would like nothing better. I was old enough to just pack my bags and leave, but I knew that I wouldn't have the strength to leave if my mother asked me to stay. I felt I was abandoning Ken and Sue, then only ten and eleven years old. It would be the hardest thing I had done in my young life.

To my surprise and relief, my mother agreed with my decision to leave. Without me, she would have no one to support her, or even to take her around, as she had never learned to drive. It was a measure of her love for me that she could let me go. We had to sell an old family dining room set to raise money for my bus fare. I think in a way she saw my departure as vicarious fulfillment of her own dreams. She knew I would see the ocean; I would be free.

Two weeks after I arrived in Maine, I attended a Navy picnic with Larry, and he introduced me to his best friend, Tom Clark. Tom was from Illinois, four years older than me, and had dark hair, a quiet manner, and a pleasant, reassuring presence. I loved Tom and felt safe with him almost from the first moment I saw him, and I was thrilled that he felt the same way about me.

He was about to go to sea again, so only eight weeks after we first met, we were married on Christmas Day, 1964. Tom was assigned to the U.S.S. Tinosa, a nuclear submarine. We lived in Maine, Connecticut and New Hampshire in the months to come.

Sue spent the summer of 1965 with us in New London, Connecticut, and was with me when I called my mother to tell her that I was expecting a child. My life was rich and complete. In February of 1966, my mother came out to stay with us, and it was a happy time for all. She played cards with Larry and Tom, fussed around the house, and helped choose new clothes for the imminent arrival of our new baby.

My first son, Ron, was born on the seventh of February, after a long and difficult labor, at the Navy base hospital in Groton, Connecticut. Everything in my life changed at that moment, and I was overwhelmed with happiness. I found it hard to believe that the same crazy world was going on outside the hospital, minding its own business instead of stopping to admire my son with his deep dimples and big blue eyes.

Just over a year later, on the sixth of March, 1967, my mother was back to help with the arrival of our second son, Daniel. I gave him the middle name of Lawrence, after my Pop. I could not imagine two children ever meaning so much to anyone. I had never seen my mother as happy or proud as she was with her infant grandsons.

Tom was frequently at sea for three months at a stretch. When he was away, I would often set up a portable crib in the back of our new Chevy and drive straight through to Indiana with the music blaring, singing loudly and off-tune, with my sons in the back seat. I was happy to be alive. I felt as if I had escaped some terrible fate.

My mother was holding down a job at Singer's Dry Goods Company, a landmark in Peru. From there, she could walk across the street for her liquid lunch at the Eagles Lodge. Ken and Sue were both doing well in high school and devoted to her, and we all deeply loved my two boys.

I was embarrassed that I had never graduated from high school, so in 1968, I took a Navy-sponsored GED course. I passed the test with flying colors, which proved to me that I had the ability to assimilate educational curriculum and not just Bible texts.

Tom was nearing the end of his second enlistment. I had assumed that he would make the Navy his lifelong career. I encouraged him to apply for a transfer overseas, and he soon received notice that his next assignment could be in Crete, a Greek island in the Mediterranean Sea. I was in heaven. I spent hours looking through travel magazines and perusing books about Crete in the library. I was in love with the idea of taking my family to that warm, sunny, exotic land. I knew we would be happy there. I started mentally planning for the trip.

However, it was not to be. In one of his most decisive and firm actions during our marriage, Tom told me that he wanted to leave the Navy. He wanted to move to the Quad City area in northwest Illinois, where we would be near his family. I was heading back to a place buried even deeper in the Midwest.

Within a month of our return to civilian life, Tom was hired by IBM. My growing hunger to travel was temporarily assuaged when we accompanied Tom to Minnesota and then New York, where IBM sent him for extended training sessions. We were very much the all-American family.

I began to take an interest in the education that had escaped me in earlier years, and took evening classes at a local community college. Suddenly, I loved school. I started with psychology classes.

The next course was ostensibly sociology, but the instructor was very much opposed to the war in Vietnam and made it the focal point of our studies. Until then, the war had been a distant event to me. I was vaguely aware of the buildup of troops in Southeast Asia, and it was hard to ignore the growing antiwar protests at home. The Paris Peace Talks were by this time a daily news item, though the negotiators hadn't yet advanced beyond arguing over the shape of the table.

In class, we were divided into four groups. Each of us was assigned to research the position of the side we were given, then argue it before the class as a whole. The class was divided into the Americans, the North Vietnamese, the South Vietnamese and the Provisional Revolutionary Government (Viet Cong). I was picked at random to become a member of the PRG.

I was approaching all of my college courses with enthusiasm, intent on proving to myself and others that I was not a high school dropout; I was a college student as well as a mother. Eager to earn a good grade, I studied everything I could find on Vietnam. Like many college students in those days, I grew far more knowledgeable than friends and family about the war. I invested a semester of hard work, studying the Viet Cong side of the talks. The class ended with the students conducting our own peace negotiations and presenting terms of how the war could be ended.

I earned an "A" in that class, as I did in most classes, but I took away far more than a good grade.

The college sociology course had a profound impact on me. In the "real world," I was attracted to Robert F. Kennedy's presidential campaign because of his antiwar stance. Soon I began actively participating in antiwar demonstrations, taking Ron and Dan with me on candlelight marches and challenging the police when they accused us of mounting illegal rallies. I read everything I could, trying to make some sense of America's involvement in Vietnam, but the more I read, the less I understood it.

When Martin Luther King, Jr., was assassinated, I wept for our country. I watched the television as Bobby Kennedy walked into the crowds in an attempt to quell racial violence, and shook hands and said, "A white man killed my brother too."

I learned that Bobby's whistle-stop train campaign would stop in Peru, so I drove the three hundred miles with my boys to see him. When the train arrived, I hoisted my sons in my arms and drew as close as I could possibly get. For one glorious instant, Bobby's eyes locked with mine. Perhaps thousands of other people felt the same way, but as I stood there in the sun with Dan on my shoulders and Ron in my arms, it was my sons and me he was looking at. He then waved and smiled at us. His two promises to stop the war and to work against the racial division in our country were some of the finest words I had ever heard. I placed in him my hope for a better world.

I had found a new cause and volunteered for any project that would help secure a Kennedy victory. I worked relentlessly for the campaign. We had to win; for me, he was the solution to all of America's wrongs.

In the early morning hours of the sixth of June, 1968, Tom was working at another training program, and I was watching TV in our tiny rented apartment in Rochester, Minnesota. I was rejoicing that we had just won the California primaries when, suddenly, I was stunned by the sound of bullets and the confusion on the television as another Kennedy fell to the ground.

When the news came through that Bobby was dead, murdered by a lone gunman, I sat alone in the living room, crying in my anguish and loss. I wandered outside, sat down, and wept for the entire world and for all my lost dreams.

Along with millions of Americans, I watched Bobby Kennedy's funeral on television. I cried as the Kennedys paraded before us in their grief, just as they had at JFK's funeral only five years earlier. Those days and weeks imprinted themselves on my life, and it took time for me to recover my equilibrium. I took to heart Ted Kennedy's words when he beseeched us to remember Bobby as a good and simple man "who saw a war and tried to stop it."

As the summer of 1968 passed, escalating protests against the Vietnam War were playing out on the nightly news. This would be the first presidential election that I would be eligible to vote in. Overcoming my sorrow, I forced myself to again take an interest in politics. After much deliberation, I joined sides with Hubert Humphrey, the Democratic nominee in the presidential race against Richard Nixon.

Each day when college classes finished, I gathered Ron and Dan and took them to the local Humphrey headquarters, where the boys played while I made telephone calls on behalf of the candidate. When Humphrey lost to Nixon, a man I genuinely feared, I was deeply saddened.

Education and motherhood became my equal passions. I continued to enroll in classes, and in a burst of confidence took an intensive biology class. The idea of becoming a nurse was growing within me. When I passed that class, I knew I was on my way. I took chemistry and passed that exam too, with the second highest score in the class.

My excellent grades and test scores won me a spot in the nursing program at Black Hawk College in Moline, Illinois.

I was still attending the college full-time in February, 1970, when I gave birth to a lovely baby girl; Tom and I named her Elizabeth. Mother was there for her arrival on February sixteenth and told me that every girl should have an older brother. Beth was doubly blessed with two.

We often made the three-hundred-mile drive to northeast Indiana to visit my family. We were all there applauding when first Ken graduated high school, and then, a year later, Sue. I felt such pride in them. Their upbringing had not been easy; still, they had somehow managed school and helped my mother as best they could.

In April of 1971, my mother became ill and was admitted to the hospital for tests. Doctors removed her gallbladder and warned her that her liver was badly damaged. Years of drinking had taken their toll on her body. Easter Sunday fell a few days after the operation. We visited her in the hospital along with my grandmother, Larry, Ken and Sue. We all arrived with Easter gifts and spent a special day with her. She looked thin and weak, her health broken.

Days earlier, I had learned that I was pregnant again, but I decided that I couldn't tell her just then. Each of my pregnancies had been progressively more difficult, and I didn't want her to worry.

On the ride home that evening, Tom and I expressed our concern that my mother seemed so weak. The doctors had told us that, though her recovery was slow, they expected her to be on her feet soon. We made plans that my mother would come to visit us after she left the hospital. She had told me that her greatest dream was to watch me walk across the stage to receive my college diploma.

The following Wednesday my mother died. She was forty-seven years old.

We buried her in a lovely spring dress in Denver, Indiana, not far from where she was born, near her beloved father.

The months of my pregnancy passed as if I had the weight of the world on my shoulders. Who would welcome this child the way my mother had welcomed the others? Who would take off each stitch of clothing and examine each part of its body as if seeing a masterpiece for the first time?

I went into labor while in class at the hospital where I was training; the other students looked at me with amazement as I left class to go to the maternity ward to have my child.

After my easiest labor, my precious son Brian came to us on the eighth of December, 1971. I had never missed my mother as much as I did the moment I held my new son.

Chapter Two

*I*n the early fall of 1972, I was sitting in a doctor's waiting room, idly thumbing through a copy of *Ebony* magazine, when an article caught my attention. Reading the story, I learned for the first time of the plight of half-black, half-Vietnamese children born in Vietnam.

The children, I read, had no place or future in the strictly traditional Vietnamese society and little hope of being adopted by American families. The article struck a chord deep within me, as I knew intimately the pain of feeling unwanted.

With the help of Tom's family, we had built a lovely new home outside the small town of Geneseo, Illinois, on three wooded acres. Each day, a yellow school bus would collect Ron and Dan, and their faithful collie Stormy would wait patiently for their return home. Tom's work with IBM was secure, and Sue had come to live with Tom and me after our mother's death. Together Sue and I took care of the children and attended college. Sue went to school in the evenings so that I could continue my nursing classes during the daytime.

My political antiwar fever had not diminished. I had become an officer in the League of Women Voters and the Chairman of the McGovern/Shriver Campaign for Henry County, Illinois. Sue and I had rented a storefront in downtown Geneseo that we painted in red, white and blue enamel, and decorated with posters of George McGovern, the new peace candidate.

Nixon had campaigned against Humphrey four years earlier on a platform to end the war, but after he was elected, more Americans had died in Vietnam on his watch than under Johnson's presidency. Sue and I worked relentlessly toward McGovern's election. We kept our politics simple; for us, the Vietnam War was the only issue that mattered. Despite all our efforts, the vast majority of Henry County voted for Richard Nixon—along with the rest of the country. He won in a landslide victory.

My Pop and my immigrant grandfather had instilled in me a belief in the American democratic process. I still believed in the system, but it was beginning to feel like a lost cause. Polls showed that only thirty percent of the American population supported any kind of war effort in Vietnam, but those opinions weren't translated into votes.

The war had been front-page news for so long that now, with the American troops withdrawing from Vietnam, it wasn't a story that people were interested in. With no young Americans dying, people simply did not care what America was doing in Vietnam.

Oddly enough, in the course of this long war, America had killed more South Vietnamese, our allies, than we had the enemy. The chemicals that we sprayed and the forests we burned ravaged the very land we were supposedly defending.

I felt helpless, fighting for a cause that most people didn't even care about. Up to that point, nothing I had done about the war had made one bit of difference. The thousands of hours spent in pushing for peace—candlelight marches, demonstrations, and the political campaigning—had accomplished nothing.

Gradually, the thought struck me that perhaps I could make a single, small contribution and make a difference in the life of one person. Maybe that would help the world become a better place. I recalled the magazine article I'd read and thought about the poor, unwanted children.

I brought up the subject with Tom one night. I asked him how he would feel about adopting a mixed-race child from Vietnam. It felt as if this was the only way I could do something for the most innocent victims of the Vietnam War. Along with that came the joyful anticipation of adding a new child, a sister for Beth and the three boys. To my great pleasure, he agreed; there was room in our hearts and our home for one more.

I set to work, researching the subject of international adoptions. I came across the name of a Minnesota-based organization called OURS, which was raising money to assist the orphans in Vietnam. When I told them that we were interested in adopting a mixed-race child, they referred me to Naomi Bronstein. Naomi worked with Families for Children, a Montreal-based group that arranged international adoptions for Vietnamese children.

Naomi patiently explained her mission. She told me of two Australian women, Rosemary Taylor and her assistant, Margaret Moses. I learned that, with worldwide assistance, they were raising money and supplies for the Vietnamese orphans and accomplishing miracles through their love and concern.

From our first telephone conversation, Naomi made it clear that there were others who found homes for the Vietnamese children. Her entire focus was to help the Afro-American children, who she believed were the most desperate of the war orphans. She was a great help and outlined the procedures we would have to follow to adopt a child from Vietnam.

The formalities seemed daunting, but we threw ourselves into the project wholeheartedly. We had to check Illinois state and county adoption laws. A social worker would conduct a "home study" to evaluate our ability to parent a child of a different race and help prepare us for the process.

We compiled a dossier containing copies of our marriage and birth certificates, financial and medical verifications—all to prove that we were fit to be adoptive parents. We gathered letters of recommendation from our priest and local congressman and added them to our dossier.

We were also required to write a special letter, humbly requesting South Vietnam's President Nguyen Van Thieu's permission to adopt a child from his country. It seemed uncanny that I was carefully and with great respect composing a letter to ask his help to adopt a child, when for years I had been attacking his American-subsidized presidency.

Naomi told me that she would travel to Vietnam just before Christmas of 1972, despite being pregnant and having a large family with adopted children at home. She offered to hand-carry our paperwork with her and promised to give our document package personally to Rosemary Taylor. She told me to include a letter to Rosemary that would help her understand our desire to adopt a child from her care. Almost as an afterthought, Naomi reminded me to enclose a self-addressed, stamped envelope. Rosemary had friends with APO addresses. Perhaps that would speed up a reply.

I was so grateful to Naomi. Despite her workload, she never faltered in her efforts to help. I was deeply impressed with the gentle spirits that powered the international movement to rescue the forgotten children of war.

Nothing in our precious dossier of documents was as important to me as the letter I composed to Rosemary. I thoughtfully chose the stationery and wrote innumerable draft versions of the letter. I was becoming educated about the adoption process. My initial motivation to adopt a child was rapidly changing as I met others with children from Vietnam. Now I longed for a child's arrival in our family for the person that she would be, not because of a war that I could not stop.

❦

Our home was decorated for Christmas. We had a huge tree, filled with lights and decorations that our children had made. We were all looking forward to receiving some news that a child had been selected for our family. My attention was now focused on Vietnam even more, if that was possible.

We were dismayed to see television newscasts that Christmas of the mass bombing of civilian areas of Hanoi, the capital of North Vietnam. We watched, enraged, as images of thousands of civilians fleeing a city in flames filled the screen in our cozy living room. Months earlier, Nixon had campaigned vigorously with promises of his secret plan to end the war. Once reelected, he unleashed unparalleled bombings that destroyed hospitals and the residential areas of the city.

I wept for the lives of the innocent people that were killed and became more firmly committed to this distant land that seemed to hold me captive during my waking hours and even in my dreams.

As the weeks went by, the waiting for news from Vietnam grew more arduous—for all of us, even the children. I lived in suspended hope. I went through days at college and took care of my children with my mind focused on the war, and now, more importantly, the children of the war.

My world broadened as I spoke by telephone with other adoptive parents who had gone through the same intense waiting experience. I was cautioned repeatedly that the adoption process could take many months, sometimes a year, or even more. It was unbearably sad to learn that so many children died before the adoption process could be completed. Instead of embarking on long, fulfilling lives, they lay in unmarked graves.

Nothing in the experiences that I had gone through with pregnancy had prepared me for this longing for a child that I had never seen. We had no idea how old she would be, or how she would look, but suddenly our family conversations seemed to be enveloped by this child, as if she were a cherished member of the family who was simply absent. And every telephone conversation I had with another potential adoptive family left me with the feeling that I had found a kindred soul.

When at last I opened the mailbox and saw the self-addressed envelope that I had sent to Rosemary, I knew that our life was about to change forever. The child Rosemary called Thu Loan was born just two weeks before

Brian. They were both fourteen months old. The picture was one that any waiting adoptive parent would long for. A smiling nun was holding Thu Loan, who was wearing a white frock. Her face was clear and perfect. Her hair was curly and her eyes bright.

When Tom finally arrived home from work, I gently took the small picture from the hands of my children and ran barefoot out into the snow to greet him. I was oblivious to anything but the absolute miracle in which we were participating; our entire family was enchanted by this child.

I entrusted the care of the picture to a local photographer who promised to keep it only overnight. He would make copies, so that I could send the photo out to my brothers and other family members. I had it enlarged, hoping it would somehow reveal more about our new daughter. Our family decided that we would name our newest member Jennifer Loan.

Some weeks later, in Rosemary's absence, Margaret wrote requesting a new paper that was required to complete the dossier. She ended her letter by saying, "Your daughter is well." These simple words, confirming that this child was ours, brought infinite joy. They proved that this was not a dream.

In early 1973, weeks after we had received the first news of Jenny, I was surprised to find another letter in my mailbox from Vietnam. This one was decorated with colorful stamps from Vietnam and not sent through the APO boxes that Rosemary's staff used.

I carefully opened it and was bewildered to find a photograph, not of our child, but of a different child with a sad expression. The letter was from a woman named Michelle Wentzell, who worked at the Sacred Heart Orphanage just outside of Da Nang, where one of America's largest military bases had been located.

Michelle had received word from Rosemary that we were looking for a child to adopt. The letter told us that the little girl in the picture was in dire need of a family. Her name was Cam Van and she had been born in Chu Lai before arriving at the Tam Ky Orphanage.

The sisters at Tam Ky were skeptical and uncertain of adoption, Michelle wrote. The only way she had been able to convince them to allow it was to show them the letter I had written to Rosemary. In addition, she had shown them the highly supportive letter from our priest. Because she had found

25

a Catholic family willing to adopt a black child of this age, the nuns allowed Michelle to move the child to the Sacred Heart Orphanage in Da Nang. Michelle wrote that we were "truly a gift from God." The child so desperately needed a family.

I was confused. Margaret's recent letter had confirmed that Thu Loan's adoption process was well under way.

Michelle had written that the child she had found for us, Cam Van, was four years old. Looking at her photograph, I could not imagine that was true. The poor child appeared to be hardly more than an infant.

When Tom arrived home from work, we studied the letter.

Cam Van was obviously dear to Michelle. She had worked so long to find a family, and she wanted to be as honest and as open as possible. She wrote that she had feared she might never find a family who would come forward to adopt Cam Van and also be approved by the sisters.

Cam Van was burdened with problems that had made her placement for adoption very difficult. Besides being four years old and half-black, she had been so deprived that she may already have suffered permanent physical and emotional damage. She was so weak that almost any insignificant illness could kill her.

From the picture, we could see that her stomach was bloated and her spindly legs could not support her upper body. I wondered if the poor child would ever walk.

Michelle wrote that Cam Van means "a cloud of velvet" in Vietnamese. The sisters had baptized her shortly after her abandonment; her baptismal name was Mary.

Tom and I discussed the letter and looked at the picture late into the night. We were sure Cam Van was meant to be our child, just as Jenny was. By the time we went to bed, exhausted with the emotions of the long day, she had captured our hearts.

The next day I sent Western Union cables to Michelle and Rosemary and briefly explained that we had two referrals, and that we had mailed letters confirming our desire to adopt both children.

It was weeks before we received an apology from Rosemary and an explanation of what had happened. Rosemary had written to Michelle about us and even forwarded our letters to her. When Thu Loan arrived in her nursery, she thought of our family immediately without thinking further of her request to Michelle to find us a child. The confusion was understandable; they were all working very hard and under a great deal of stress.

By that time, it did not matter. Cam Van, whom we named Joanna, after Tom's grandmother and my aunt, was as much ours as Jenny.

Our greatest concern was for her health and safety. She was not in Saigon under Rosemary's care, but in Da Nang, closer to the war and living in an overcrowded and underfunded orphanage.

In January of 1973, the United States and North Vietnam agreed to a cease-fire, a way out of a poor military and political situation that President Nixon labeled "peace with honor." South Vietnam angrily rejected the agreement, which did not call for the withdrawal of North Vietnamese troops from the South. But for America, the war was over.

Our prisoners of war were coming home. I watched them on television, vicariously experiencing their happiness as they were reunited with their families. That joy was shared by every household in America. As I witnessed the soldiers' homecomings, I waited for homecomings of my own, impatient for my daughters to be with us.

After only a few months of what was predicted to be a very long wait, we received a letter from Rosemary telling us that Margaret would soon be escorting Jenny home. The American Embassy in Saigon had granted "humanitarian parole visas" to a large number of children in Rosemary's homes. The visa meant that Jenny would be able to bypass the long wait for the Illinois INS to process her immigration papers, and she would be able to travel home soon. Our hearts were filled with pure joy.

We learned that Jenny would arrive in Colorado and would stay there overnight before a volunteer would fly with her to Illinois. Tom and I agreed that it was impossible to wait the extra day; we decided to fly to Denver to get her ourselves.

In Denver's Stapleton International Airport, I was surprised to find a large number of people at the gate where the plane would arrive. They too were waiting for the flight, and the air was filled a sense of expectation. The flight was delayed, and while we waited, we struck up a conversation with Cheryl and Mick Markson, volunteers with the Denver-based Friends of the Children of Viet Nam (FCVN).

We learned that FCVN had been founded in 1967 by a Denver doctor who had served in Vietnam and been moved by the plight of the orphaned children.

He was soon joined by others who cared, and they incorporated FCVN as a nonprofit, humanitarian organization to send medicine, food, and trained personnel to Vietnam to help the infants and children. FCVN also supported individuals and organizations that were placing children for adoption.

The Marksons introduced us to the others who were waiting for the flight, and we exchanged names with people active in this humanitarian effort. The large gathering was composed mostly of parents who had adopted children from Vietnam. Cheryl explained that many other families waiting at the gate were adopting with the help of FCVN.

The Marksons were beginning the process of adoption, and they hoped to soon have a child referred to them. The volunteers spoke of the acute need to help the Vietnamese orphanages, and I promised I would do my part once we were back home.

We were pleased Jenny's arrival would be celebrated by others who understood so completely the waiting we had endured. Many of them had come to thank and applaud Margaret Moses, one of the women who had made it possible for them to adopt, and who had helped so many others.

Margaret and Rosemary were heroines in the cause of international adoptions. They worked ceaselessly to save the lives of the children who came to them. It was a rare opportunity for the families to meet Margaret and be able to express their appreciation personally.

As the plane landed, I watched anxiously through the crowd standing at the huge window; it seemed to take forever for the plane to draw up to the ramp. Finally, I heard a murmur that grew louder, heralding the arrival of the passengers.

At last, I saw a tired woman walking toward us with a small child on each arm. I was surprised to see that she was so young, and she looked exhausted and frail. She was carrying my Jenny, who was wearing a faded yellow stretch suit.

Margaret gently lifted Jenny into my arms. In that single moment, I bonded as deeply as I had at the birth of my children. This was going to be our daughter forever. Jenny was smiling as she placed her hand on my cheeks, now wet with tears. Tom wrapped his arms around us both in a loving embrace.

Jenny's skin was the color of milk chocolate, her hair black curly ringlets. She was smiling at us, and I saw she had beautiful dimples, something I couldn't tell from her picture.

After thanking Margaret and showing Jenny to everyone, Tom and I simply wanted to be alone with our new daughter. We walked out of the

airport with the same feeling we had had leaving the hospital with Ron—
that feeling of being totally entrusted with and responsible for this small
person. We couldn't take our eyes off her; she was truly ours, to cherish and
bring up in our family. This certainly was a miracle.

In the hotel that night, Jenny became frightened and started crying. To
comfort her, we took her out of the crib and laid her between us. We desperately wanted her to know that she was safe. Neither of us got much sleep as
we watched her sleeping.

It had taken the miracle of her survival and the wonder of her photograph to bring us together. There was no doubt in my mind that in a moment as full of chance as the moment of conception, this child was destined
to be our daughter.

Our thoughts were also for the woman on the other side of the world
who had given birth to her. We spoke of her and somehow wanted her to
know that we would always love and cherish this child.

❧

We had another child still in Vietnam. Jenny's arrival made us long for
Cam Van even more. She was in much worse physical condition, and every
day that she remained in the orphanage, I felt she was in peril.

We had been spoiled, because Jenny's adoption was one of the fastest on
record. We hoped that Joanna's adoption would be accomplished as easily
and quickly. The four-month wait to receive Jenny had been unbearable,
but now I was to learn what patience really meant.

Word of progress on Joanna's paperwork was excruciatingly slow. Rarely
did we receive any word about her from the orphanage in Da Nang, and
what we did learn brought us no comfort. Epidemics regularly swept through
the orphanage, killing many infants and toddlers. Even mild illnesses could
take the life of the malnourished children.

With my nurse's training, I understood that because of Joanna's weak
condition, any illness could prove fatal. The next letter would be as likely to
inform us of her death as it would the status of her adoption. As winter
turned to spring, I became increasingly concerned at the passage of the
months.

Jenny's assimilation into our family was so easy. She arrived home already able to walk and climb and was amazingly well coordinated. We gave

her all the love that we had to offer, just as we had promised in our letters to the people in Vietnam.

Brian and Jenny played in their toddler world, always laughing and inseparable. They were constantly together, and we nicknamed them "Thunder and Lightning." Brian would sooner crawl than walk, and Jenny would take him by the hand and pull him behind her. Often she climbed into his crib at night, and we would find them there in the morning, cuddled close together.

Relatives who had been skeptical about the adoption were enchanted with Jenny's flashing eyes and laughter that accentuated her dimples. Watching my children play, I thought of my mother often, and my heart ached with the loss. I knew how much she would have loved these two children she had never seen.

I was now in frequent telephone contact with the FCVN people we had met in Denver. Cheryl Markson introduced me to Carol Westlake, whose husband was the president of FCVN, and we got along remarkably well. Tom and I kept our promise to do what we could to help the children in Vietnam, and in early 1973, Tom and I founded the Illinois chapter of FCVN.

We wanted to help other children in Vietnam who were living in the orphanages and surviving with only the barest of essentials. I approached every group I could think of to solicit money, clothing, and medical supplies. I prepared slide presentations and gave shows wherever I was welcome. I spoke in Protestant and Catholic churches, the American Legion, and the Junior League. As the slides flicked across the screen, I added a commentary to describe the plight of the war orphans. Sometimes I saw tears when I spoke of the difficulties facing the children that our American soldiers had left behind. I knew that my efforts were worthwhile. I was helping the children in Rosemary's care as much as I could.

Naomi called with the news that she had arranged for an airplane load of supplies to be airlifted by the Canadian Government to Saigon and Rosemary's nurseries. Tom and I packed boxes of donated medicine and supplies and rented a U-Haul trailer. Then we drove, with our five little children, all the way to Canada to deliver the valuable goods that we had collected.

Our family became the focus of Quad City newspapers. They helped spread the word of our adoption and our ongoing activities to help other children in Vietnam. Soon we were not alone, and other families joined in to help us raise money and supplies; some even made plans to adopt children themselves.

Many nights, I arrived home very late from giving slide shows, exhausted but unable to sleep. I wandered through our silent house, touching my children, drawing comfort from the knowledge that they would never be alone, hungry, or desperate for attention. In Beth's room, I would stand looking at Joanna's unoccupied bed, wondering if she would ever sleep in it. Every night I went to bed praying that there would be some news in the next day's mail. Every morning my vigil began anew.

When word finally came, we were brokenhearted. We were told there were problems with the paperwork that could not be overcome. Joanna could not be released for adoption.

We were devastated. For all this time, we had been thinking of her as part of our family, just waiting for her to arrive. We had even bought matching clothes for our three little girls. The room—in our hearts as well our home—was ready and waiting for Joanna. I cried for days and would not let go of the picture of her. I could not imagine what fate awaited the child that I already thought of as my daughter. I was inconsolable.

I knew that Michelle felt deeply committed to Joanna and that she had done all she could, but she wrote that the obstacles were simply too great for the adoption to go ahead. The Vietnamese authorities had forbidden Cam Van's move from Da Nang to Saigon. We had already named the child, and she had a place in our heart and family. How could we just let this child go?

The sisters in Da Nang also wrote. They told us they understood and sympathized, but, ever practical, they told us to put the idea of adopting Cam Van aside. They asked us to remember that there were hundreds of mixed-race children who needed families. They told us there was nothing they could do to help us.

I wrote to Rosemary and explained what had happened and asked if there was any way that she could possibly intercede and help us. She wrote back that she knew of the situation but felt it was hopeless. Echoing the words of the sisters from Da Nang, she encouraged us to look elsewhere for a child to adopt. She reminded us that the sisters in Qui Nhon, whom we were very close to since Jenny's adoption, had other children in need of families.

Every part of me rebelled at giving up on Joanna, and I grieved.

❦

After some time, we were able to discuss the prospect of filling the empty place in our hearts, and felt ready to ask for another child. We discussed the great need for homes for boys since the preference for most adopting families was for girls.

Perhaps there was a boy who needed our family. Maybe news of another child would help me get over the loss of Joanna. Although I had never held her or seen her, I felt as if something precious had been taken away from me. I worried incessantly about her poor health. Her picture remained in a frame on my bedside table, and I looked at her sad face each morning.

Finally, we took the advice of Rosemary and the sisters and wrote to Qui Nhon. Sister Marie wrote back almost immediately with the news that they had a special child they wanted us to adopt. They did not send a picture but wrote only that he was "one and wonderful." Our spirits lifted with this news, and we began to make plans to add a new son to our family.

In the midst of my continuing sorrow over losing Cam Van, I began to bond with the little boy, who I knew was in the same room where Jenny had spent the first year of her life. I chose the name Thanh and wrote to the Sisters to ask their approval. If Cam Van was truly not meant to be our child, then I must put my pain aside and love this little boy. Soon I began to long for him just as I had for Jenny and Joanna.

Our circle of friends and contacts in the adoption world was growing. By now, we were writing regularly to the sisters in Qui Nhon, and we introduced other families who wanted to adopt children from them. Many of these new friends became part of the Illinois chapter of FCVN, and others started their own chapters in the states where they lived.

One spring morning, a letter arrived from Da Nang with unbelievable news. Michelle, who had a special place in her heart for Cam Van, had refused to accept the failure of our adoption efforts, and, unbeknownst to us, had continued to try to overcome the bureaucratic problems that had blocked the adoption. Her efforts were eventually rewarded, and she informed us that the adoption could now go ahead. Cam Van would soon be on her way to Saigon and Rosemary's nursery. Although I was very happy, I decided to keep a close rein on my emotions. There was no guarantee, but at least there was hope.

With the constant emotional highs and lows of the adoption process, the slow mail between the countries, and the confusion wrought by the war, our lives felt like a roller-coaster ride. One letter made us ecstatic, while the next made us cry. We decided to proceed with the thought of adopting both Joanna and Thanh, but we were uncertain if either of them would ever make it home.

❦

In early summer, I received yet another unexpected letter from Vietnam. The letter was from an Illinois native named Steve Johnson. His parents, who lived not far from us in Geneseo, had sent him a newspaper clipping about Jenny's adoption and our money-raising efforts for the orphans. Steve wrote to congratulate and encourage us in our efforts. He had served with the U.S. Army in Vietnam and now worked for International Telephone and Telegraph (ITT) and was based in Saigon.

Steve wrote of the needs of the Vietnamese people and closed with an offer to be of assistance should we ever require any help. We were touched by the compassion and offer of help from a complete stranger.

I replied to his letter and told him at length about our involvement with the orphans, and about Rosemary's nurseries. I also told him that we were trying to adopt two children still in orphanages in Da Nang and Qui Nhon.

In the weeks that followed, Steve became our main link with Vietnam. He went to visit Rosemary's centers in Saigon and became close friends with some of the nurses who worked there. He wrote of the despair, the deaths, and the tireless struggle of Rosemary's volunteers, who toiled against the odds to keep the young babies alive.

Steve wrote almost every day and sent lists of urgently needed supplies. He allowed us to send supplies via his APO address, which expedited the deliveries of the items the nurses had placed at the top of their list.

His long, descriptive letters and beautiful pictures changed my viewpoint of Vietnam and the people. I began to see Vietnam as a country and not just a war zone. His letters brought the people to life for me, and I could see and feel Vietnam through his words.

It was Steve who first informed us that Cam Van, whom he called Miss Clark, had at last reached Rosemary's Allambie Nursery. He visited the nursery and later sent an envelope full of pictures.

In the early summer of 1973, Steve wrote that he had made plans to travel to Qui Nhon with one of Rosemary's nurses. He wanted to meet the sisters, see Thanh, and take some photographs of our son for us. Travel to Qui Nhon was difficult and dangerous because of the ongoing war; the roads were not safe and the best way to travel was by plane. Tom and I were very thankful for his unselfish help.

Weeks after Steve's journey, we received a thick envelope containing pictures of Thanh and a long, detailed letter about life in the orphanage. He wrote of other children waiting for families in Qui Nhon and of the sisters' tireless efforts to care for the abandoned children.

Steve painstakingly described each detail of Qui Nhon and the orphanage. Reading his letters was like taking a walk through that distant place. He also enclosed a photo album filled with pictures of Thanh, the sisters, the South China Sea, the cathedral, and the nursery.

The pictures of Thanh showed a beautiful child. Though he was frail and covered with boils, to us he was perfect, with huge round eyes. Finally we had a glimpse of the son that we had so longed to see.

During his trip to Qui Nhon, Steve discovered that the problem that was causing the delay with Thanh's adoption was that he simply didn't have any papers. He had been abandoned in such terrible condition that he was not expected to live, and the sisters had not wanted to waste precious money to file for a birth certificate. So, although Thanh was now about fourteen months old, his birth was not registered and, legally, he did not exist.

After the sisters had offered him to us for adoption, they repeatedly visited the civil servant that should have prepared Thanh's birth certificate, but he refused to type the scrap of paper. His obstinate refusal meant that none of the other documents necessary for Thanh's adoption could be processed.

That frustrating state of affairs lasted throughout the summer. Our only real hope was that I had Steve in Vietnam willing to help. Rosemary and her staff were working hard to cope with the influx of orphans from all over the country. They didn't have the resources to try to resolve every problem that arose.

During the summer, we met the McGee family from Iowa. They too were trying to adopt a son, and we comforted and reassured each other through the months of waiting. The little boy they were going to adopt had been in the same orphanage as Joanna, and he had been taken into Rosemary's center as well. He was in the same room as Joanna in Saigon, while we, waiting in America, shared the same fears and frustrations.

In the fall, Steve wrote that he was going to Qui Nhon again. Weeks later, he surprised us with a telephone call in the middle of the night. I heard Steve's voice for the first time, although it was badly distorted by static. Despite the poor connection, I got his message. He had brought Thanh from Qui Nhon to Saigon; he was now at Allambie in the very same room as Joanna. Tom and I were so thrilled that we talked about our future family until dawn broke outside the bedroom window. Just maybe, this really was going to happen.

Thanh's move had been made possible because the sisters had taken matters into their own hands. To overcome Thanh's lack of a birth certificate and circumvent the petty official who refused to issue one for him, the sisters employed a small, not unprecedented ruse to beat the system.

A newborn baby was abandoned at the orphanage, and they applied for a birth certificate, but gave Thanh's name and assigned the document to him. He was already a year old, but when the birth certificate was issued, he was officially a newborn. With the birth certificate, the adoption could at last proceed.

By the time winter arrived, my desire to see and hold my two children became unbearable. I simply had to go to Vietnam and attempt to untangle the paperwork. I had heard about other adoptive parents who had made the trip to Vietnam and managed to shake their child's paperwork loose. Nearly a year had passed since we had first learned of Joanna, and although some of her adoption paperwork had cleared, she still did not have a passport.

After much discussion, Tom agreed that by traveling to Vietnam, I might be able to bring the children home. Gloria Johnson and the McGees, our friends in the adoption world, offered to take care of my children while I was away.

In November of 1973, knowing my children were safe with friends, I arranged to travel to Vietnam. The flight to Vietnam would be my first international plane trip. It would be the journey of a lifetime, and I was excited and apprehensive, but fortified by the confidence that when I returned, I would be accompanied by our two new children.

Chapter Three

*T*hrough the window of the descending Boeing 747, I peered down at the long coastline of Vietnam. From that height, the country looked serene and peaceful. Below us stretched miles of rice fields. Small houses appeared dotted among the fields, and as we neared Saigon's famous Tan Son Nhut International Airport, more and more properties appeared until they filled my view; they all seemed to be jumbled together, one against the other. In what I supposed was the downtown area, stately looking yellow buildings with red tile roofs lined impressively wide boulevards.

There were only a handful of passengers left on the Pan Am flight into Saigon; most of the others had disembarked at the last stopover in the Philippines. Not many people wanted to fly into a war zone.

The plane touched down and slowed quickly, taxiing past graffiti-covered hangars filled with warplanes, stark reminders of the troops that had recently pulled out of the country. The peace symbol was painted everywhere, alongside army unit names and good luck messages.

As the door swung open, a blast of hot, humid air swept into the plane. Vietnamese soldiers carrying heavy-looking machine guns rushed into the plane. The sudden appearance of the soldiers was disconcerting; I'd never seen fully armed soldiers close up before. They walked up and down the aisles, closely scrutinizing each passenger, as if they were looking for someone to take away.

When we were at last allowed to disembark, I walked down the metal steps onto the hot tarmac. I'd done it—I'd managed to get myself safely into this country I'd dreamed of for so long.

There was no luggage carousel. We lined up to collect our luggage straight off a small tractor-driven cart that stopped near the open-air Customs and Immigrations counter. After a cursory inspection of my passport and visa and a quick glance at my bags, I was allowed to pass through the barrier, and with little formality, I entered the real Vietnam.

The arrivals hall was packed, hot and noisy. I wandered through the crowd, pulling my two heavy suitcases behind me. I listened to the singsong rhythm of the Vietnamese language all around me. Feeling a little scared, being alone in a sea of foreigners, I scanned the crowd looking for Steve Johnson, and spotted him almost at once. He stood out in the crowd, tall among the Vietnamese men who surrounded him.

Steve made his way toward me, and we greeted each other shyly, despite the almost daily letters we had exchanged over the past months. He took charge and immediately started explaining the way the airport transport was set up. Ignoring determined taxi drivers, who tried to snare us into their rusty, beat-up cars, we made for the exit. On the way, Steve explained that commercial taxis were not allowed in Tan Son Nhut Airport. "Airport limousines" was the lofty name for the assorted, battered old Chevy sedans parked outside, which cost too much for a ride downtown. He suggested walking to the main road in the airport to hail a Lambretta, which would take us to the main gate, where we could hire a taxi.

Steve carried the large, heavy suitcases I'd brought; they were filled with medicine for the orphans and clothes and toys for Joanna and Thanh. I struggled along behind him, wading through the sea of people. The heat and humidity were like a hot, wet blanket, oppressive and sticky, something I would have to get used to in this strange and different land.

We reached the road, and within minutes, Steve had brought me up to date with all the latest news about Joanna and Thanh. Steve knew them so much better than I did that I felt strange calling them "my" children.

Our ride arrived; it looked to be already filled to capacity. The Lambretta was a strange-looking vehicle, a little like a miniature bus. It was boarded from the rear, and passengers sat facing each other on wooden seats along the sides. The passengers slid along the seats to make room for me and Steve to sit. Then they helped us pull the huge suitcases in as well.

Just outside the gate of the airport, cab drivers milled about, hoping to snare a foreigner who would pay twice the customary fare for a ride into town. Their small taxis were all painted blue and yellow. Rust, dents and scratches covered every surface.

Steve began bartering with the drivers in Vietnamese, and they reluctantly lowered their prices as they bargained for our business. Finally, with a price agreed on, we climbed into one of the rusty cabs. Looking down, I saw that most of the floorboard had rusted away, exposing the pavement beneath. Steve casually leaned back, his feet straddling the hole in the floor as the taxi lurched away. He seemed indifferent to the pavement whizzing by just inches from his shoes.

Almost immediately, he pointed to a street that he identified as Vo Tanh.

"Your children are about two blocks away from here. We'll drop off your bags at the hotel first, then we'll go to Allambie."

I couldn't believe I was so close to my children. After waiting so long, I was now more impatient than ever to see them.

The driver maneuvered his way down streets filled with crowds of people, all scurrying about on bicycles, in vehicles and on foot. Hundreds of noisy motorbikes mingled in the pack, jockeying for position with cars, trucks and buses. The smell of the exhaust fumes wafted into the hot interior of the cab and made my eyes water. A bus in front of us belched out great gouts of dense black smoke that momentarily obscured our view of the road ahead. The smoke was so thick I could taste it.

On every street corner, using carts on wheels, people peddled steaming hot food to those who passed by. Plucked chickens, head and feet still intact, hung in glass cases on top of the carts, ready for the next round of meals.

We rolled along, jerking and swerving through the streets, heading towards a downtown hotel. Steve pointed out places of interest along the route. He talked loudly to be heard over the racket coming through the windows and the scratchy sounds coming from the car radio.

Occasionally, we passed large groups of happy-looking children in school uniforms, walking on the sidewalk. Their lovely faces brought me joy, for I had seen too many photos of Vietnamese orphans with sad faces.

We crossed over a road bridge and, looking down, I saw long rows of wooden shacks built over a small body of stagnant water. I could see the grinding poverty, just below street level. Gangs of children picked over garbage heaps, looking for anything of value in the trash.

I was relieved when we arrived at the Caravelle Hotel. The taxi ride had exposed me to Saigon's streets, and my mind was reeling with an overload of images—it was too much in too short a time.

Steve pointed out the Continental Hotel across the street. He told me that it was the favorite haunt of most of the war correspondents. Some famous stories had been written right there, he said. I saw a large, open terrace filled with tables, and could easily imagine reporters hanging about in that open space, looking out at the noisy street.

Along with the withdrawal of American forces from Vietnam, there was also a significant withdrawal of the reporters who had covered the war. On the flight over, I'd read an article that claimed American people were not interested in stories about Vietnamese killing Vietnamese. The war, perhaps the most heavily covered in history, was no longer interesting. Too bad it hadn't been canceled due to lack of interest as well.

Inside the lobby, the hotel seemed dark after the brightness in the street, and my eyes took a few minutes to adjust to the interior lighting. The hotel was air-conditioned and seemed cold, dark and drab after the color and light of the streets. I checked in and left my bags with the porter, anxious to get to the nursery and see my children.

Emerging again into the noisy commotion of the street, we were immediately surrounded by an effervescent group of street vendors. They offered us everything—chewing gum, cigarettes, postcards, and magazines. One man followed us, chanting mantra-like in my ear, "Change money, Madam. Change money, Madam." Although I showed no interest he persisted, staring at me as if I might suddenly produce a wad of dollars.

Brushing them off, Steve insisted we travel to the nursery by a *cyclo may*, a type of small, converted motorbike, a three-wheeled taxi unique to Saigon. He held out his arm and shouted, and within seconds, our transport pulled up to the roadside with a jerk.

It was a motorbike with a passenger seat, on the front, supported by two narrow wheels. We climbed aboard, and I realized that the driver could hardly see over or around us.

"In Saigon's traffic, it's better if one cannot see," Steve laughingly assured me. He seemed impervious to the heat, noise, bustle, and obvious danger. I wondered how long one had to stay here before the street sounds became mere background noise.

We set off and just missed colliding with a portable soup stand before the driver settled down, and we retraced our route back towards the airport. After another hot, colorful, and exciting journey, we came to an abrupt halt outside Allambie.

The nursery was in a converted villa, surrounded by a large compound with a high wall. A huge barred gate provided the only access to the interior. Steve rang the bell, and after waiting for several minutes with no response, he mumbled something about the bell not working if the electricity was off. Without another thought, he scaled the fence and dropped inside.

Finally, the gate opened and Steve reappeared, carrying my child, Joanna, in his arms. I reached for her. She looked at me curiously, and then buried her head in Steve's shoulder. I knew that I was a stranger and she was afraid of me, but I had to hold her in my arms, if only for a moment.

Steve whispered to her in Vietnamese, explaining that I was her new mother. She looked me over, shook her head no, and then turned away again. I touched her hair and her soft black skin, but she quickly brushed my hands away.

Though Joanna resisted, Steve put her in my arms, then moved away to let us share the moment. Joanna's body was rigid, quivering with fright—or was it anger? She stared at the ground and ignored me. At that moment, I felt she resented my intrusion into her life. I felt I should apologize to her.

As we walked into the center, she pounded her tiny fists on my shoulder and chest. She kicked me, then slid to the ground and began to scream. Her cries scared me, and I was at a loss as to how I could tell my new daughter that everything would be all right now. Joanna was scared of what her future held. She didn't know that I was going to love and nurture her; she saw me as a threat to her new world here at Allambie.

Steve led me to the lunchroom while a child care worker tried to comfort the howling Joanna. Other children were seated at long wooden tables, eating their lunch. We talked about Joanna's first reaction to me, and Steve told me it would take a while for her to accept me, just as it had taken a long time for her to accept him into her life. I nodded, comforted by his kind words, but deep in my heart, I knew that it was not going to be easy.

Steve pointed toward some small tables where the children were eating, and I immediately spotted my son. He was tinier than I'd imagined. A child care worker was feeding him rice and vegetables. He looked content and did not take any notice of me as I walked over to him. I knelt down next to the woman to get a better look. He was so beautiful. His hair was cut very short, and I could see hundreds of tiny scars on his scalp, reminders of the boils that had once covered his entire body.

More than anything, I wanted this meeting to go well. I sat quietly, just watching him eat his meal. When Thanh finished eating, Steve told the worker who I was. She smiled and hoisted Thanh into my arms. He offered no resistance, just rested his tiny head on my shoulder as his eyes followed the worker's every move. Relief and confusion flooded me in equal parts. Tears of joy rolled down my face and onto my son, but he took no notice; his attention was fixed on the worker.

The child care worker, finished with her chores, turned to walk away, and a tiny whimper escaped Thanh's lips. She turned, smiled sympathetically at me and took him from my arms. I felt rejected. The moment I had anticipated for nearly a year had come at last, but when it arrived, the greeting had not gone as I'd expected. This was normal, I reminded myself, and it was foolish to expect more. I'd heard the stories from many adoptive parents who had initially felt rejected when their new children didn't warm to them immediately. Time and love would make the bond grow stronger. I realized that Jenny, who had bonded to me so quickly, was the exception rather than the rule.

❦

Having met my two new children and experienced their indifference, I felt low. Steve cheerfully greeted the American volunteers and introduced me, then asked if he could take me on a tour of the nursery. They quickly agreed, and I began to cheer up.

Allambie was then one of Rosemary's new centers. It was a perfect place for the hundred or so toddlers waiting to go to their adoptive families. The nursery was well run and clean, with a warm and happy atmosphere. It was quiet now; all the children were lying down for their afternoon naps. Steve quietly led me past the various rooms, each named after a different country that supplied aid.

In one room, Steve pointed out Ellen McGee's son, and I walked over and picked him up. It was strange; I was holding her son while Ellen was taking care of my children in distant America. Adam was in good health and smiled sleepily as I stroked his hair.

We returned to the hotel and had an early dinner with Ray Ebbets, a good friend of Steve's who also worked for ITT. We had a wonderful meal, and afterwards I went to bed early, tired after my long flight. Weary as I was, sleep did not come easily. Memories of the day's events ran repeatedly through my mind like a newsreel. The sounds in the streets stopped abruptly at curfew, and in the ensuing silence, I could hear the sounds of a war being fought in the distance. Eventually I dozed off into a dream-filled sleep.

❦

The following morning, the ringing of the bedside telephone dragged me from my jet-lagged sleep, and Margaret Moses' crisp Australian voice welcomed me to Vietnam. We chatted for a few minutes, and I told her that Jenny, whom she had placed in my arms, had blended perfectly into our family.

42

Moving right to the point, she told me that she knew I was a nurse and asked me if I could help out at the To Am nursery, as they were very short-staffed. Of course, I would be delighted to help with the babies. Then she asked me if it would be possible for me to leave the hotel and move into the nursery immediately.

She explained that Elaine Norris, was working alone at To Am. Ilse Ewald and Birgit Blank, two German nurses, were busy caring for the most fragile of infants at the newly opened Hy Vong ("Hope") Nursery. They urgently needed another nurse to assist Elaine at To Am. I was taken aback and very excited.

To be invited to work alongside the nurses that I so deeply respected was exciting. I had only recently completed my nursing degree, and I had little nursing experience in a ward. I was thrilled to be asked to help out, but apprehensive, and hoped I could live up to their expectations.

I assured Margaret that I would like nothing better, thanked her for the opportunity, and told her that I would arrive in the early evening. Excited beyond measure, I checked out of the hotel. Steve once again proved a perfect friend, and helped me take my bags and move into the nursery.

I didn't know at the time, but Margaret's telephone call was a momentous event in my life. From the moment I was invited into the nursery, my life changed, and I would never be the same again. Just as a butterfly emerges from a chrysalis, all my experiences crystallized at that one moment in time and I became a more mature person, able to draw on reserves I never knew I possessed.

❦

Later that day, when Steve and I arrived at To Am, I entered through the gates with a sense of purpose. In the compound, the first sight that greeted us was an open porch crowded with dozens of infants, all sleeping soundly in the cool night breeze, their baby bouncers covered with one huge mosquito net.

For the first time, I met Elaine Norris, the nurse from Colorado, who greeted me warmly. Elaine had sent me letters about Joanna when she had first come down from Da Nang. I immediately liked the quiet, soft-spoken young woman. As we talked, I could see she was exhausted; small wonder that Margaret said they needed more staff.

Elaine explained that the flow of children into the nurseries was increasing daily, and this center was filled to overflowing. They had no more room inside, so they had to accommodate the extra babies wherever they could, even outside on the open porch. They couldn't turn a child away, for they knew to do so would mean certain death.

The villa's living room had been pressed into service as a makeshift intensive care unit. The room was filled with very sick babies; many of them were receiving IV fluids from bottles hanging from nails driven into the walls. Nothing in my training had prepared me for such a sight, and the enormity of the task ahead took me by surprise.

Nervously, I confided in Elaine that I wasn't sure that I was competent to help nurse so many babies. Elaine smiled and told me that she had only been there a few months herself. The Vietnamese staff was excellent and knew the babies well. She assured me that I would learn quickly.

She showed me where I would sleep, a small bedroom on the second floor. Birgit had just moved to Hy Vong, leaving the room empty for the time being. Elaine and I talked while working with the babies; then, bone tired, I crawled into bed. As I drifted off to sleep, I listened to the night's serenade: babies crying, gunfire in the street below and explosions in the distance.

I woke before dawn and went to look for Elaine. She was working in one of the rooms. Quietly, she pointed to a tiny baby boy and told me she had been up all night nursing him. The baby was due to travel to a new family soon, but he wasn't going to make it.

The sight was traumatic for me. Before that moment, I had never seen a baby die; now I was a part of it. I stayed with Elaine, and we comforted the baby until he passed away. I was crying so hard, I was sure that I couldn't continue to work. The emotion was too much for me, but I couldn't leave the nursery. Elaine was exhausted after a full night's work—she needed me to get back in control.

I urged Elaine to rest and told her that I would take over while she slept. Alone, I gazed about the room, frozen by the awesome responsibility I had just agreed to take on.

Suddenly I was in charge of a house full of babies. There was no doctor and no other nurses, only the Vietnamese staff, who spoke little English. There was nobody I could turn to for advice or guidance; it was up to me to make the decisions.

A child care worker soon approached me with an infant in her arms. She pointed to the child's forehead. I saw his flushed face and felt his forehead; he was burning hot with fever. Together we sponged the baby with cool water, and slowly the fever diminished. When the baby was sleeping soundly, the woman gently slipped him into a crib.

I followed behind the workers as they made rounds, quickly seeing how well these women knew their small charges. Though we couldn't converse, we communicated through the needs of the babies.

A nurse pointed to a baby whose IV had infiltrated, and the area was red and puffy; I had to do something. I knew what should be done, but there was no doctor to do the job, and I would have to do it alone. My hands shook as I pulled out the IV needle and correctly re-inserted it into the tiny girl's vein.

It was the first time I had ever started an IV, and I was relieved when I saw the fluid begin to flow into her vein. I fretted, checking the IV every few minutes, and was amazed that it continued working well.

As I went from child to child, my nursing skills came to the fore and I knew what had to be done. No sooner had I finished with one child than another would need my attention. The hours blurred into a constant round of nursing different babies. I started recognizing the individuality of each one, and soon could identify them as the unique little people that they were.

I looked up to see Elaine smiling and watching me; she looked refreshed and rested.

"You're a natural," she told me.

Suddenly I realized how hungry I was; I hadn't eaten since checking out of the hotel the day before. We walked to the kitchen, and Elaine picked up what looked like a loaf of French bread. She told me it was called *banh my* and was a staple in Saigon, sold on every street corner. We covered the bread with peanut butter and washed it down with warm Coke. The bread was to become an integral part of my diet.

Later that day, I volunteered to collect medicine the babies needed from the nearby Hy Vong Nursery, which was on Truong Minh Giang Street. Elaine wrote down directions, and I set off on my first solo street journey in Saigon.

Hy Vong was a specialized nursery where the sickest babies were nursed. Ilse, who had become famous in adoption circles for the miracles she worked, was the strength behind the nursery. For months I had collected supplies for this nursery, and I was eager to see it for myself.

When I arrived at Hy Vong, I met Ilse, who had just returned from the Mekong Delta, a large region south of Saigon. Ilse introduced me to Birgit Blank, who also worked in the nursery.

Ilse had just brought twenty babies back with her from the Delta. Although she knew the nurseries were already full, she simply had to bring them. Ilse explained that the death rate of babies in the Delta was very high, and the sisters in the remote orphanages begged them to take more babies or else they too would die.

The first twenty-four hours working in the nurseries were a revelation to me. I was tired and aching, but I knew that I'd found my calling. I went to bed that night feeling eager to sleep a few hours and then return to the nursery to relieve Elaine. I was exhausted. The explosions and gunfire didn't keep me awake anymore.

Though there was a war being fought throughout Vietnam, and we could hear the sounds drifting through the night air, I was no longer bothered. I was now part of another war—helping babies and trying to save lives. This was a war that seemed far more important to me.

Each day, I managed to visit my children at Allambie and start the bonding process. I tried to penetrate Joanna's reserve, but she was afraid and withdrawn. Her protective shell was a natural response to the events of her short life. Although only four years old, she had been moved four times to different orphanages before arriving at Allambie, where she was loved and cared for. Perhaps she feared that I had come to take her backward, to a place of hunger and loneliness from which she had escaped. It would be a challenge to gain her confidence, one that I knew would take time and love.

Thanh was younger and not as frightened of change as Joanna was. He allowed me to hold him during my visits. As he became more comfortable with me, we ventured outside the center. Eventually Joanna was comfortable enough to join us too. I took both children outside, and as we walked down busy Vo Tanh Street, their eyes widened in excitement as they took in the traffic and the colorful bustling of the crowds. We were making progress in building a trusting relationship; I instinctively knew that we would be happy together, but that it would continue to take time.

As the days passed, I became more familiar with the sights, sounds, and people of Saigon. I spent my free hours exploring the busy streets on my own, and took side trips during journeys between the nurseries. I quickly learned to use motorbikes for transportation; they were quicker and cheaper than taxis. But I had to negotiate the fare I was willing to pay with a new, primitive sign language that I was rapidly learning.

Often I stopped to buy food and drinks, again communicating by sign with the smiling vendors and shopkeepers. I started to recognize different people and smiled back at them whenever our paths crossed. The city was vibrant and alive with its own force. I felt drawn by its energy and pulled into its magnetism; it was like nothing else I'd ever experienced.

I felt so alive, and my adventurous nature came to the fore. I wanted to tell everybody about what I had learned and seen. There was a whole world more to this country than just the suffering and tragedy shown on American television. Suddenly the slide shows I'd presented for months, when I was proud of my vicarious knowledge, seemed shallow. I had thought I'd captured life in Vietnam, but now that I was directly experiencing it, I realized that there was so much more to this country than could ever be conveyed by a series of photographs.

One of Rosemary's nurses offered to take me with her on a visit to one of the orphanages in Saigon. So far, my experience was limited to Rosemary's centers, and though I'd been shocked by the sheer numbers of babies, I recognized that the care they received was the best that could be made available under the circumstances. I had yet to step inside the orphanages that I had spoken about so knowledgeably in Illinois—and I had no idea how unprepared I was for the sights that would soon greet me.

The first orphanage I visited was in the center of Saigon. It was no different from any other property on the block. The place looked forbidding, with a tall rusted gate and a high concrete wall. Inside the fence was a simple, concrete two-story house, with paint peeling from the walls.

I opened the gate and ventured in. Once inside, all I could see at first were freshly washed clothes blowing gently in the afternoon breeze.

My eyes were pulled towards twenty or more babies, all close to a year in age. Each naked child was half-seated and half-propped in a small plastic pail. They looked so uncomfortable as they sat there; many of them were crying. They looked as if they had been stuffed into pots with their spindly legs hanging over the side. All of them were hunched over, motionless and sad-looking.

As we walked inside, the nurse who had taken me there explained that the children were brought outside once a day and placed on the pots, where they were left for hours at a time. Their visit outside served to give the toddlers a chance to get some fresh air. It was also an opportunity for the over-stretched staff to enforce a rudimentary toilet procedure.

I looked carefully around at the toddlers; many of them were malnourished. Flies and ants crawled on them, gathering at the open sores scattered all over their bodies.

Inside the building, we were led into a dark, depressing room that was home to the toddlers who were now sitting outside. The small room was overcrowded. There weren't enough cribs, and many toddlers now lay listlessly on straw matting on the filthy floor, staring into nothingness.

A small narrow stairway led upstairs to an unlit, cobweb-covered, squalid room filled with babies. The windows were closed, heightening the smell of urine, feces and sour milk. In the oppressive heat, the odors mingled to make me nauseous.

Inside the small room, more than fifty cribs were packed side by side, each filled with a tiny life, bereft of hope. I walked past the cribs, appalled that humans were reduced to living in such a situation.

The babies were pale, a pasty white, with empty bottles propped in their mouths to keep them quiet. I watched a tiny baby sucking intently on an empty bottle, wasting what little strength remained in his body.

In the half-light, I could see that all of the babies' heads were shaved. Many of them were covered with skin rashes and had angry-looking boils clustered on their bodies.

They lay there weakly, lacking the energy to brush the flies away from their eyes, nose and mouth. I was appalled. The place didn't come close to anything like I'd described in Illinois. I had been fervently asking for donations to help, but until that moment, I had simply had no idea how desperate the situation really was.

It was obvious that many of these children were dying. If they survived this adjunct of hell, they could only look forward to another version of it when they were transferred downstairs. There they would lie in the filth of the room until they made their once-daily trip outdoors to sit on a plastic bucket.

I was told that the sisters in charge of this orphanage did not believe in international adoption and felt it was God's will if a baby lived or died. No heroic lifesaving efforts were conducted here. The children either survived or they didn't. I thought of the priest who had explained the Church to me when I was only sixteen; the God he had described could never have been so callous.

As we left the room, I glanced at the children's Vietnamese caretakers, sitting in a corner with a deck of cards, oblivious to the crying of their charges.

When we departed, my emotions were in turmoil; I was angry and sad at the same time. The odds against the children surviving were so stacked against them, it was horrendous; yet the mothers still streamed into the orphanages, handing over their babies with mind-numbing regularity.

Distraught as I was at the waste of human life, it was not too difficult to pinpoint the reasons that gave rise to the tragedies.

The poverty in Vietnam, created by the war, was crushing. Many people had little or no food to eat, and the hardship of introducing another mouth to feed from the same small pot was too much. Therefore, the mothers willingly gave up their offspring, thinking that by doing so, their existing families would manage better on their meager resources, and that the baby would have a better chance in life. Little did they know that when they handed their precious children over to the orphanages, they were all too often handing them a death sentence.

As the war spiraled ever upwards and battlefields covered greater areas, families were separated, and thousands of soldiers and civilians were killed. Many of those who fell were the breadwinners for their families. Without a provider, families fell apart, and young babies were often the first casualties. Mothers hung on to their elder children and willingly gave their infants into what they saw as a safe haven.

Very few Vietnamese families were willing to accept the child of an unmarried mother, particularly if the child had an American father; those children were nearly always brought to orphanages soon after their birth.

The children's pathetic existence brought to my mind the critics of international adoption, who vehemently spouted that children were better off left in their own culture. I thought about the dying babies and could still smell the foul air. How could any adult condemn an innocent child to live in such squalor? There was certainly no "culture" in this building.

Outside, I breathed the fresh air, and wondered how I was ever going to be able to go back to a life in suburban America, knowing that such tragedies and injustices prevailed. I knew I would never be able to turn my back on these children.

❦

Back in To Am, I thought about what I had seen in the orphanage. The situation was desperate and would continue to get worse as long as the war forced more mothers to give up their babies.

I worked with the children each day and night until I was exhausted and bone weary. Every night, my last task was to write to Tom about the day's events. The writing served as a vent for my frustrations as I grappled with the enormity of the task that faced those who worked here. I had traveled to Vietnam on a three-week return ticket. I would soon be leaving this country behind me, but in my absence, the plight of the suffering children would continue unabated, their only help coming from the selfless volunteers that gave up their own way of life to help the little unnamed infants of war.

In my letters, I told Tom that I missed our children so much that I was dreaming about them. I also reported that the wait for passports for Joanna and Thanh was proving tedious and frustrating. I had no way of knowing what progress was being made.

My letters were like a diary. I recorded my thoughts to Tom, struggling to find words to express my feelings. The death of a single child caused a depression that would hover over the nursery like a dark cloud, only lifting when another baby rallied or showed some small sign of improvement. It was impossible to focus too long on the sadness; there was always another baby demanding help, another chance to save a life.

Steve dropped by To Am almost every day to collect my outgoing mail and dispatch it through his APO box. His friendliness and good humor lifted everyone's spirits and made our days a little easier to bear.

Chapter Four

Qui Nhon. The name had meant so much to me for more than a year and had conjured up vivid images in my mind—and suddenly, at last, I had an opportunity to visit the orphanage there.

Some of the supplies that I'd sent from FCVN's Illinois chapter via Steve's APO box had been stored at Allambie and were to be delivered to Qui Nhon that week. Christie Leivermann, one of the American nurses, invited me and Steve to help her take the supplies and visit the sisters on her next trip.

The roads from Saigon to Qui Nhon were treacherous; the coastal road was made virtually impassable by the war raging in the countryside between the cities. The only safe way to travel there was by air, and Steve kindly made the arrangements.

At Tan Son Nhut Airport, we saw the Air Vietnam plane that would fly us to Qui Nhon; it looked like a rattletrap to me. Inside the cabin, I saw a small plaque fixed to a bulkhead, proudly announcing that the plane had been reconditioned by the U.S. Air Force in 1954.

Steve explained to me that many of the Air Vietnam planes had been donated by the U.S. Air Force. His explanation did little to alleviate my anxiety. The plane we were entrusting our lives to had been reconditioned almost twenty years before. God knew how many miles it had flown since then. I was quickly coming to realize that I just had to go on faith. There was no way that I could see and do all that I wanted to, and at the same time worry about safety or the consequences. I made a vow to simply look forward.

The plane ride was bumpy, and we remained strapped in our seats the entire flight. There was no cabin service, and I spent the flight looking through the clouds trying to spot the greenery below. Finally, the plane landed in Qui Nhon and I offered up a prayer of thanks for our safe arrival. Though apprehensive, I was excited as well, knowing I was just minutes away from the place where my children had lived, a place I'd dreamed of many times during the long nights in Illinois.

It was raining hard when we disembarked, and in minutes we were all soaked to the skin. We quickly hired three bicycle cyclos for the trip to St. Paul's. The drivers packed each cyclo with boxes of supplies, and we crawled on top of the bulky boxes as best we could, scraping shins and bottoms on sharp edges. The drivers covered the passenger areas with pieces of rough canvas to shield us from the driving rain.

The area was quieter than Saigon; gone was the bustle and incessant throb of motorbikes zipping in and out of stalled traffic. This setting was more rural, and I savored the views as well as I could through a small opening in the canvas, as we were pedaled slowly through the wet streets.

The roads were deserted, residents driven indoors by the rain. Our drivers struggled to pedal along side roads turned muddy by the cold rain. Dusk was falling when we turned a corner and, in front of the cyclo, I saw St. Paul's Cathedral, a familiar landmark in the city. The Cathedral's spire earned it the distinction of being the tallest building in Qui Nhon.

The orphanage was inside the Cathedral grounds, so we were almost at our destination. We passed quickly through the sandy courtyard, and I remembered how close we were to the beaches that border the South China Sea. Finally, after a year of dreaming and waiting, I'd fulfilled one more of my dreams—I had made it to Qui Nhon. Suddenly I felt a very long way from home in Illinois.

As the gate to the orphanage opened, I saw the nuns, dressed in traditional habits, waiting on the porch. They rushed out with umbrellas, chattering happily and welcoming me. They helped unload the supplies as we all rushed to get out of the pouring rain.

The nuns were excited to see us. I had written to them from Saigon, and they had been expecting a visit from me since my arrival in Vietnam. They all spoke French, and I wished that I could converse with them. Sister Theresa spoke English, so she served as the translator.

They were eager to please. We sat down in a waiting room, and they served us hot tea. While we drank, taking pleasure from the warmth of the piping hot liquid, the sisters paged through the photo album I had brought along, exclaiming with delight at the photos of Jenny with our family. Looking around, I could see the pictures that I had sent to the nuns. It was a strange feeling to see photographs of my family proudly displayed on their walls, thousands of miles away from my home.

After we drank the tea, they guided us on a tour of the orphanage. The rain was still beating down, and the temperature had dropped even more. It was November, and there was a distinct chill from the cold drafts that blew through the cracks in the old building. The orphanage was unheated, and I thought of how the cold would affect the sick children. I could hear the coughing and the bronchial wheezing of children with chest infections. This was a different sound, something I hadn't heard in warmer Saigon—another life-threatening ailment that was a serious hazard to the children in Qui Nhon.

First, we visited the toddlers' room. The old roof leaked and rain poured into the room, splashing loudly onto the stone floor. The cribs had been moved to one side of the room to avoid the pouring rain. Despite these disturbances, I saw that the room was in much better shape than some of its counterparts in Saigon. The place was clean, and though the air felt damp, it was better than the smell of dirt and unwashed babies that permeated the atmosphere in many of the Saigon orphanages.

Despite the differences in surroundings, the children still had a lackluster look. They stared silently at me as I walked past their cribs. These children were clean, well fed, and dressed in decent warm clothing, but they still seemed deprived of any form of stimulation or contact with the outside world. The poor nuns were struggling to cope with too many children, and they didn't have the time or staff to give every child the attention and love they deserved and craved.

We spent hours holding the children and playing with them. They all responded to the human contact and seemed happy to be held and talked to. Each one of them protested loudly when they were returned to their cribs.

The baby room seemed so familiar; I'd sat for hours poring over photos of this room in the comfort of my kitchen in Geneseo. I asked the sister if she remembered which crib Thu Loan had slept in, and she laughingly shook her head; too many babies had come and gone since then. She did remember where Thanh had slept and pointed to a crib on the far side of the room.

I walked over and looked at the crib; this was where my child had spent the first year of his life. I was both happy and sad, an emotional mix that was becoming familiar during my stay in Vietnam. I ran my hands over the crib, absorbing the feel of the chipped and faded paint. The baby boy who now occupied the crib looked up at me with huge, appealing eyes. As I picked him up and stroked his hair, I felt a lump in my throat; the boy in my arms now could so easily have been my Thanh. I hoped that this little one would find a family too.

We were all tired after our journey. We retired to the sisters' dining room, where we were treated to a good, hot meal. The need for sleep was growing, and Christie and I trudged up to the third floor, to a guestroom that had been set aside for visitors. Steve walked down the road to spend the night at a hospital where he had made friends on previous trips to Qui Nhon.

The room was small and simply furnished, but impeccably clean. I climbed onto my cot and pulled the mosquito netting around the bedding. Within minutes, I was asleep, despite the sounds of warfare echoing from the surrounding hills.

I awoke a few hours later to hear a baby crying below. I listened for a while; the baby's cries were louder than the hammering rain and the distant explosions. Unable to bear it any longer, I dressed and went in search of the source of the pitiful weeping.

I found a little boy in the babies' room, crying with all his heart. I picked him up to have a closer look at what ailed him. He was at least a year old, but weighed no more than ten pounds. His skin was tough and dry, and he was so dehydrated that when he cried, no tears fell. His body felt like bones connected by old, leathery skin. He was thirsty and hungry, and when I picked him up, he reacted immediately, seeking food. He was a very sick baby. I cuddled the child and looked carefully at him. He looked like a wizened old man, with a wrinkled face and an ancient air about him.

I looked for a feeding bottle, without success, so I woke an old woman sleeping in the corner who was supposed to be the "night staff" for the hundred or so infants crowded into the nursery. I showed her the baby and indicated that he needed a bottle. She shook her head and pointed to the clock, counting off six with her fingers. Her meaning was clear. It was two o'clock in the morning and the babies would not be fed until six.

I was determined that the "old man" baby would have a drink before the morning, and after a lot of cajoling, by expression and sign language, she finally relented and shuffled off into the darkness. After what seemed an eternity, she returned with a none-too-clean bottle, coated with soured milk on the nipple. It was filled with lukewarm water. Having done her extra duty, the old woman went back to her seat and immediately dozed off again, her interest in my nighttime activities taking a poor second place to her need for sleep. I found a chair and sat down to feed the baby. The baby was stronger than I thought. He sucked the bottle vigorously and, pacing himself, continued until it was empty.

As I held the baby, I looked at his wizened face, wishing for him a life I feared he would never enjoy. I wanted him to live and laugh and feel sunshine, but I knew he was a very sick baby. Sad and tired, I returned upstairs to lie on my cot.

As I lay down, I suddenly realized that the guns were silent. The war had been fought to a temporary halt. Did the war stop in the early hours of every morning, I wondered, just before sleep claimed me.

In the morning I dressed quickly and ran downstairs to the nursery, concerned and wanting to check on the little boy. His eyes were sunken, as was his fontanel. He had bad diarrhea and was dehydrating before our eyes. His lips were dry and cracked, flecked with traces of dried blood; I feared he would die without proper medical treatment. He desperately needed an IV.

We asked Sister Marie if the baby could go with us to Saigon. Perhaps Ilse could work another miracle. The nun shook her head sadly and told us no. His mother lived in a leper colony miles outside the city, and like her son, she was gravely ill. The child had been cared for by an elderly aunt, who had sold all of her meager belongings to feed him. The aunt came to visit him almost every day, and she loved him very much. I felt grateful for this much. At least he had someone who cared.

Sister Marie told me that the child was eighteen months old. I could see decayed teeth in his mouth, but I was disconcerted that a child of that age could weigh less than ten pounds.

Sister Marie and Christie would choose three babies to take to Rosemary's home in Saigon. Christie walked silently with the sister past each crib, forced to accept the untenable, choosing only three to travel south with us to new lives. They would have a better chance in life, while those who remained behind would have to continue playing in this dismal lottery of life and death. Christie passed up the reasonably healthy newborns and instead chose the sick, those that needed immediate medical attention.

Once the choices had been made, we prepared to leave Qui Nhon. The sisters seemed genuinely sorry to see us leave, and I hugged them all dearly, just like old friends. I thanked them so much for their help in caring for Jenny and Thanh and promised to continue sending whatever aid I could from America. They would continue to write to us, and we tearfully said our good-byes.

The flight back to Saigon was depressing. The plane bumped and swayed, much as it had on our outward journey, but by then I was used to the uncertain movements of the old aircraft, and I had other things on my mind.

The rain beating down nonstop while in Qui Nhon had taken the edge off my mood. I felt downcast, and the feeling was made worse by having seen firsthand the enormity of the task that faced the ever-cheerful sisters. I respected their courage and tenacity, but I wondered how long they could continue to save babies without dramatically increased funding. I resolved to redouble my fund-raising efforts in America.

The mood in the plane's cabin was somber; we sat silently, lost in our own thoughts. Finally, Steve suggested that we name the babies. Christie invited Steve to do the honors, and Steve, trying to lighten the atmosphere, proposed naming them "Winkin," "Blinkin" and "Nod." We thought about the nursery rhyme and cheered up a little. Looking at the babies, we all agreed, and so three more babies were named.

I looked at the tiny baby, now called Blinkin, asleep in my arms. It seemed strange that such a little baby belonged to no one. Blinkin was on the first stage of a journey that could take him to another country and a loving family. I was grateful to have participated in some small way.

The morning after our return from Qui Nhon, I awoke early and lay in bed, thinking about all I had seen in the last few weeks. I listened to the sounds of Saigon awakening after the curfew ended. Hundreds of motorbikes, cars and trucks kicked to life within a few minutes. Engines coughed and roared, horns blared, and the chatter of people on the move began in earnest.

The city's public address system started playing scratchy patriotic music through tinny loudspeakers mounted on street corners, reminding the populace that another day had begun. Within a few short minutes, life in Saigon was moving forward at its usual frenetic pace.

The center was stirring around me. Babies cried, and I heard child care workers chatting as they bathed the infants and gave them their morning feeds. Another day had begun at To Am. I luxuriated in the warmth of the bed for a few minutes longer, thinking about my day's work. I thought of Joanna and Thanh. I decided to visit them immediately and find out what progress had been made in obtaining their passports.

After a quick piece of bread smeared with peanut butter, I found Elaine and told her I was going to Allambie to check on my children and would be back to help later in the day.

I took a motorbike across the city and arrived at Allambie charged with enthusiasm. Inside, I went to visit Joanna and Thanh. Perhaps it was my imagination, but Joanna seemed friendlier that day. At least she let me look at her without throwing herself to the floor in tears. Thanh was shy, but beginning to enjoy my attention.

After playing with Thanh for a while, I carried him inside and went in search of one of the nurses. I asked about the children's passports, and a nurse suggested that I should speak with Sister Mary Nelle, who worked at another of Rosemary's centers, called Newhaven.

After a quick good-bye to the kids, I went to Newhaven, where Margaret and Sister Mary Nelle Gage, from Colorado, oversaw the adoption paperwork. Rosemary was out of the country, so they explained what had been done and what must yet be done to obtain passports for Joanna and Thanh. They were very busy with so many adoption cases and trying to ensure the smooth running of the centers in Rosemary's absence, so I told them I would do the legwork if they pointed me in the right direction.

Sister Mary Nelle hesitated, then explained that dealing with the bureaucrats could be a very frustrating job. She said they were all very sure of their own importance and fiercely protected their fiefdoms. The best approach was to be courteous and polite, respectful and obsequious. Being pushy never worked. They had the ability to delay the issuing of passports for months if they thought an applicant was insulting their position.

I listened carefully to her advice and promised to make the applications on my own, being careful not to upset anybody in the Ministry building.

I traveled by taxi, timing my arrival to coincide with the end of the siesta, a daily ritual in Vietnamese life. The taxi ride took more of my rapidly dwindling funds, but I was anxious to move the applications along faster so that I could take my children home.

When the taxi pulled up outside the Ministry of the Interior building, I was surprised to see a decrepit, one-story structure, surrounded by sandbags, barbed wire and armed soldiers. The place looked like a poor man's fortress. Taken aback by the shoddy appearance, I walked diffidently toward the entrance, watched by a number of soldiers. They let me pass without comment, and I entered the gloomy interior.

Inside, I followed Sister Mary Nelle's instructions and entered the first door on the right. The small room was filled with other passport applicants, milling around the dozen or so desks jammed into the cramped office. The room was very hot, and the swirling fans made no impression on the cloying heat, other than requiring every piece of paper to be weighted down against the hot breeze.

I watched from the doorway, trying to make sense of the scene before me. Officials sat imperiously behind desks while desperate applicants told their stories. The stone-faced bureaucrats seemed indifferent to the begging, pleading applicants, all speaking rapid-fire Vietnamese as they sought to gain attention for their own case. The sights and noise nearly defeated me before I started. What chance did I have of getting two passports when I didn't even speak Vietnamese?

I sucked in my breath and approached one of the desks. The man sitting behind it saw my approach and jumped as though his chair had been electrified. Without looking at me, he walked away. I stared after him in despair, but was determined to stand my ground until he, or somebody else, came back. Finally, a young uniformed woman approached and asked in hesitant English if she could help.

Relieved that at least somebody official could understand me, I blurted out my story. I told her that I was adopting two young Vietnamese orphans, and I needed to get their passports and exit visas so that I could take them to America with me. From the look on her face, it was obvious that my simple speech had exceeded her limited English comprehension. One or two words must have been understood, and she repeated "adoption" and "America." Frowning, she told me that it would take three months. As she turned to go I fought back tears, feeling I had failed at the first hurdle. Suddenly afraid, I carefully moved toward the departing official and politely asked her if I could see the person in charge. She looked at me for a moment, then simply pointed to swinging doors at the end of the office. She turned on her heel with an air of finality—I was on my own.

Determined to salvage something positive from my trip, I walked through the doors and entered a smaller, quieter office. In the corner, a man worked at some papers on his desk and looked up at me with an inquiring expression. I walked over to him and told him that I needed to talk to him. He ignored me and returned his attention to the paperwork littering his desk.

I walked closer to the desk and stood there silently looking at him. After a few minutes of embarrassing silence, it became apparent that I wasn't going to leave. He sighed and motioned for me to sit. I sat on the edge of the hard seat and explained my plight. As I conveyed my predicament, I handed him the pictures of my children, hoping they would touch his heart. The minutes passed slowly as he peered at the pictures.

When I had finished my story and made my plea for their passports, he considered things for a moment before telling me that it might be possible to get their passports in a month or so. I responded that I had to get the children to America soon because they were sick. Suddenly, he interrupted my flow of words with a jerk of his hand. He told me that a statement from a doctor confirming that the children were sick would be of great help and would allow the Ministry to process the passports immediately.

I was so happy, I could have kissed him. I smiled and told him I would get the statements and come back soon. I left the Ministry building with a feeling of elation, sure that I could get the necessary statements from a doctor.

I caught a passing motorbike and whizzed back to Allambie, where I explained to the nurses what had happened. They were very encouraging and told me that I should take Joanna and Thanh to Hoan My Clinic, where the doctors were familiar with Rosemary's children.

I gathered up the kids without taking the time to pay attention to their sensitive feelings; I didn't want to undo the spark of trust, but I had to get them to the doctor's office as soon as I could. Within minutes, both children were screaming, Joanna because she was afraid, and Thanh simply because Joanna was.

After a hot taxi ride to the clinic, I took the two scared kids inside and carried them, wailing and squirming, into the examining room. The doctor stood there, obviously unhappy with this disorderly invasion of his office.

I explained about our need for a medical statement confirming that the children were sick so that the government would issue passports for them. I passed him their medical notes that I'd brought from Allambie, and reading them closely, he nodded sagely. It obviously wasn't the first time he'd made such an examination.

He started with Joanna. After looking at her briefly and listening to her heart, he looked up triumphantly and pronounced that she had a heart murmur, a condition that needed urgent attention. It was enough. Joanna would get her statement. And then the doctor turned his attention to Thanh.

After looking Thanh up and down and noting his frail condition, he consulted Thanh's medical notes before listening to his chest. I told him that Thanh had tuberculosis and was about to start a course of treatment. The doctor was satisfied. He wrote a note confirming that the children needed to leave the country immediately for urgent medical attention.

It had been a long, hard day for the three of us, but at last I had the key that I hoped would unlock the door, allowing my children to start their journey to America and their new family.

Early the next morning, I walked purposefully into the supervisor's office. He looked over at me, and I handed him the doctor's note, written on official stationery. He read the note and nodded. He picked up the birth certificate that had been submitted with the application for Thanh's passport. He looked at the certificate and studied one of the small black-and-white passport-sized photographs that lay on his desk.

It was obvious that he saw the deception. Thanh was small, but he couldn't be only two months old, as claimed on his birth certificate. He asked me if I could explain the obvious discrepancy between the age on the certificate and the age of the boy in the picture. I took a deep breath; it was make or break time, and it struck me that now was the time to tell the whole truth.

He listened to my story about dying babies, obstinate clerks and the nuns' desperation to help this sickly child. He nodded as I was talking, and I felt I was getting a sympathetic hearing—I wasn't telling him anything he didn't know. Finally, he told me that everything would be fine. He signed a couple of forms and stamped everything in sight with an official-looking red seal.

Last of all, he penned a short note in Vietnamese on a scrap of paper that he placed in my hand, before waving me away and wishing me good luck.

I walked out of his office, back through the swinging doors into the rush of the general office. I was elated and knew that the elusive passports would soon be within reach. I didn't know how to thank my benefactor enough.

I looked around the busy office, not knowing where to go next. A clerk came up to me and reached for the files, and I gave him the supervisor's note. He read the note and seemed to decide that he would be my guide through the rest of the application procedures.

He took me from desk to desk, each time handing over the files and rattling off instructions to the person sitting in the chair. At each desk, another clerk added yet more rubber stamps to some form or another. With more visits to clerks still to come, my guide looked at me. He must have noticed how flustered and hot I looked, or maybe he was tired of having me tag along.

He took me to a wooden bench and pointed to it. Gratefully, I sat down as he rushed off to get more stamps in the files. I soon lost sight of him in the melee of bodies in the room. I had resigned the fate of my kids to this unnamed clerk who seemed to have made it his purpose in life to help me get the passports we needed. I didn't know how much progress was being made. Yesterday I'd been told the applications would take three months, and the supervisor had told me one month. I wished that someone could have told me how much progress the efficient-looking clerk was making. Was he saving me hours, days or weeks?

As lunchtime approached, I was getting anxious. I had no idea who this man was, and the thought of going back to the supervisor with another hard luck story was daunting.

Just as my nervousness was peaking, the clerk reappeared through the press of bodies. He quickly walked over, smiling, as he waved two green passports in his hands. Proudly, he opened each passport and showed me the names and the photographs, as if assuring me that he had got it all right. Then he pointed out the red stamps of authority—the exit visas. He pressed the passports into my hands.

What could I do to thank this super clerk? I could never have succeeded without his help, and I thanked him profusely, nearly crying with delight. As I was leaving, I turned back, smiled, and waved. He turned away, and I feared that I had embarrassed my Good Samaritan.

Later that evening, back at To Am, Elaine and I celebrated my good fortune. We feasted on some luxuries that I'd bought on the black market: Ritz crackers, V-8 juice, and a tin of sardines. Steve came by, anxious to share our good news, and wanted to see the passports for himself. He was amazed at how fast I'd managed to get them, knowing how slow officialdom usually moved in Vietnam.

Steve and Elaine pressed me to tell them the story, so I recounted the day's events, highlighting the help of the supervisor and the super clerk who had guided me through the process. Steve was amazed and asked me how much I'd paid the clerk for his help. Suddenly I remembered the man's stare as I left the office, and it hit me that he had expected me to pay him for his help! I had never even considered the thought of it. My face went red in a deep blush as I realized my blunder. Bribing an official was something that had never entered my mind.

Word had spread quickly to the other nurseries, and everybody knew that I had the passports for Joanna and Thanh. Nurses from the other centers telephoned and congratulated me. I booked an international call to Tom to tell him that everything was completed and that we would all be home to celebrate Thanksgiving together. I went to bed that night feeling elated. Soon my family would be united.

The following morning, Margaret telephoned and asked me to visit her at Newhaven; she had a favor to ask. When I arrived, I was shocked to find her pale and resting on a cot, an IV attached to her arm. She smiled wanly, assuring me she would be up and about in a few days.

She explained that the centers were desperately short of money, more so than usual, and that they had no money to buy milk for the babies. She went on to ask if I would cash in my return ticket so that they could buy the milk they needed. They could get me a free escort pass home on a Pan Am flight if I would escort another three children, along with Joanna and Thanh, to the States.

One problem, she added, was that the other children wouldn't be ready to leave for a few more days, so I would have to delay my departure until then. I never hesitated, and I hid my sadness as I realized I would not be home in time for Thanksgiving with my family. I handed my ticket to Margaret and returned for another day's work at To Am.

I telephoned Tom and relayed the news to him. He was very pleased that I had the passports for Joanna and Thanh, but not so happy when I told him that I was delaying my return. I explained the problems at the center, which he quickly understood and he told me that he realized I had to stay and help. He reassured me that our kids were fine but missing me greatly, and looking forward to meeting their new brother and sister.

The delay proved to be a blessing in disguise. Within hours of my returning to To Am, the nursery was struck by a deadly round of illness that ran through the babies like wildfire. Vomiting and diarrhea, probably from a viral infection, threatened to dehydrate them, which could easily lead to death.

Ilse arrived to help and surveyed the situation. Looking at all the sick babies, she prescribed boiled carrot water, claiming that the vitamins and the liquids would give the babies the strength to get through the infection.

Following Ilse's instructions, the Vietnamese staff rushed off to buy carrots. Soon the nursery smelled of boiling carrots. The staff mashed them and strained the bright orange liquid into sterile bottles. Ilse told us to feed each baby only carrot juice until the diarrhea stopped. One by one, the babies responded and were getting better. I couldn't help but wonder what my nursing instructors would have to say about this.

Elaine and I were busy all Thanksgiving Day with the sick babies. As we worked, we reminisced about other Thanksgiving Days spent in more normal circumstances. The day passed in a blur of sick babies, and in the late evening, Elaine and I sank into chairs, exhausted.

We heard the bell ringing at the outer gate. Wearily, we walked together through the compound and opened the gate. Several American women stood outside, smiling and holding two aluminum foil-covered plates which they offered to us as they wished us a happy holiday. They told us they had decided to share their Thanksgiving dinner with all of the nurses in the centers.

We thanked them for their hospitality and kindness; their appearance made us think more of home and the families we were missing. We ate the meals quietly, savoring the American-style food, convinced that no Thanksgiving dinner had ever tasted so good.

On the day of our departure, I arrived at Allambie early to prepare my children. Joanna had been told by the staff that she was leaving, and I sensed her fear. The young Vietnamese woman who had acted as mother to Thanh for the last three months cuddled my son one last time before handing him over to me.

Our departure from Tan Son Nhut Airport was harried. Another American escort was taking five orphans, and I had Joanna and Thanh as well as the other three orphans I was escorting. Nurses from the center helped us through the maze of the airport, handling check-in and immigration.

As we walked towards the departure gate, Steve appeared and reached to take Thanh Steven Clark into his arms. I watched them as they said their final good-byes. I shook his hand; he would never know how grateful Tom and I were for his help and comfort during the past months. We promised to keep in touch, and I said I would send him photographs of all my children together.

All too soon, the loudspeaker announced that it was time to depart. We walked across the hot tarmac to the waiting plane and entered the comfortable, air-conditioned interior. The nurses were allowed on board to assist us, and a couple of stewardesses helped us settle the ten children into the seats before the nurses had to leave. We heard the cabin door slam shut, and the plane readied for takeoff. The babies were all crying, and I only had time for a quick glance out of the window toward the airport.

The screaming babies demanded our attention as the plane rolled down the runway. I was sad to be leaving Vietnam, yet eager to see my family again and to bring Joanna and Thanh home at last. There was no doubt in my mind that I would return to Vietnam. I had intended to make only a brief visit to arrange for my children to leave, but the country and the people had captured my soul.

Ha Thi Thu Loan (Jenny) in Qui Nhon, Vietnam 1972.

Tom and Cherie Clark (center) with FCVN volunteers, waiting for Jenny's arrival at Denver's Stapleton Airport, February 15, 1973.

Cherie and Jenny meeting at Stapleton Airport.

Jenny at home in Illinois.

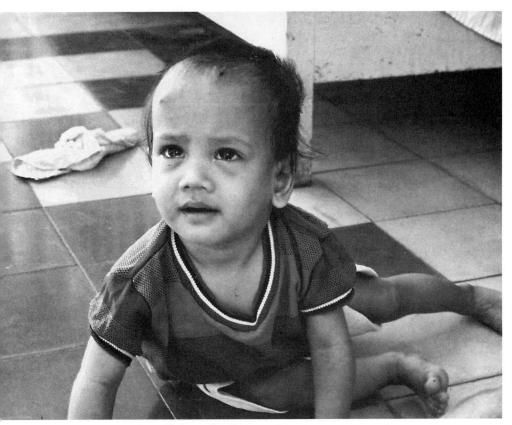

Nguyen Phuc Loi Thanh, Qui Nhon 1973.

oanna at Allambie Center in Saigon with
teve Johnson.

Joanna at Allambie Center.

Steven Johnson with Thanh in Qui Nhon.

Ross Meador

Children in orphanages of Vietnam.

children in orphanage.

Steven Johnson with Minh, (Andrew Pettis).

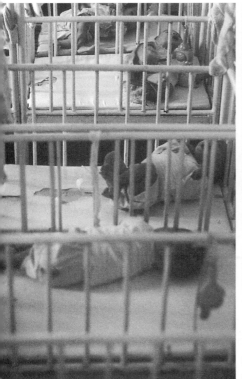

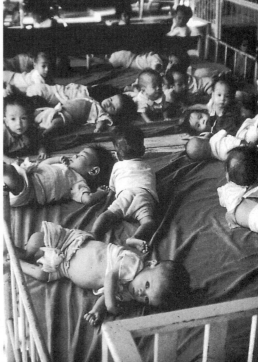

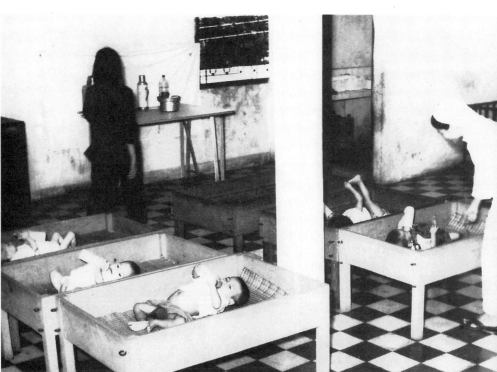

Rosa de Lima Orphanage on the outskirts of Saigon.

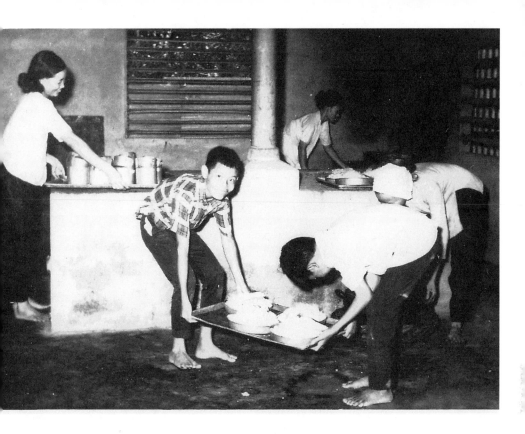

Rose de Lima Orphanage.

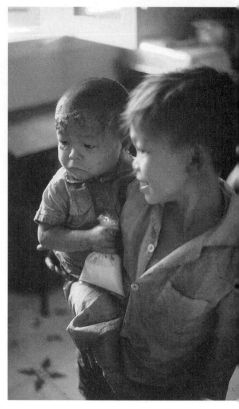

Ross Meador

Children in orphanages.

Ross Meador

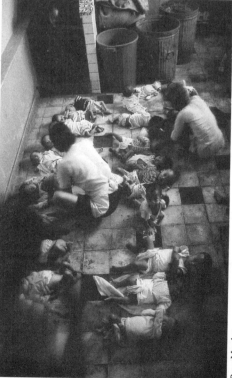

Ross Meador

Christmas 1973 in Illinois: (from left) Ron, Beth, Tom holding Brian and Jenny, Cherie holding Joanna and Thanh, Dan standing.

Chapter Five

*A*fter their arrival in America, both Joanna and Thanh spent a month isolated in the hospital; both of them were very sick. Thanh's tuberculosis was worse than we had thought, and Joanna had multiple medical problems that needed close supervision. It took a toll on Tom and me as we juggled work, hospital visits, and kids at home. However, with excellent medical care, the two children began to thrive.

We were very happy when the doctors gave them the all-clear and we brought them home from the hospital. As busy as we were with so many small children, our lives were rich and full. Now our family was comprised of Ron, Dan, Joanna, Beth, Jenny, Brian and Thanh. We were a complete unit, and over the next few weeks we worked hard to help the latest newcomers adapt and feel loved.

Everything was new to them. They had arrived in mid-seventies America from a life in a deprived and war-torn Vietnamese orphanage. Little things were so important. They could have juice or fruit whenever they wanted; they played with real toys, and for the first time in their short lives they watched and laughed at cartoons on television.

Joanna took an instant liking to Tom, and adjusted more easily than I would have predicted to life outside the center, although her moods continued to swing easily between laughter and an anger generated by fear. Thanh thrived on attention, and fortunately, we had plenty of family members with the time to provide the loving care he so desperately needed.

As the weeks passed they both learned English quickly, mainly from their siblings. Soon they were talking, laughing and arguing with the other kids; orphanage life seemed only a distant memory to them.

Tom had progressed to a good job as an IBM field engineer and provided well for us. I attempted to adapt to the role of homemaker, but after my trip to Vietnam, I was restless. I watched other mothers and women in the supermarkets, chattering in the beauty shops, and sharing opinions at PTA meetings. I tried to join in with them, but I felt removed from suburban life. After the vibrancy and excitement of Vietnam, I knew I could never be content as a housewife in the Midwest.

The faces of the children in the orphanages haunted me through the days and nights. I wondered how the children I had come to know and love were doing. I wondered if they were healthy and if they had traveled to their waiting families. I felt that I was missing so much.

All I could think of was returning to Vietnam. It seemed impossible at first, and for days I tried to ignore the thoughts. But the arrival of letters from Vietnam reinforced the conviction that was growing in me: I had to go back. I sat for hours, looking out over the snow-covered lawn, daydreaming about Vietnam. As time passed the idea took shape; slowly but surely I knew that I had to do something to put my thoughts into action.

During the long winter evenings I broached the idea with Tom. Initially he was hesitant—he had a good career with a major corporation, and we had seven beautiful children; why would we uproot ourselves and go to a country in such turmoil? But gradually, over the weeks that followed, he caught my enthusiasm, and from then on it was only a short step before we were discussing the practicalities of a move to Vietnam.

Just before Christmas 1973, I received a letter from the sisters at Qui Nhon, telling me that the "old man" baby I had snuggled that long night had died. Late on Christmas Eve, as the children lay sleeping and a full moon glinted on the snow outside the bedroom window, I looked at the Christmas tree and its pile of waiting presents, and I cried for his lost life.

I wrote to Steve and shared with him my dream of returning to Vietnam and bringing my family with me. The flow of letters increased as I outlined my dreams. Steve answered all our questions positively, confirming that houses were easy to come by and that the American Embassy School was wonderful. Suddenly the plan was moving forward and taking shape, becoming more of a reality.

The war seemed a distant problem, and we were confident that our children would be safe. After all, there were other families residing in Saigon, and our children would be attending the Embassy school with them.

❧

I was in regular contact with Cheryl Markson in Denver. Our FCVN chapter's fund-raising in Illinois was going well, and I was sending a constant stream of donations and supplies to them.

Cheryl was now the proud mother of a half-American child, Thi Anh, who had joined her and her husband, Mick, a few months earlier. We shared a passion for the children of Vietnam, and it was no surprise that we became close friends.

Cheryl had also introduced me to Carol Westlake, a Colorado nurse who had recently been to Vietnam and had escorted babies home to their families in America. She and her husband, Al, who was president of the FCVN board, had already adopted several children. Carol was down-to-earth, diligent, full of energy, good at organizing people, and had a great sense of humor.

Cheryl and Carol understood my dream of returning to work with the orphans and abandoned babies. Because both had adopted Vietnamese children, they knew firsthand the deep bonding between the children and their adoptive parents, as well as the mysterious love of the country where our children were born.

Meanwhile things were evolving with the FCVN adoption organization. I was unaware of the details of events in Colorado, but during the course of our phone conversations I learned that FCVN would soon divide into two separate organizations.

The offshoot organization, led by Wende Grant of Boulder, Colorado, would continue to arrange adoptions through Rosemary Taylor. Wende was well known and rightly respected for her role in helping organize the adoption of many Vietnamese children. Wende and Rosemary registered as a licensed adoption agency in Colorado, called Friends For All Children, or FFAC.

Friends of Children of Vietnam had registered as a licensed agency in 1973. With Rosemary's resignation, FCVN was left without representation in Vietnam. The vacancy came at an opportune time for me, because by now my plans to return to Vietnam were in high gear. Cheryl and Carol proposed me to the FCVN Board, who subsequently agreed that I would become one of their representatives in Vietnam. Suddenly my dreams had a concrete foundation upon which we could build.

IBM granted Tom a humanitarian leave of absence, starting the following summer. He would remain behind in Illinois to sell our new home, donating the sale profits to FCVN to help fund our work.

Tom and I accepted the titles of Overseas Directors for Friends of Children of Vietnam. Carol was appointed American Adoption Director, and Cheryl became the Executive Director. The formal titles belied the combination of compassion and enthusiasm that charged our mission. We were all one hundred percent committed to the task before us.

FCVN needed money, and we set about raising it. Fortunately, FCVN had continued to grow until we had volunteers in nearly every state. The chapters worked long, hard hours to raise money. One day Suzie Cummings, of the St. Louis Chapter of FCVN, called to tell me that they had raised the first thousand dollars toward our airfare to Vietnam. We were thrilled. Our own Illinois chapter worked diligently and, dollar by dollar, we scraped together the needed funds.

Ross Meador, a young man who had already traveled extensively in Mexico, where he'd volunteered to help the poor and sick, heard about FCVN. He visited the group in Denver and offered to help. Ross was nineteen years old, an articulate and caring person; he would prove to be an integral part of our Vietnam team.

In March 1974, Ross flew to Vietnam to arrange customs clearance of some supplies that FCVN had already sent. He did well and after sorting out the paperwork logjam, he took the supplies around to the orphanages.

My sister, Sue Walter, also departed for Vietnam in March. Sue had just turned twenty-one and was eager to join our volunteer effort. We were still gathering money to fly to Vietnam and to rent a center, but decided to use some funds so that Sue could leave in advance to join Ross and Steve.

Sue was eager and compassionate. She had been deeply touched by the plight of the Vietnamese children and had fallen in love with our three adopted children, her nieces and nephew.

The trip to Vietnam was a first for her—her first airplane flight and her first trip out of America. Her initial flight did not connect with her international flight to Saigon, so she would be arriving a day late and was worried that she would not be met by Steve or Ross. On the flight the next day, she was lucky to be sitting near Ed Bradley, then a war correspondent. Once in Saigon Bradley helped her locate "My Friend's House," a children's center where she would stay until our own center was organized.

Finally, in April, all our arrangements were made, and we had raised sufficient cash for our tickets; it was time to leave Illinois.

Leaving America was difficult for the kids. They had to leave Tom's family and all their school friends, playmates, cousins, and precious belongings behind. On the last day, the children said a tearful goodbye to their dog, Stormy. The car was filled with crying kids as we drove to the airport.

When we arrived at the Quad City airport, local newspapers and a television crew had turned up to record our leaving. The local media had been supportive of our fund-raising activities and continued their support right up to our departure.

A reporter interviewed me briefly, and I could tell from the tenor of his questions that he thought I was crazy. He couldn't understand why anybody would voluntarily leave safe, middle-class America to live in a country torn by war, knowing that America had already pulled the plug. Taking my seven children with me only compounded his inability to understand. By that time I had grown tired of trying to justify our reasons for moving to Vietnam in a way that would appear logical to anyone outside the adoption world.

Tom and I hugged at the gate, and the children crowded around us, crying and telling their father to hurry and join us. Tom promised to sell the house and be with us at the earliest opportunity. As I led my crying children away, I couldn't look back at Tom. I had to look forward—if I'd have turned around to wave a final good-bye, I'm not sure I could have left.

On the plane I looked at my children, strapped into the seats, ready for departure. Ron, at eight, was the oldest; five of the children were under the age of five, and here we were, taking off with one-way tickets and five hundred dollars in my pocket. I was hopeful that, once safely installed in Vietnam, the children would soon make new friends. I knew they would have adventures that they would remember for the rest of their lives.

We flew to Denver first and spent the night with the Marksons. This gave Cheryl, Carol and me some time to talk and make plans. The Markson and Clark kids were so close in age that they had a great time together before we departed for Saigon the next day.

The journey to Vietnam was long. By the time we reached Saigon, I was worn out with trying to amuse the little ones. The sound of the wheels lowering was a welcome relief as we made the final approach to Tan Son Nhut Airport in Saigon.

We all cheered up as the plane landed, and the kids were excited when soldiers boarded the plane and inspected the passengers; it was their first sight of uniformed soldiers carrying automatic weapons. Ron and Dan leaned forward to have a good look at the guns.

As we walked down the steps onto Vietnamese soil, the heat, sounds and sights of Saigon delighted me. I breathed deeply and felt exhilarated as the often-remembered smells brought back memories of my previous trip. The heat was far greater than during my visit in November.

We caused quite a stir at the Immigration desk as I placed five American passports on one desk and three Vietnamese on another. I had Thanh and Brian in my arms, while Joanna and Jenny clutched my legs, scared by the unfamiliarity of the situation. Ron, Dan and Beth stood nearby, exchanging stares of wonder with a crowd that had gathered to watch our unusual arrival.

An armed Vietnamese soldier approached us. He motioned to my children and said, "Are all these babies your babies?"

I nodded yes, and he shook his head in disbelief. "I see many times babies like this leave Vietnam—I never did see any coming," he laughed.

We passed through Customs and Immigration without a hitch and joined the crowd in the arrivals hall.

The kids were nervous at the press of so many people and so much noise, but excited at the prospect of seeing their Aunt Sue. While I collected the bags, the kids spotted her in the crowd and rushed forward for a joyful welcome into her waiting arms.

Steve and Sue greeted me and helped us make our way to the exit. As we were walking, they introduced me to Ross; it was good to put a face to the name I had heard so much about. Ross was a tall, lanky, smiling, mustached blond wearing a Hawaiian-style print shirt.

They introduced me to the fourth member of our reception party, Le Thi Bach Thuy, who had recently become FCVN's new social worker in Saigon. Thuy had attended college in Minnesota and her English was good. The walk to the van was very animated as everybody tried to talk at once. Steve carried Joanna and Thanh, claiming they had doubled in weight in the five months we'd been away. Ron and Dan ran around, obviously very excited and pleased with their first impressions of the country. I was so happy to be back in Vietnam, with my friends and now my family.

Thuy was a lovely person, and as we drove from the airport to the newly acquired Center in a rental van, we introduced ourselves properly. Thuy told me she was an adoptive mother also, with a daughter, Kiki, who was the same age as Beth and Joanna.

After a few minutes, we pulled into a driveway off busy Truong Minh Ky Street in Gia Dinh, a suburb of Saigon. The brief view of Vietnam's colorful and lively streets left my children bubbling with anticipation, and they wanted to explore the exciting city straightaway. I was as happy as the kids, and had watched the street scenes passing in front of us with my own barely concealed excitement. When we pulled into the driveway and I saw a small blue sign on the iron gate that read "Friends of Children of Viet Nam," I felt happier than I had in years; I had finally come home.

Inside the gates we all piled out of the van and rushed forward, eager to explore our new home. The villa was stately and large, with bright airy rooms and many windows that would catch the afternoon breeze. The bedrooms were large, and there were plenty of bathrooms. At the back of the main villa stood a separate three-story building that we immediately earmarked as the toddlers' quarters. The house was everything I could have hoped for and more.

It wasn't until I was walking through the rooms with Ross and Sue that a major drawback became apparent. The villa came complete with its owner, who, with her retinue of personal staff, would remain as our sitting tenants. An elderly French lady who had lived in Vietnam most of her life, she was a remnant of the former French colonists, with the breeding and imperious arrogance that went hand-in-hand with that historical era.

Though we were surprised by her presence, her assurances that she was about to depart for retirement in the south of France allayed our fears of using the villa as a nursery for lots of crying babies and noisy, lively children.

That first night, as we led my children into their bedrooms to help them get ready for bed, Sue and I warned them that they would hear gunshots in the street below and loud booms in the distance. We explained that for the most part the gunshots on the street were nothing to fear. The young soldiers took delight sometimes in firing their guns at rats, or did it simply to remind people that they were on watch. Suddenly my children all wanted to sleep in the same room with me!

Later I lay in bed, listening to the sounds of my children sleeping around me. The sounds of gunfire in the streets below brought back memories of my first visit. My last thought before I drifted off to sleep was of all the hard work ahead of us.

The next morning we woke early to the sounds of our new neighborhood coming to life: a rooster crowing outside the villa, and women vendors on the street below, selling food to local residents. The children were up quickly and couldn't wait to explore their new world. They bounded down the winding stairs to the kitchen, looking for breakfast.

The French woman's cook had offered to prepare breakfast, and there were mounds of fresh scrambled eggs, heavily laced with red-hot chilies. They sat around the scrubbed wooden kitchen table, laughing as they tried to eat their breakfast with wooden chopsticks.

That day we took the children on a tour of the city. They were agog at the noise, color and liveliness of the streets. It was nothing like the life they had left behind in America, and they enjoyed every minute of it.

Chattering incessantly, they pointed out the sights around them. The children were aghast when they saw the squalid houses built on stilts above the filthy water of the river and realized that entire families actually made their homes in them. The shacks were falling apart, roughly patched together with tin cans, cardboard, and scraps of wood and metal.

Later that evening, back at the villa, Sue, Ross and I had settled down for a discussion about the future when we were interrupted by screams from outside. Dan had tripped and fallen while racing with Ron. I took a quick look at his arm—it was obviously broken and we needed to get him to a doctor immediately. I had no idea where the nearest hospital was, and we had no transport available.

Ross rushed out to try to find a taxi, but to no avail. The best he could come up with was a motorbike driver willing to take Dan and me to medical help. The driver took one look at Dan's misshapen arm and motioned us to hop onto the bike. Within a few seconds we were on our way.

The clinic we were taken to was awful, but I didn't speak the language and this was the best I could find on my own. The doctor didn't set Dan's arm or even attempt to clean the dirt and blood from the injured area. I pointed out the dirty cuts, but he just brushed away my concerns. I knew that the heat and humidity would cause infection within days if the wounds weren't properly treated, but the doctor, who spoke no English, ignored my frantic sign language and applied a cast right over the unclean break.

The next day I phoned Steve and told him what had happened to Dan. He told me that the best hospital for foreigners was not far from us. Following his advice, I took Dan to the Seventh Day Adventist Hospital, a facility with competent, English-speaking staff. When we arrived and told our story they removed the cast, cleaned the wounds and reset Dan's broken bone, before applying a proper cast.

Poor Dan was brave throughout the long, painful procedure. Later at home he commented, "I wonder what my classmates will say when they find out I was wounded in Vietnam?"

❦

I was anxious to get to work. I met Ross, Sue and Thuy in the dining room to evaluate progress to date and to determine what we had to do before we could open the nursery and start accepting orphans. I'd brought a copy of the adoption license and my letter of appointment from Denver, and I thought that we were ready to start—but Ross and Sue had already run into problems.

They told me that the American government agencies in Saigon could be the biggest hurdle we had to overcome. Ross had already met with some USAID officials, and his report was disappointing. If what he said was accurate, the license on the table in front of us would prove to be worthless.

He said that the U.S. Embassy and the U.S. Agency for International Development (USAID) in Saigon thought that there were enough adoption agencies working in Vietnam, and they seemed to be determined to keep us from opening our center. That attitude made no sense to me, especially since USAID in Washington had been so helpful to FCVN. I was sure that this was simply a misunderstanding that could soon be resolved. With nearly two million orphans and abandoned babies in South Vietnam, how could there possibly be too much help?

Ross had already set up a meeting with the USAID officer in charge, and we were due to meet at his office early the next morning. I wanted to go to the meeting prepared, so we spent the day formalizing our plans on paper.

We made an outline of the existing FCVN programs. Our Foster Orphanage Program was already under way, helping to aid orphanages in the provinces. FCVN chapters across America had "adopted" individual orphanages and were sending them monthly sponsorship funds to care for the orphans.

We were eager to start an adoption center, backed by the adoption licenses already obtained in Vietnam and America. We were already supporting many children who were ready to be adopted and had families waiting for them in America.

FCVN was essentially a grassroots operation. Nevertheless, we were impressed with the way our plans spelled out when we committed them to paper. We didn't have millions of dollars to spend, but we had the backing of many families throughout America who were willing to help Vietnamese orphans and support us in our fledgling endeavors. We were sure USAID officials would also help us, when we properly explained our intentions.

Thuy, Ross and I went to the meeting at USAID with high hopes. We met with Jay Ruoff, a senior USAID official in Saigon. His office was plush and smart, a quiet, cool den that sheltered him from the noise, heat and bustle of the city. Mr. Ruoff was reserved; his greeting was formal and as cold as the temperature in his air-conditioned office.

Nonetheless, I enthusiastically launched into a description of the FCVN programs. As I was talking, I could tell that he wasn't empathizing. I wasn't making any impression on this career professional, and his dispassionate stare unnerved me. The compassion of the hundreds of American households that supported FCVN didn't move him at all. When I had finished presenting the proposal, the room was silent for a moment.

He looked at the three of us, drew a breath, and explained that USAID in Washington, D.C., had just allocated more than seven million dollars to provide to child welfare services in Vietnam and make it easier for American citizens to adopt war orphans. He told us in no uncertain terms that there were already enough organizations working in Vietnam. Many, he said, were large organizations that had access to almost unlimited funding.

He leaned forward, as if to impart a very personal message: "The simple truth is you are not needed."

I tried to explain that we were not like some of the larger agencies that were staffed with ranks of committee members and had very high administrative budgets. FCVN was made up of unpaid volunteers, with a practically zero overhead. Every dollar we received by donation went to help the orphans; we didn't have the huge administrative costs eating into a budget that was supposed to be for the children.

It was obvious that we weren't getting anywhere; his mind had been made up before the meeting started.

We collected our papers and left his office. I was trembling with anger. FCVN had been working in Vietnam since 1967 and had always been treated very well by the Washington USAID staff, who encouraged us to continue our work in Vietnam. I couldn't understand why anyone would want to block us out of the picture.

Thuy, who had remained silent throughout the confrontation, erupted with a passionate rage as we walked out of the building. She tore into Ruoff, reminding us that we were in Vietnam, a free country ruled by its own democratic government. Why did Ruoff, a foreigner, believe that he had the authority to decide who could work here?

Thuy had raised a very important point. Ruoff was an advisor and administrator—he didn't speak for the Vietnamese government. Thuy had seemed so timid when I first met her, but her eyes held a defiant spark as she declared, "Who does he think he is!"

By the time we reached her old car, "Who does he think he is" had become a battle cry. We decided we would go directly to the Vietnamese and ask them if *they* wanted us to continue our work. It would be their decision, and we would go along with whatever they decided. We wouldn't be crushed by some American bureaucrat's on-the-spot policy making.

We drove from the USAID offices to the Ministry of Social Welfare to ask their opinion of our projects. Throughout the rest of the day, Thuy and I visited countless offices, talking with different administrators, until their faces and names blurred together in my tired mind.

The Vietnamese officials smiled so much, I had no way of knowing if they were impressed with our plans and programs or were just being polite—but at least they listened to us.

The rounds of impromptu meetings continued until the offices closed for the day, but the next morning we were back again at the Social Welfare Ministry offices, waiting for them to open. Our first meeting of the day was with Madam Quoi, a Vietnamese official, handpicked for her post by USAID. She politely offered us tea, but little else. In response to our presentation, she replied that she had already heard about us from USAID. She repeated Ruoff's message that we weren't needed because there were already enough adoption organizations in Vietnam.

Her reply only made us more determined. We left her office and continued talking with other Ministry officials. Throughout the day we kept moving up the ladder of officialdom. We met with Mr. Hien, the Director of Planning, who told us that the FCVN license was valid. He sent us to see Dr. Cao Xuan An, a senior powerbroker in the Ministry. We knew we had reached a very important official, and it was make-or-break time.

Dr. An, a cultured, attractive man with laughing eyes, listened intently to the outline of our plans. We finished by telling him that the local USAID office didn't want us to continue our work. In response to our pleas he picked up the telephone and began making several calls. He encouraged

Thuy and me to relax and assured us that this was a problem he could sort out. Most of the conversations were in Vietnamese, but I didn't need to understand the language to know that things were going our way. He and Thuy were both enjoying the discussion, and the atmosphere was light.

His final call was to USAID. The conversation was short and direct. Barely civil, Dr. An told the Americans that the FCVN license was valid, the Vietnamese government wanted us to work with the orphans, and that they should back off and not interfere with our plans. We were here with his Ministry's blessings.

As he hung up the telephone, he smiled at us. Then, as if it was the easiest decision of the day, he calmly said that we should continue our work in progress and begin our other programs immediately. We were triumphant and knew we had won the right to work in this country from the people who mattered the most—the Vietnamese.

Showering Dr. An with our thanks, we left the office and rushed back to the Center to share our good news with Ross and Sue. I had gone through some sleepless nights, concerned that this dream wasn't going to take off. The way was now clear for us to do the work that we knew was so desperately needed.

Now that we had established our legal right to work in Vietnam, I knew that we would stay in the country as long as possible. I quickly set about sorting out my own family's domestic arrangements. I enrolled Ron and Dan at the American Embassy School, which was located in a converted villa near the city's center. For my younger children, I found a small but excellent Montessori School, not far from our Center, that had American staff. The journeys to and from school would become the high spots of the day as they passed through the teeming streets.

With the government's blessing for our operations, we began furnishing the nursery and hiring staff. Sue had the responsibility for interviewing and hiring new employees. Among the new hires were two young women who were to become indispensable nurses: Hong, who had worked in the pediatrics ward at a Vietnamese hospital, and Anh, a third-year medical student. We planned that these two would train other women to become child care workers.

We bought some cribs with money that Steve's friends at ITT had donated. Carol had sent dozens of matching gowns and baby blankets from America. Ross had learned of a supply of surplus office equipment that had been left behind when the American military had pulled out. The equipment was available for the asking, so Ross applied for some of the things we needed. Soon we had an abundance of desks, tables and chairs. We painted some of the desks bright colors and installed them in the nursery.

Within three weeks of our arrival in the country, everything had come together, and our nursery was ready for occupation. We had decided that the first children we would bring in would be those who already had adoptive families waiting for them in America. While the rest of us continued preparations at the Center, Steve traveled to Qui Nhon to escort the first group of children down to Saigon. These children would then live at our FCVN Center until their paperwork was processed and they could leave Vietnam for America.

We knew each of the children from pictures that Steve had sent to us. Vu, a bright, smiling, curly-haired fellow, was awaiting his papers before flying to a family in Wisconsin. Two shy, half-Caucasian toddlers also had families waiting for them. One of them, Minh, was as blond as my children and was due to be adopted by the Pettis family in Colorado. The other boy, Ky, was going to be adopted by Gloria and Ron Johnson, founders of the Wisconsin FCVN chapter, who had cared for my children when I traveled to Vietnam to collect Joanna and Thanh.

The Larsens, who had founded the FCVN chapter in Massachusetts, were also waiting for their child to join them. The youngest child that Steve would bring down was a little baby girl, Hong, who would ultimately make her home in Florida with a doctor and his family.

As we waited for Steve to bring the children, I wandered about the nursery, thinking about the struggles we had all endured to make this day possible. The frustrations, anger, sadness and joy would all merge the next morning as the nursery finally came to life with the sounds of young children. I knew all my dreams would be realized as the nursery filled. Although some people had made it obvious that they thought FCVN wasn't needed, the evidence of the children in our nursery would be proof that FCVN had an important role to play.

When Steve arrived with the children we were all excited and rushed outside to greet them. They were tired after their journey from Qui Nhon, and we took them inside to prepare them for their stay with us.

We bathed and deloused all the children, then dressed them in new clothes and fed them before bedding them down for the night. We felt a great closeness to them, even though we'd never met them before. I had spoken for hours with their new American families, and felt greatly honored to have their sons and daughters entrusted to our care. While they remained with us at the Center, we would look after them and teach them basic English so that their transition into America would be easier.

Chapter Six

*T*huy was proving to be a real blessing. She was already a well-known and popular social worker. Her work often took her to orphanages around Vietnam, some in the cities and some in the provinces. She seemed to know everybody involved with orphans and adoptions, from the care workers up to the Minister of Social Welfare. Her obliging attitude and determined spirit were a great door opener, and she was a huge benefit to the FCVN team.

During my first weeks in Vietnam, she took me with her on a tour of some orphanages in Saigon. We saw the best and the worst. Each of my trips with Thuy would show me yet another facet of life in the Vietnamese orphanages.

Some of the unlicensed ones were little more than Victorian poorhouses. The children were dirty and ill fed, and exploited by the managers, who siphoned off benefactors' donations into their own pockets.

Others were well run—the children were clean, well fed and cared for. It was easy to tell the good orphanages from the bad. In some, it was obvious that the children attended school and bonded with workers who cared for them, while in others, children of eight years old were pressed into service to look after babies.

Donations from the FCVN chapters started filtering through to us in Vietnam. We wanted to use the funds to help as many children as possible, so we carefully selected orphanages where we knew the money would reach the children in the form of food, clothes and medicines, and not line the pockets of the directors.

From the outset we encouraged orphanage directors to send photographs of their orphanages and children to America, and to write a monthly letter outlining their programs, to help the photographs come to life. Ross started the ball rolling by taking pictures and sending them to America so that fundraisers and donors could actually see the children their dollars were helping. I had discovered, after our Illinois chapter had sponsored the St. Paul's Orphanage in Qui Nhon, how important it was for the chapter volunteers to feel a direct bonding with the orphanages and children they were sponsoring.

Thuy introduced me to Father Olivier, an elderly Canadian priest who ran several orphanages in Saigon. We got along well right from the start. The condition of his orphanages was very poor, but he was a genuine man with great compassion for his young charges. He was happy to join in with the FCVN sponsorship program, and we knew it would greatly enhance the care in his needy orphanages.

❧

Word of our adoption center spread, mainly through Thuy, who told everyone of our program. Soon other children joined the initial group in our Center, many coming from orphanages around Saigon. Some of the directors wanted us to take their mixed-race children, believing that being half-American, they would have a better chance in life if we could arrange for their adoptions.

Within a few short weeks our Center was a home for many Amerasian children. Some of them were nearly ten years old and, until they came to join us, had always been outsiders. Now all the children played with my kids and melded together in the garden as one big, happy family.

Among the new arrivals were two mixed-race boys from Saigon, Hung and Man. They quickly formed a lively group with Ron and Dan, and I often heard them teasing my sons because they couldn't speak Vietnamese. My boys took the ribbing good-naturedly and soon picked up some Vietnamese words. Perhaps it was no coincidence that the first words they learned were *quan doi,* "soldier," and *may bay truc thang,* "helicopter."

The Center was soon filled with the sound of happy, laughing children; our dreams were becoming reality. We were all working hard, but the effort was well rewarded. Every time we picked up a baby or played with a child, the look in their eyes made everything seem worthwhile.

Not long after Steve had brought the first children from Qui Nhon, two of the sisters came down to visit Thanh and Jenny, bringing with them two more orphans. Both girls were half-black American. Cuc was about eight years old, cute and with an impish grin. She was an extroverted tomboy who soon joined in the games and loved to rough-and-tumble with the boys. Everyone knew when Cuc was around—she streaked through the center screaming and laughing, and chasing the others around. She rarely let little Diem, who had come down with her, out of her sight. Diem was extremely shy when she first came, always crying for Cuc, but within weeks we had nicknamed her "Evil Woman" because of her guileful sense of humor, unusual in one so young.

Father Olivier began to send us small babies from his orphanages; our new cribs were being put to good use. Some of the babies were in poor physical condition, weak and vulnerable to infections. Their mothers had had virtually no prenatal care, and many of these babies had been abandoned soon after birth. It was obvious that they would require a great deal of nursing if they were to survive.

The arrival of each baby placed an extra burden on our small staff, and before long, we were all working around the clock to cope with their needs. We had to hire new employees every week just to look after the infants. We'd all been looking forward to this work—the arrival of the infants was welcome and we all shared the same feelings of joy in naming babies, nursing them to health and watching them grow. But we grew more tired with each passing day and fell exhausted into our beds at night, albeit with a sense of fulfillment.

Ron and Dan spent a lot of their free time after school helping in the nursery, where Beth was by now a permanent fixture. They all loved holding and nursing the babies, but they did something much more important. My children gave the babies the warmth and love they so desperately needed. I was sometimes surprised that my children would rather play in the nursery with the babies than run about the lawn with the older children.

Our French owner-cum-landlady was still firmly entrenched in the room she had annexed upon our arrival, while her retinue made their homes in various corners throughout the villa. Despite her earlier promises to leave Saigon, Vietnam and us for France, she still showed no sign of packing her bags. Indeed, as the Center filled, she took to whining and complaining endlessly about the children and their noise, like an argumentative old grandmother.

Her constant remonstrations in French only increased the tension between us, and we soon felt like the interlopers in her house, despite the dollar bills we were feeding her on a regular basis.

❦

Once the Center was up and running and staffed with care workers, we were ready to visit other orphanages outside Saigon that were already being sponsored by FCVN chapters.

We decided to make a trip to the famous Mekong Delta. Having no transport of our own, Thuy rented a van and driver for our journey. Early on the morning we were scheduled to leave, I dressed quietly and went outside. The rented van was waiting in the driveway. It was an old beat-up Ford, with no air-conditioning, that looked as if it wouldn't even make it across the city. The driver, Thanh, was an enthusiastic young man with a bright smile. He assured me that his battered van was more roadworthy than it appeared.

We loaded up the diapers, medicine, food and some clothing, and embarked on the risky journey to the Delta. Despite Thanh's assurances, I knew we were in for a long, arduous trek.

Before Thuy and I left, I checked on my children, who were still sleeping upstairs. They had learned a valuable lesson from their Vietnamese friends; they were sleeping on the bare tile floors to stay cool during the hot nights. I also looked in on the nursery, where the care workers were already hard at work, feeding the early risers.

We drove out of the city through the early morning rush hour. The roads seemed even more frenetic than usual; suicidal drivers were cutting in front of trucks and buses with abandon. On the outskirts of the city we encountered the street vendors as they made their way to Saigon's markets. Incoming bicycles and cyclos were loaded with every sort of produce—fruit, vegetables and mountains of *banh my*, my favorite Vietnamese bread. Chickens hung from bicycle handlebars and livestock were in cages bound for market. It seemed that half the city was on the move, and our progress was slow as Thanh negotiated his way through the crowd.

As we left the relative security of Saigon behind, the mounting evidence of military activity was a stark reminder of the war being fought in the areas we were visiting. Only a few miles outside the city we came face-to-face with the Vietnamese Army. Soldiers guarded a strong point and barrier at a bridge over a dirty river. Vehicles waited in line while each was inspected by heavily armed, unsmiling soldiers.

The road was heavily fortified. Tanks stood menacingly by small roadside encampments, heavy machine gun barrels jutted out from sandbag emplacements, and the whole area was filled with rolls of evil-looking barbed wire. The checkpoint had become a mini-fortress, and soldiers seemed to be everywhere, on tanks, in guard posts; some were still sleeping in hammocks slung in nearby trees, and even underneath military trucks. It was like driving into a movie set.

Our papers were briefly examined and Thuy explained our mission to the disinterested guard. He waved us through and we moved along slowly as the machine guns seemed to follow our passage. Once clear of the road-block, I breathed a small sigh of relief. Those were the soldiers who were defending Saigon—they were on our side!

As we progressed southward towards the Delta the military presence increased dramatically. Heavily armed soldiers guarded each turn in the road. Jeeps and heavy military trucks, all painted in drab green camouflage, were parked alongside the road, and soldiers watched our slow progress.

It was almost impossible to pass a vehicle on the narrow two-lane road. When we came upon a long army convoy we were forced to creep slowly behind it. These convoys were prime targets for Viet Cong rockets, and we all felt uncomfortable. The tension mounted inside the van as we tried to pass.

Eventually our driver managed to find a gap in the oncoming traffic, and swung out to pass some ammunition-laden trucks. We had to swerve back into the line as more oncoming traffic appeared. Soon we found ourselves behind a truck filled with young soldiers going to the front. Thuy and Thanh began to talk about them, and Thuy turned to me to translate. She said they were discussing how healthy the soldiers looked—they were new recruits. Many of them would be dead soon, she added in a distressed voice.

We were sandwiched in the convoy. Slowly we worked our way up, taking the chance to pass more trucks as an opportunity arose. By now I knew why Thanh had so much confidence in our rattletrap van—at the speed we were going, rarely over thirty miles per hour, the van would last forever.

In spite of the military all around us and the undercurrent of danger, I felt excited to be making such a journey. This was the first time I'd ever traveled outside Saigon by road, and it was good to see the land up close.

The countryside was colorful, with a vast array of fields filled with green-ery. The landscape was dotted with tombs that at first glance seemed to have been placed haphazardly in almost every field. Thuy explained that the farm-ers and their families buried their dead in their own fields whenever pos-sible. She said that local fortune-tellers determined the actual placement of the tombs in the fields according to very old traditions. It was a strange sight for my Western eyes, and the large number of new graves was a grim re-minder of the war zone we were driving through.

The road wound through villages of small wooden huts and I watched the village life unfolding before us. We saw women shopping at local markets, barefoot children playing in the roadside dust, while fishermen tended their nets strung out across small streams.

Hours later, we reached the banks of the Mekong River and stopped behind a long line of vehicles waiting to board a ferry. The sun beat down fiercely on the van's metal roof; no breeze came through the open windows to help us cope with the stifling heat. While we waited in line, an endless stream of vendors tried to sell us their pathetic goods. They knocked on the windows and pounded on the sides of the van, eager to attract our attention and entice us into buying pieces of sugarcane or fly-ridden pineapple sticks and watermelon.

We sat there in the heat and humidity for two sweltering hours before we were finally motioned to drive onto the ferry. We passed blind and war-wounded beggars, some amputees, all holding out begging cups and hats. Soldiers with lined and weary faces, guns slung over their shoulders, their dark green uniforms thick with dust and caked mud, made their way onto the ferry alongside us.

The embarkation area was packed solid with vehicles and foot passengers, all jostling for a place on the old wooden ferry. We drove down the wide riverbank and up onto a rickety loading ramp. I nervously watched the muddy brown water swirling underneath as our van slowly crept along the open sides of the ramp; one false move and we would tip into the river.

As we bumped onto the ferry deck an irritated crewman directed us to draw up close behind a row of vehicles. Other trucks pulled up on either side of us, and soon we were completely hemmed in; I couldn't open my door more than a couple of inches. If the ferry had been attacked and sunk, we would have drowned, trapped in the van.

When the main deck was packed to its fullest capacity with trucks, cars and vans, the waiting foot passengers were allowed to embark. They swarmed aboard, carrying babies, packages, bicycles and all kinds of belongings. Every square inch of the ferry was packed like sardines in a can, with hot, sweating, noisy humanity. Finally the loading ramp was pulled up, and we set off on the trip across the Mekong River.

The current was swift and the old engines labored noisily as they forced the ferry across the water. Because the vehicles were packed so tightly, we didn't get any breeze inside the van. I could see the foot passengers relaxing for the trip, their hair and clothing blowing in the wind; we just sat still and sweated, knowing we had to make a second ferry crossing some miles further down the road. The excitement we had felt at the start of the journey had waned, the heat and time taking their toll on our enthusiasm.

Finally, after a hectic disembarkation, we drove through the dispersing passengers and made it back onto the asphalt road to continue our drive to the first orphanage. By now we had lapsed into a listless silence; we just wanted to reach our destination and start our planned visits.

We made our first stop at Diem Phuc, an orphanage just outside Vinh Long, which we hoped would become the next addition to FCVN's Foster Orphanage Project. Thuy had sent news of our trip, so we were expected. The dirt driveway was lined with children, who formed an impromptu welcoming committee. The director was in Saigon, and the nuns who had been left in charge greeted us with the children. Their black habits were dusty and they looked hot and weary, tired by their exhausting duties.

The director of this orphanage had written several long and descriptive letters to FCVN, and Cheryl and I had formed a special feeling based on those letters. We knew they were in need of FCVN help, and I intended to report to Colorado and try to include them in the sponsorship program.

After greetings and the customary offer and acceptance of unsweetened, lukewarm tea, we entered the orphanage for a quick tour. The rooms where the older children lived were crowded. The nursery was in a tiny room upstairs; inside we saw several young girls in charge of about twenty babies. The air smelled of dirt and disease. I walked past cribs filled with sick babies, lying in rough, dirty diapers. Their bodies were red and sore, and they were so wasted away that their bones were visible through the skin.

Another, larger room held perhaps fifty children of toddler age. There was one small, barred window, which let in some sunlight, but the room was hot and stuffy. The children lay in cribs with wooden slat bases; there were no mattresses to cushion their frail bodies. The toddlers wore no diapers, and their urine and feces dropped through the slats to the filthy floor, which obviously had not been cleaned for at least hours, maybe days. Thuy explained that the staff cleaned the floor and cribs by washing them down from time to time with buckets of water.

The room was full of flies that flew between piles of waste and the babies' faces, no doubt spreading infections throughout the room. Seeing the conditions in the orphanage, it was no surprise to me that many of these places had a mortality rate of eighty percent.

I was drawn to two black-American children lying in a corner crib. I reached into the crib and examined them before picking one of them up.

She was too weak to hold her head up and she rested quietly against my shoulder. Her curly hair and huge black eyes reminded me of Jenny.

Next to her, the other black child was burning with fever, her eyes glazed and tormented. She had a mass of scar tissue on her lip, perhaps from an untreated wound, but even that did not detract from her potential beauty.

"What are their names?" I asked. The sister gestured toward the sick baby in the crib and said her name was Minh Trang; the other child, she said, shrugging toward the baby in my arms, had no name.

I learned that both of the girls had been abandoned just after their births. I decided that when we passed again on our way back to Saigon I would ask the director to allow them to go with us.

After completing the tour and giving the sisters what supplies we could spare, we said our reluctant good-byes and departed, to continue our journey.

Next we visited the Good Shepherd Orphanage in Vinh Long, which was located in the city proper. That orphanage was run by Irish Catholic nuns, many of whom had been in Vietnam for twenty years. The orphanage was already sponsored by FCVN and other organizations. The grounds were immaculate, the sisters cheerful, and the children clean, well stimulated and healthy.

Sister Ursula, a nun from Malaysia who seemed to have a permanent smile on her face, escorted us through a very clean, well-run nursery. After we had toured the rooms, the sisters invited us for lunch in their dining room. The atmosphere was bright and the conversation animated. The sisters told us about the training programs they had introduced for the children. They had ambitious plans for their charges, and it was obvious that the sisters bonded very well with them.

Although we were in a hurry to leave before nightfall, when the fighting would recommence, the sisters encouraged us to take the time to stop at yet another orphanage, St. Paul's, also in Vinh Long. They told us the orphanage was poor but, despite the lack of funding, the staff took excellent care of the children.

We took their advice and soon found St. Paul's, where we arrived unexpectedly. St. Paul's director, Sister Marie Christine, led us to a clean, pleasant sitting room that opened onto a playground. The sister was short and plump, and wore gold-rimmed glasses. She was eager to tell us about her orphanage. She had heard of us from other nuns from her Order who ran the Qui Nhon nursery.

Again, we were served the ubiquitous tea as children ran through the room, showing off for the strangers. After the tea and some polite small talk, we were ushered into the large, baby-filled nursery. An elderly nun led us past each crib and gave us a running commentary about each baby. Thuy translated; it was obvious that the nun knew each child personally.

Before we left, the sisters confided that they had to water down the children's daily formula so there would be enough to go around. At night, they only had rice water to feed the babies. Thuy and I agreed that we should start helping these sisters who were doing so much with so little. We walked out to our van and again gave freely of our dwindling supplies. Before we left, keen to cross on the next ferry before it closed at dusk, the nuns asked us to take some of their babies to Saigon, and we agreed to call in on our return trip.

Driving as hard as we could in the late afternoon, we made it to the second river crossing just in time. We waited in line for less than an hour and crossed on a ferry remarkably similar to the one we'd used earlier in the day.

It was dark when we arrived at the Providence Orphanage in Can Tho, the southernmost point of my first trip to the Mekong Delta. Sister Eugenia, the director, greeted us with a bright smile and a warm welcome. She wore the white robes and large wooden cross of the Sisters of Providence, and a few gray hairs peeked out from under her veil. She embraced Thuy, who was an old friend, and enthusiastically pumped my hand.

The children were all asleep and the building was quiet. The nuns showed us to guest quarters at the top of a spindly staircase. The guest room was simple but clean. The nuns had kindly carried in buckets of water, and I thankfully shed my dirty clothes and washed down. Just being clean and wearing fresh clothes seemed a luxury after spending the day cooped up in the hot, dusty van.

We ate an evening meal with all the sisters. They had really tried to lay a good spread, and we were grateful for the filling meal. We all chatted for a while, and the sisters told us of other orphanages, deeper in the Delta, that were even more desperate for help. Those orphanages were rarely visited by any outside agencies; they were overloaded with infants and their resources were stretched to the breaking point.

When I went up to bed and lay in the darkness, the war seemed very close. I could hear gunfire and the noise of rockets being fired in the nearby jungle, exploding with loud crashes. Tired after the long journey, I fell asleep to the sounds of war.

The next day I awoke early. Birds were singing in the nearby garden, and the smell of fresh flowers drifted into the room. Feeling refreshed, we ate a cooked breakfast before touring the orphanage.

The older children were already up and about, laughing as they prepared to go to school. I saw them running around the yard and playing on the swings and slides. It was a far cry from some of the orphanages I'd seen in Saigon.

The baby room was small but clean. The babies slept in little hammocks suspended over their cribs, to keep them cooler. Each crib was decorated with colorful mobiles. Despite the good care, many of the babies were very sick. The sisters explained that sometimes as many as twenty babies would arrive in a single week. Often they had been abandoned in the maternity hospital, where they lay unattended for several days before arriving at the orphanage, sick and dehydrated.

Outside the nursery, we saw bookshelves filled with photograph albums of children who had left this nursery and been adopted. The pictures attested to the nuns' belief in adoption. They knew that the adoptees were likely to become bright and healthy in their new lives, unlike many of the sick and dying that remained behind.

Before we left, the sisters asked us to take four infants with us to Saigon. Three of them were tiny baby boys and the other was a little girl called Kim Hoa, with thick black hair and lovely eyes. She had a cleft lip and palate, which we knew could easily be repaired by doctors in America.

After giving out the last of our supplies, we hastily made some changes to the interior of the van. We hadn't planned to take children back to Saigon, and we had no traveling cots or cribs with us. Thanh removed one of the rear bench seats and we laid several blankets on the floor. Thuy and I would sit on the floor and care for the babies during the long drive back to Saigon. We said a hurried farewell to the sisters and promised to return soon.

Once we were on the road, Thuy and I named the boys. All four infants were in poor physical shape; all were less than a week old and none weighed more than five pounds. In any Western country, the babies would have been in intensive care nurseries with a staff of skilled doctors and nurses caring for them.

The journey was slow and the hot sun was beginning to dehydrate the sickest of our charges. Waiting for the ferry, we were forced to sit in the heat, watching the life slowly ebbing from our four babies. Thuy and Thanh managed to get the attention of somebody in authority and finally—after waiting a couple of hours for an important military convoy to be ferried across—we were given priority and took the next boat over the river.

As promised the day before, we stopped at St. Paul's. The sisters had four babies for us to take. Now we had eight tiny babies to care for on the road to Saigon, and we still had one more stop to make. The nuns had tears in their eyes as they bade farewell to the little ones they were entrusting to our care.

We hurried on to Diem Phuc, the first orphanage we had visited the day before. The director had returned from Saigon and greeted us warmly. We asked her if we could take the half-American children back with us to Saigon. The director looked at the other babies in the van and had a brief discussion with some of the other nuns. Thuy warned me that as far as she knew, the orphanage had never placed children for adoption, and told me that I shouldn't get my hopes up, especially as the nuns had never seen me before.

Nevertheless, a few minutes later the director and some other nuns arrived, carrying the two Amerasian girls we had seen yesterday. The director motioned for one of the tired sisters to give Minh Trang to Thuy. She explained that the child had a fever again. Another nun handed me the other baby, and we carefully set them side-by-side on the blankets we had laid on the floor. Thuy told the sisters that I wanted to name the little girl after my own adopted child. The nuns nodded enthusiastically at my suggestion, and so Thu Loan was named.

We thanked the director profusely for her trust and promised to do our best for the children. By now the heat of the day was building and the temperature inside the van was climbing even higher. We took our leave of the sisters and started our homeward journey.

The trip seemed to pass very quickly despite having ten babies to care for. We fed them and tried to keep them cool in the hot van. Once we were moving on the road, the circulating air quieted them, and the rhythmic swaying of the van helped lull them to sleep.

When we reached the second ferry crossing, Thuy went up to the soldiers who controlled the flow of road traffic. She flashed them a vivacious smile and asked them if we could have priority because we were carrying sick infants. The soldiers followed her to our van and peered in at the now crying babies. They were amazed—they obviously hadn't expected to see a van full of babies on the road to Saigon. They smiled, and within minutes we were at the front of the line.

The last leg of the journey was dreadful. By then the babies were uncomfortable and in need of proper medical attention. Driving along a bumpy road in the hot van was extracting a high price from them. Even we adults were exhausted by the journey and felt bruised by the constant bumping. We were thirsty, hungry and ready to get home.

When we finally pulled into the driveway, I was so happy to be home. I wanted to get the babies into the nursery and see my own children.

Sue, Ross and the nursery staff rushed out to greet us, happy to see us safe and well after our trip into the Delta. When they looked into the van and saw Thuy and me surrounded by so many tiny babies, they were taken aback. We had brought ten children, eight of them infants less than a month old, many of them sick and in need of urgent care. The babies were whisked off into the nursery and Thuy and I thanked and paid Thanh, who told us he was happy to be of help in our great work.

My first trip into the Mekong Delta was an experience I will never forget. We were surrounded by the war and sometimes we feared for our safety. However, we had seen the need for outside help and had enjoyed meeting the sisters. We knew we would make many more trips in the days to come.

Chapter Seven

*B*ack in Saigon, events had been deteriorating quickly during our two-day trip to the Mekong Delta.

Relationships with the French woman had become more strained as the number of infants increased, and now her constant complaining was becoming a real thorn in our side. The arrival of the eight infants and two toddlers was a real shock to her, although the rest of us were thrilled, and everyone quickly had their own special baby.

Whatever happened, we couldn't stay there with her on the premises—and we desperately needed more room to expand our program. Even knowing how great the need was, we simply had not imagined that we would be asked to take so many children so quickly.

Sue, Ross, Thuy and I sat down early one morning for a conference. After a couple of hours discussing the problem we came to the reluctant conclusion that the FCVN Center would have to be moved as soon as possible. I called Colorado and explained our situation and the need for larger premises.

The Board of Directors met and telephoned their enthusiastic approval. Our FCVN chapter in Illinois was working hard to raise money for a larger place. Thrilled, we asked our staff to put the word out, and within days we had a list of potential properties to view. Ross and Sue visited several prospects but finally settled on a building located near the main gates of Tan Son Nhut International Airport on Bui Thi Xuan Street.

The place was huge but had some drawbacks. Everyone was concerned about the massive black market that operated every day in the small lane outside the courtyard gates. The market was well known and always busy, and we thought that the crowds would restrict our access to the gate.

The facility included two parts. There was a three-bedroom concrete-block house with a flagstoned yard and a round, shallow fishpond that would serve well as a wading pool for the children. Next door, a five-story apartment building would provide good accommodation for the staff and visitors we anticipated arriving from America. We planned to convert one of the apartments into an office.

A large nursery could easily be accommodated in the building, and the separate apartments would enable us to isolate the infants according to their specific needs. The ground floor could be used for the toddlers and older children, who would have access to the adjacent pond and yard area.

We negotiated the lease and moved at once. We hired and trained more staff and supplied them with uniforms—bright yellow tops and black pants. The new building gave us a real chance to show off our capable staff. Our plans were now coming together.

Ron and Dan were doing well in school and making friends. My younger children were all enjoying the nursery school with its bilingual staff, and the children's command of the two languages increased daily. They quickly got used to the idea of waking early in the morning and having a structured routine to their days.

Every day we received requests from our friends in the FCVN chapters to visit other orphanages that we sponsored. Additionally, the orphanage directors were calling us, obviously eager to meet with us as well.

Thuy and I decided to fly to Da Nang to visit the Sacred Heart Orphanage, which was run by Sister Angela, a favorite of many in adoption circles. Sister Angela was a great believer in adoption for mixed-race children. She traveled to many of the other orphanages in the distant northern provinces and encouraged many nuns, reluctant to participate, to release their half-American children to adoption programs. Sister Angela then collected the children and cared for them at her Da Nang orphanage until homes could be found for them or they could be moved to Saigon.

Of course, I also wanted to travel to Da Nang to meet Sister Angela for personal reasons. Sister Angela had cared for Joanna in her orphanage during that long wait before she was able to travel to Allambie. Thuy called ahead and we were welcomed, just as soon as we could get there.

The flight arrived at the Da Nang military base. During the American involvement in the war, Da Nang had been one of the largest military bases in the Pacific. It was like a city in itself. The place was massive, with giant runways stretching in every direction. Mammoth concrete and metal hangars lined the landing strips.

As we got off the plane a group of friendly soldiers approached and asked the purpose of our trip. When we told them we were delivering medicines and supplies to the nearby Sacred Heart Orphanage, they kindly offered us a lift. We climbed into a jeep and raced across the tarmac. The soldiers' ride saved us the hassle of trying to find cyclos outside the base while managing the boxes that we were delivering.

Our arrival at the orphanage caused a great stir. We piled out of the jeep and rushed into the doorway, lugging the heavy boxes. The sisters all greeted us effusively, especially Sister Angela, who treated me like an old friend.

We stayed in the orphanage that night, talking and showing photos of Joanna and other children. The next morning we toured the orphanage and looked at the two hundred children. I was surprised to see that so many of them were half-American. Sister Angela explained that many of them had been moved here from an orphanage in Quang Ngai because of the heavy fighting in their area. Despite the overcrowding, the center was clean and well run.

Sacred Heart was in a beautiful location, just yards away from a beach fronting the South China Sea, in a place that the American forces had dubbed "China Beach." We took the opportunity to visit the beach and spent a short time strolling on the pure white sands.

Sister Angela asked us to take five children back to Saigon; all of them were older and of mixed race. One of the children was a beautiful black girl of about seven named Thuy. She was very shy and didn't talk much at first. We soon nicknamed her "Little Thuy."

After promising to return to Da Nang as soon as we could, we left the orphanage and headed back for Saigon, where the new center was looking even more organized. The five children we brought from Da Nang joined the ever-swelling ranks of babies and children in our spacious new accommodations.

Carol Westlake had been planning a trip to Vietnam. When we got back from Da Nang there was word that she would come soon to help set up the nursery. Afterwards she would escort some children to the United States to join their new families. I looked forward to seeing her again, and knew her nursing experience would be of great help.

Carol arrived on a Pan Am flight a few days later and went to work with a will. What a joy it was for me to have my friend by my side! From the first moment, Carol fell in love with Little Thuy, one of the most beautiful children in the center. After a call to her husband, she soon began making arrangements to adopt Thuy.

Many of the babies coming into the Center were very sick, and it was obvious that they needed more than just good food and loving care. We took some of the sickest ones to a clinic and others to Vietnamese hospitals around the city. Within days, despite our close monitoring and love, the babies would die. We were devastated by each death. We had brought the babies in, named each one, and nurtured them as well as we were able, and yet we were powerless to help them further and felt so hopeless each time one of them died.

We had a meeting, and there was no question in anyone's mind that our babies would have a better chance of survival if we had better in-house medical facilities. We had to start our own intensive care nursery. We would need more qualified nursing staff and equipment. FCVN quickly agreed to our plans and started the wheels turning to provide more volunteers.

The influx of babies, many of them sick, meant that we were all working long hours. Day by day the staff gradually became more tired until we were all dropping from exhaustion. Finally the endless rounds of nursing, traveling and administrative duties proved too much for me, and I ended up in the Seventh Day Adventist Hospital, suffering from exhaustion and viral hepatitis. I had lost more than thirty pounds in two months and I looked half-starved myself. I spent a week in the hospital on IVs while my body recuperated, just enough so that I could jump back into the same work as before.

Tom heard that I was ill and forwarded his plans to join us. He'd sold our house and belongings and was just about ready to come to Vietnam. When I left the hospital I was pleased to find our team working as hard as ever, and they greeted me with the news that Tom would arrive later in the day.

Our kids were ecstatic to see their father; they showed him around the Center and introduced him to the staff and children. Later they wanted to take him around Saigon on a *cyclo may* and show him the delights of the city. The Center rang with laughter as the older kids joined in the festivities. Pop music blared from our old radio; Elton John's "Crocodile Rock" and Gladys Knight's "Midnight Train to Georgia" echoed around the front yard of our home.

After we had left Illinois, Tom had stayed in close contact with FCVN in Denver, and spent time chatting with Cheryl and Mick on the phone. He got to know them well and knew they had started the paperwork to adopt another Vietnamese child. In the Center Tom met Lan Mai, a charming little three-year-old girl who was to be adopted by the Markson family.

In the days to come Tom was a great help. He relieved me of many of the tiresome administrative duties, which allowed me more time to nurse the babies and travel to the provinces.

Paperwork consumed more and more time, time we would rather spend saving lives. Many of the babies came to us without names, let alone a birth certificate. To give those children a legal existence, and so a chance at adoption, we had to create Vietnamese identities for them. In some provinces, the authorities refused to process the "Birth Judgment" for the little abandoned babies unless they had a mother's name. In those cases, since no one had any idea who these women were, we fabricated that name as well.

More than ninety percent of our babies arrived without paperwork, as abandoned orphans. In the few cases where children were officially relinquished to the orphanages, we were fiercely protective of their paperwork so that it might be possible for them to know their origins.

The paperwork and administrative duties grew, and we soon hired two secretarial staff, Phung and Mai. They were bright young ladies who kept pace with the papers and other clerical duties throughout the Center.

Soon after I came out of the hospital, the promised FCVN support arrived. John and Terre Super from Colorado joined us and went to work, helping cope with the ever-growing numbers of orphans. Shortly thereafter two nurses joined us from America, Chris Mosher and a newly married couple, Kathy and Duane Frisbee. Their joint help was much needed—by then the FCVN Center was caring for more than one hundred babies, many of them sick, and fifty older children.

We hired Dr. Cong, an excellent Vietnamese pediatrician, who visited the Center daily. His cheerful good humor was infectious and he brightened the atmosphere, even in our new critical care room where the sickest babies fought for their lives.

Steve Johnson had become an unofficial part of the team. Though he was still working for ITT, he devoted every spare moment to helping us. He made frequent trips to the northern provinces and often brought children back with him. He was so involved with the children and the Center operations that we invited him to move into the apartment building.

We had managed to scrape enough spare cash together to buy an old, rusty Ford van, which was a great benefit to us. On weekends Steve and the others took the children to the U.S. base at Tan Son Nhut airport, where they would eat ice cream and popcorn, watch movies and swim in the base pool.

Many of the officials at USAID had thawed toward us over the months, and we gratefully received their donations of food and excess property. We also managed to obtain free passes for flights on Air America within Vietnam. Although we didn't know it at the time, the airline was operated by the Central Intelligence Agency (CIA). What mattered to us was the free transportation.

The passes allowed us to visit far-flung destinations and take much-needed supplies to some of the poorest orphanages. On many a morning Thuy and I would simply go to the airport, loaded with boxes of supplies and medicine, and fly to whichever city an Air America plane happened to be visiting that day. We didn't know where we would end up during the day, and we had to trust that Air America would get us home.

The planes we hitched rides on were military aircraft, and many of the flights were "mail drops." On those flights, we watched in wonder as crew members dropped parcels and crates through open hatches in the floor. We never asked what they were dropping, or who the intended recipients were—we were just thankful for the ride.

Sometimes we didn't make it home or got "bumped" on the way to our destinations. On one trip we were able to spend a few days in Nha Trang with Thuy's extended family. I fell in love with the pristine beaches and the aqua blue water. I told Thuy that when I was an old woman this is where I would retire.

On one flight, we met a group of un-uniformed but obviously military Americans escorting a few small wooden crates. They told us confidentially that the boxes contained the remains of American soldiers who had died in the war. Looking at the small boxes, I felt a rush of sadness when thinking of the loss of the lives of these men. They had given their life to a war that proceeded on, oblivious to their sacrifice.

Thus far, all the children at our Center had been given to us by orphanages or hospitals. It came as a great surprise when a man appeared at the Center one day and, through Thuy, asked me to help his young niece and two nephews. He explained that the children were from Da Nang, that their soldier father had been killed in the fighting, and their mother subsequently had become insane. The man had a large family himself and was unable to feed the extra mouths.

The three children were all named Nguyen Phuong, though each had a different middle name. The oldest was a girl of about thirteen, and her brothers were nine and eight years old.

I listened to the man's story and looked at the sad children standing quietly at his side. Feeling sorry for the children, I decided to discuss his unusual request with the staff before making a decision.

I knew the Vietnamese government prohibited adoptions of boys over ten years old, as they would soon be conscripted into the army. If I accepted them, we would have to find them a family as soon as possible.

Everybody wanted to take them in and I didn't need much prompting. After a few days of thought and a quick call to FCVN in Colorado, I accepted the children. They were a welcome addition to the Center and enriched our lives. Like the other kids, they clamored for American names and we soon called them Tanya, Nick and Paul.

Carol, who was by then back in Colorado, soon found a family for them, Bill and Charlene Smart of Oregon, who came to Vietnam to meet their three new children.

In July I escorted three orphans to Colorado. When I returned to Saigon, I found out that an epidemic of "Saigon measles" had swept through the nursery and killed twenty of the most vulnerable babies within days. Even some of the toddlers became critical. Brian, my son, had fallen victim to the epidemic and was seriously ill. Chau, the woman who cared for our children, never left his side.

Little blond Minh, from Qui Nhon, was so sick that he had to be admitted to the Seventh Day Adventist Hospital, and Sue spent days at his bedside nursing him. Minh was ready to travel to meet the Pettis family in Colorado, who had named him Andrew, but the sickness delayed his departure and it took a few weeks for him to convalesce and regain his strength. He finally reached America on the eighth of August 1974, the same day that Richard Nixon resigned the presidency.

Nixon's resignation was a time of personal celebration for me, and many of the others showed their happiness when the news came over the radio. Later that night Tom, Sue, Steve, Ross and I went out to hear Steve's fiancée, Carol Kim, singing at one of Saigon's top nightclubs.

❦

During the summer, Thuy and I made another of our frequent trips to Qui Nhon. That night, after dinner, Sister Marie and her staff told Thuy and me a long story about three brothers in her care: fourteen-year-old Tho, his brother Thanh, and their younger brother Nhan, who was eleven years old.

As we listened to the sad story, the normally stoic Thuy began to cry. The brothers had been living near Pleiku with their mother when she gave birth to her fourth son in 1965. Their father, a soldier, returned home to see his new child. Shortly after he left, word reached them that he had been killed during fierce fighting in the Mang Yang Pass.

The mother struggled on as best she could, trying to feed the four children, but the baby eventually died. The sisters told us that soon after, the boys' mother was killed while she was crossing a bridge near their village. The three boys, now orphans, were taken to St. Paul's, where they had been living ever since.

The sisters asked us if we could take the two elder brothers to a training center in Saigon. During that trip we also arranged to bring back with us another boy, Thanh, who had been abandoned at birth and lived all his life in the orphanage.

We agreed to take the boys to the training center, and they traveled down a few days later. I made some inquiries and soon discovered that the so-called training school would simply be a precursor to the boys joining the army.

We quickly grew to love the boys. I asked the sisters in Qui Nhon if we could keep them with us in our house rather than chancing them being taken off to the army. The boys were eager to join our family life, and although they were older than Ron and Dan, the five of them enjoyed countless days exploring Saigon and teaching each other more of their own cultures.

The two brothers soon asked for American names, so I called them Jason and Jeff. We enrolled them in school and they picked up English very quickly. We bought them a guitar and nearly every night Jason played it for us, as we sat around and sang John Denver songs.

Several months later, their younger brother, Nhan, whom we named Jeremy, joined us as well. The boys rapidly introduced my sons to a real Vietnamese lifestyle. They toured the city on their bikes, eating at street stalls and mixing in with the throngs of people. Soon we felt the brothers were truly part of our family, and the other boy, Thanh, fit in as well.

Jason recounted stories of how painful their life had been as orphans. They had received a good education from the sisters, but the children at the nearby Catholic schools, cruel as only children can be, often teased them because they lived in the orphanage.

When fall came, we celebrated our first real holiday in Vietnam, Tet Trung Thu, the annual Mid-Autumn Festival. All the staff enjoyed the short break in the never-ending routine. This was a beautiful festival that all of the children took part in. In the evening we lit paper lanterns with candles inside, and the children walked in a circle in the courtyard and sang songs. My children joined in the festivities. Tom and I were certain that much of our success with the staff was due to their natural love for our children.

We took time in the following days to talk about our successes and our failures; we took stock. Tom and I attended a USAID meeting where statistics were discussed regarding the adoption programs of everyone working in Vietnam. It seemed tragic, at least to us, that in the month of September, USAID claimed that thirty-nine children had left Vietnam for adoption while another thirty-nine had died waiting for their paperwork to be processed. Considering the number of adoption agencies working in Vietnam, it seemed that processing was going very slowly. The reality of those statistics was frightening. It seemed that there was always another deadly epidemic lurking around the corner.

Our Center now had close to two hundred children and babies, and a good number had already been placed overseas in adoptive families. Some of our longer-term residents who had been with us since our arrival had found families closer to home.

Betty Beaird arrived in Vietnam to do a photo essay on orphanages, and ended up volunteering to help at the FCVN Center. During her time with us, she fell head over heels for two of our special children. Man was one of our first children and a great friend of my boys, and Tam was a beautiful three-year-old who had come into our care. As a single parent, Betty was to face innumerable obstacles before her sons were allowed to travel to America.

The restrictions on single parent adoptions at that time resulted in some parents having to persuade a senator or representative in the U.S. Congress to sponsor a private bill to allow the children to be adopted. For Betty and many other single parents, it literally took an act of Congress to bring their children home.

Adoptive parents could only adopt two foreign-born children. Those who chose to adopt more children faced similar hurdles and would often wait for a year for the U.S. visa to bring their children home. We were fortunate that Jenny had arrived on a parole visa, so we were still able to process Joanna and Thanh through regular INS channels, or our wait for them would have been far longer than it was.

A pediatrician from California, Dr. Frances Sharkey, had come to Vietnam to work with the Barskey Unit, a group that specialized in plastic surgery. During her stay in Vietnam she would volunteer at our Center whenever possible, and even took the long trip to the Delta with me. While visiting FCVN she fell in love with and adopted Cuc, our little live wire. When Cuc traveled home, Ron and Dan spent days trying to imagine how she would feel, seeing all the new and exciting things in America.

As our programs expanded, we hired more staff and, as all too often happens, there were soon problems with one of the women. We discovered some thefts, and eventually suspicion fell on one woman. When we shared the information with the staff, they told us in whispers that they didn't trust her. We initially dismissed their warnings as some kind of prejudice, but one day we caught her stealing red-handed and fired her on the spot.

The next day Dan came up and told us that Beth had just left the compound with a woman he didn't know. Then Ron came rushing into the room, screaming, "Beth's gone!" Terrified, Tom and I ran outside onto our balcony. Looking over the black marketeers and their customers crowding the street, we could just see Beth at the other end of the crowded alley, about to disappear from sight. We all shouted loudly and the staff came running. From the vantage point of our high balcony we were waving and screaming, and we quickly attracted the attention of the crowd below. The Vietnamese shouted to the vendors and explained that the woman was taking Beth. By that time Beth was out of our sight and was being pulled to the main road. Within seconds the crowd understood, and about thirty men surrounded a taxi that the woman had hailed. She was trying to push Beth inside when they caught her.

We ran out into the street, pushed through the crowds, and made our way down the lane as fast as we could. When we reached the knot of people surrounding the taxi and the now-frightened woman, Tom grabbed Beth into his arms. Within minutes the Saigon police surrounded us.

Although the woman protested her innocence, the crowd insisted that she was kidnapping my daughter. Her guilt was obvious and the police pushed her roughly into the back of a jeep before driving off to the downtown precinct house; I knew she would be in for a well-deserved rough time.

I asked Thuy and the police what the woman would have done with Beth, and their answers were the same: she would have sold her. Her blonde hair and blue eyes would have made our four-year-old daughter a prize. I cried, thinking how close we had come to losing Beth forever. For days after, I was terrified to leave the children alone, even for a minute.

Beth's kidnapping was not a chance event. The connection between the kidnapper and the fired employee was confirmed when witnesses came forward and identified them as close friends. From that moment on we hired a man to guard the gate, and stepped up security around all the children.

A few weeks later, despite my reservations about leaving my children, I had to escort another group of adoptive children to Colorado. I intended to spend a few days meeting with the FCVN Board of Directors, who were coordinating money-raising activities that funded our projects.

The board was pleased with our progress, and FCVN was now accomplishing its goals. It was also agreed that we would seek another property in addition to the existing Center, so that the older children could attend school and have more space to play. Our small front courtyard was far too small for the large number of children coming into our care.

I was pleased with my reception in Colorado, and my spirits were higher than they had been for a long time. I started making plans and thinking about suitable new premises. I called Tom and shared the good news with him. Everything was good in my world.

Tom called me late that night while I was staying at the Marksons' home. The ringing telephone woke the entire family. I knew immediately that there must be a problem. Cheryl handed me the phone.

The connection was as bad as usual, but I could faintly hear Tom yelling down the crackling lines. He had been trying to get a connection for hours. "Come back quickly," I could make out. "Brian's fallen from the balcony!" My heart stopped. I envisioned the five-story apartment building next door and knew that all the children loved to spend evenings there enjoying the cool breeze. I could only think the worst.

Broken bits of sentences came over the phone line: "Villa...balcony... intensive care." I shuddered, knowing exactly what intensive care meant in Saigon.

When I finally hung up the phone, my knees were weak and I was crying uncontrollably, afraid that my baby was going to die.

Mick and Cheryl realized I had to return to Saigon quickly, and they called friends at Pan Am to reserve a seat for me on the earliest possible flight that could take me to Vietnam. I had traveled to Denver on a free pass, which now added to my problems—passengers with such low-priority tickets were given seats only as space was available.

Flying via Los Angeles and Honolulu, I made it as far as Guam, only to find that I had been bumped from the final leg of my journey, and the next flight to Vietnam was days away. Devastated, worried, and tired from the long journey, my spirits were at an all-time low; all I could do was sit in a corner and cry.

After waiting nearly five hours for an international phone connection, I finally managed to get a call through to Tom from the airport. Luckily the connection was better but I was dreading hearing the latest news. He told me Brian was still in intensive care and had been x-rayed from head to toe; thankfully they had found no broken bones.

Tom broke down and could hardly speak as he told me that the major problem seemed to be little Brian's face. He was unrecognizable. After the call had ended, my small reserve of strength evaporated and I started crying again.

Later the same day I managed to get a flight to Hong Kong, and from there made a connection to Saigon. Altogether the flight home had taken me seventy-two hours and had left me physically and mentally exhausted.

Tom met me at the airport; he too was exhausted from his vigil at Brian's bedside. Since I only had a carry-on bag we rushed from the airport to our van, Tom talking as we walked.

He had good news. The team of doctors had given a good prognosis. Brian was doing as well as could be expected. The downside was that Brian had a great deal of swelling in the brain, and they couldn't predict the long-term effects of it.

As we speeded from the airport to the hospital Tom related how the accident had happened.

It was a warm evening, and Tom and the children were sitting on the balcony, enjoying the pleasant breeze. Tom was in a chair with his back to the metal railing, reading a newspaper. As usual Brian had been climbing all over him, and he simply leaned over to look down at some children playing in the pool below.

Suddenly, with no warning, he just toppled over and through Tom's arms, which had been surrounding him as he held the paper. Tom broke down as he told me that one minute he was there and then he was gone.

Later I learned that the staff and children screamed in terror as Brian tumbled over and smacked, head first, onto the concrete below. Tom ran down the stairs in record time and reached Brian, seeing with horror the blood splashed around his son's head. He scooped him up, and without waiting for help from anyone, he put Brian in our van and set off for the nearby hospital. As usual, the lane outside the center was packed with people shopping and bartering in the market. Tom screamed and honked the horn at the crowd, and they slowly cleared a path.

Just as Tom finished recounting the story, we arrived at the hospital and ran quickly up the stairs to the Intensive Care Unit. I steeled myself for the first sight of my darling baby. Tom's words had hardly prepared me for the sight that greeted me. Brian's head was still swollen and his features were distorted. Under his eyes, huge bruises covered the skin all the way down onto his cheeks.

I picked him up from the crib and laid him gently in my arms, crying warm tears. He whimpered "Mommy," over and over, as I held him close. Feeling my despair, Brian patted me on the back as if to comfort me.

I was grateful to be home with my family again, and over the coming weeks we nursed Brian back to full health. For a while our home life revolved around his convalescence, and we were oblivious to events taking place outside our two worlds of family and work.

Nineteen seventy-four was drawing to a close. So far it had been an eventful year, each day bringing a mix of surprise, sadness, pleasure and new learning experiences. But fate had some more twists in store for us, and the year wasn't destined to end quietly.

Since September, we had been dealing with Madam Quoi in the adoptions office at the Ministry of Social Welfare. Once a child had an adoptive family and all the other paperwork had been completed, we had to apply for a passport and exit visa, the final step in the long, convoluted process. The situation was made worse when Madam Quoi was interjected as liaison officer between the two ministries involved.

Before we could submit passport applications, she had to check and verify the paperwork. She delighted in her work; a pettifogging bureaucrat at best, she took delight in picking holes in each and every paper that passed before her. No detail was too small to escape her attention, and she almost gleefully rejected submission after submission.

The paperwork rejections caused innumerable delays, as the papers came back to haunt us time and time again. By October the flow of children leaving our Center was reduced to a mere trickle, but the tide of incoming babies and children never ebbed. Soon our large Center was becoming overcrowded. There seemed to be little we could do to ease matters along.

In late October, street rioting broke out across the city as the general population protested against the South Vietnamese government. The riots quickly grew in scale and turned ugly. From our vantage point on top of the apartment building, we watched as fighting broke out down the street. Windows were broken, jeeps and cars were overturned and torched, while crowds of people fought each other with homemade weapons. In our locality the riots lasted for days and normal movement became impossible.

The black market in front of our building seemed to be a rioters' heaven, and we watched as fights broke out up and down our lane. Finally squads of soldiers and police cleared the lane using sticks and the threat of weapons, before erecting formidable barricades at each end of the street.

One morning, when things had calmed down, we sent Ron and Dan off to school. But riots broke out again, and Tom and I pleaded with the soldiers to let us pass. In the end, after a long conversation and a little money, the soldiers grudgingly let us pass so that we could collect our sons.

We drove across town by circuitous routes, through back alleys and small side streets, to avoid bands of rioters and jumpy police patrols, and eventually reached the American Embassy School. All the other pupils had long since gone home, and the boys were watching for us through the windows.

We loaded them into the van and retraced our way back toward the FCVN Center. We were nearly there when we suddenly found ourselves surrounded by a group of rioters. The van rocked back and forth as they beat against its sides. The kids were scared, and though I reassured them, I was scared too. I had visions of the van being tipped over and set on fire with us trapped inside. Tom kept his hand on the horn and slowly we drove through the rioters; as soon as we were clear we made for home.

It was dusk by the time we arrived back at our lane, where we had to satisfy the soldiers again before they allowed us to pass through.

Back in the relative safety of the Center, we all stood on the top balcony and looked towards the city. Through the darkness we could see pockets of flames reaching into the night sky as rioters continued their mayhem, heedless of the nighttime curfew.

The riots lasted for a few days, and even when they had stopped, sporadic fighting and demonstrations flared up around the city for several days more. We all tried to stay off the streets as much as possible, although our staff had to contend with the constant threat of being caught up in the violence as they made their way to and from work.

During the rainy season of October and November, the Center was ravaged by a savage attack of a virulent strain of pneumonia. The damp, chilly air and driving rain that penetrated almost every room combined with the weakness of the babies to make the Center an attractive target for the pneumonia germs. The infection ran rampant through the nursery and there was little we could do to check it. By the time the epidemic was broken, forty of our babies had died. We were devastated. Everyone had worked so hard, but the babies were beyond our help. We cried over each of the deaths, feeling as if a part of us was dying also.

The other centers fared no better than we did. Babies were dying daily, and USAID called an urgent meeting to discuss the situation. Dr. Andre Noe of the International Rescue Committee attended the meeting and praised the efforts of all the adoption agencies that were battling pneumocystis carinii. I soon began to realize that the look of the "old man" baby in Qui Nhon was very characteristic of babies with this condition. It attacked the weak and the most vulnerable. Once the babies caught it, the outcome was usually fatal. It probably caused more deaths of infants in Vietnam than any other disease. We had help from American doctors, who also did autopsies of babies and confirmed the diagnosis.

USAID, realizing the seriousness of the situation, allocated funds to the Seventh Day Adventist Hospital for the International Rescue Committee to set up a critical care unit for the use of all the agencies.

The meeting also proposed that foster programs should be instituted as soon as possible. Fostering would take the children out of the centers and reduce the risk of cross infection. While some of the adoption agencies were not happy at the thought of releasing their charges, we thought it was a great idea and we put plans into motion almost immediately.

We began by fostering a baby we called Beth with Rosie, one of our favorite workers. Rosie was a well-trusted employee with a very caring attitude, and she lived just across the street from the Center, which meant we would be able to monitor baby Beth's progress.

The experiment with little Beth, who ultimately traveled to the Vermiere family in Illinois, was a great success. The arrangement also benefited Rosie, as she stayed home to look after Beth and spent more time with her own children.

Following this successful pilot, we decided to expand the foster program quickly to prevent another fatal pneumonia epidemic from sweeping the Center. We selected babies that were reasonably healthy, having survived the rigors of abandonment and the pneumonia epidemic, and made arrangements to foster them out to stable homes and families we knew in the area.

The foster parents were supplied with a "start-up" kit consisting of such useful items as a baby basket, a hammock, diapers, clothes and milk. Our staff members visited the foster homes every few days to ensure that the babies were accepted into the families and to check that the babies' health continued to improve. FCVN paid each foster family ten dollars per month and provided milk and vitamins for the baby.

The death rate among the children, which had run close to thirty percent at times, dropped dramatically when the foster care program took effect. Some babies still died, those that were simply too weak to take food or to benefit from any help we could offer. But overall the foster program became a great success, and within months we had one hundred children in foster care, many of them housed with former staff workers from our nursery.

❧

The disparity in the ages of the kids in the Center became a problem. The older children needed more space to vent their energy, and due to their increasing numbers, that was no longer possible in the small compound available at the Bui Thi Xuan center.

We located a villa in an area called Thu Duc, about twenty miles outside of the city. The villa had been used by officers of the Bien Hoa military base and was in good condition, with a swimming pool and substantial rooms that could easily house all the children and the staff. Because of its location, the rent was less than one hundred dollars a month. The accommodation was superb, but security that far out of the city was questionable.

Sue, Ross and the Super family moved into Thu Duc with the older children, where they quickly established themselves as an almost independently run unit. Arrangements were made with a local school, and all the Thu Duc children who were old enough were enrolled and attended classes daily.

The black market activities outside the Center were a continual inconvenience, made worse by the young men attracted to the shady dealings. Many of the teenagers were petty thieves, generally called "cowboys," who quickly decided that we represented a great target of opportunity. Time and time again they ran raiding parties into the Center and made off with almost anything that wasn't bolted down. Even if we saw them there was little we could do because they would scamper over the fence and blend into the market crowds. The police told us that they were virtually powerless to help, as the thieves were generally street kids—the Vietnamese called them *bui doi*, which means "the dust of life."

With the departure of so many of the babies to foster homes, and the opening of Thu Duc, the Center was soon virtually empty. We no longer needed the space afforded by the current Center—and that had been its only advantage for us.

We needed to locate a central property more suited to our current and anticipated needs. The ideal house would have enough space for our family and the four boys from Qui Nhon, administrative offices, an intensive care nursery, and a place from which we could monitor the blossoming foster care program.

Finding such a dream house wasn't going to be easy. The husband of one of our nurses, Dao, finally located a large, French-built villa that stood in its own gardens. It was located on Tran Ky Xuong Street, off Chi Lang Street in the Gia Dinh district of the city. The location was a little too far from the center of the city, but it was within striking distance of the places we needed to visit regularly. It wasn't easy to find a suitable property nearer the city center, especially one that had all the space we required.

The house was near a school at the end of a narrow dirt road that was just wide enough for our small van to pass. Behind the property was the entrance to one of Saigon's slum areas. Steve and others advised us against taking the house because of access and security problems. The fence and gates were low, unlike the fencing I'd noticed around other similar properties, but we didn't think security would ever be such a major problem for us again. We were keeping our gate guard and were leaving the black market crowd at the former Center location.

The house was occupied by a single maid who told us that it had been empty for twelve years. That didn't seem important at the time; we just thought that the low rent was a great bargain. The house had become run-down and had a neglected air, and the small swimming pool was filthy with mud and accumulated slime, but we could see the potential through the layers of dirt.

The landlord agreed to paint the interior and refurbish the neglected fittings. We all pitched in to clean the outside, the gardens and the pool. We quickly turned the downstairs living area into an intensive care nursery for thirty babies. After a week's hard work the house was ready, and we moved our family in, including the four older Qui Nhon boys. We hung the FCVN sign on the gate and moved in, just in time for Christmas of 1974.

Quad City Airport, leaving for Saigon: (back from left) Cherie holding Thanh, Ron, Dan, Jenny suitcase, Joanna, Beth, Brian and Tom.

Bui Thi Xuan Center in Saigon with house wading pool and apartment building.

Black market just opening up outside gate of Bui Thi Xuan.

Unloading supplies at Bui Thi Xuan Center.

FCVN Secretary Mai looks on as Cuc helps out.

Betty Beaird with her two sons, Man and Tam, with Clark children and others in Saigon, 1974.

Children playing at FCVN.

Ross Meador and Terri Super with Minh Morris, Loan Cotton, Hai and Luke.

Ross holding Jenny Clark, Lan Mai Markson, with Cuc in front.

Sue Walter playing with the children.

Cherie and Tom Clark with the orphans at the Bui Thi Xuan Center.

Ross Meador

Terri, Jane and Chris looking after babies at Bui Thi Xuan.

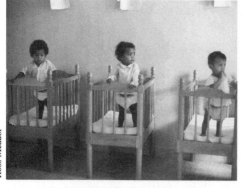

Ross Meador

Thriving children and those who are struggling at the FCVN Center in Saigon.

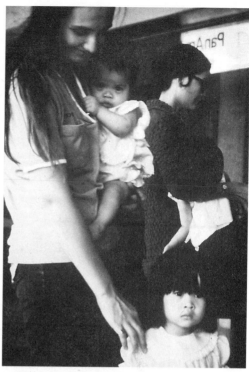

Chau who dearly loved all the children, with Thanh.

Saying good-bye at Tan Son Nhut Airport, August 1974: Sue and Thuy with Lan Mai Markson and baby Hong.

Cheryl Markson with newly arrived baby in the United States.

Bernie Mantey

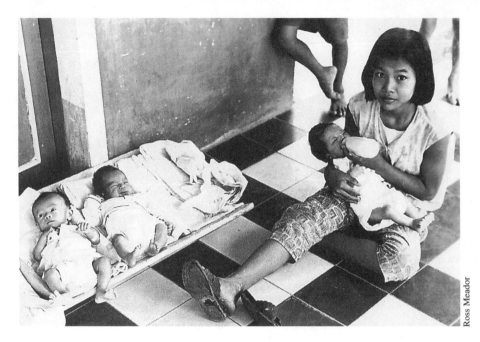

Trip to the Mekong Delta, 1974.

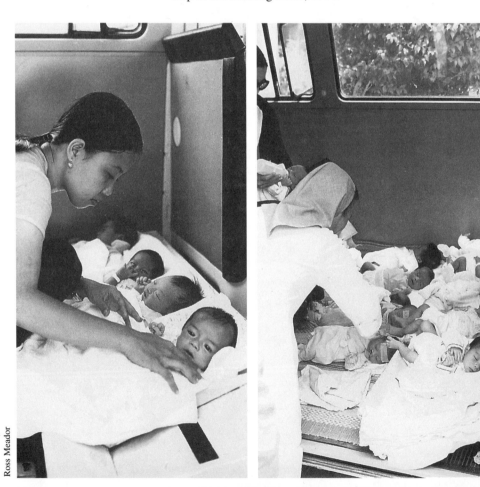

Thuy with sister in Vinh Long.

Father Olivier, Saigon.

Mick Markson

Providence sisters in Soc Trang.

Theosophic Orphanage in Saigon.

Beth in Saigon.

Two Phuong brothers Nick and Paul Smart.

Ron, Thanh (destined for Australia), Dan, Jeff and Jason.

Sue Walter enjoying local transport.

Sister Theresa

Sister Nancy with the younger Thu Duc children.

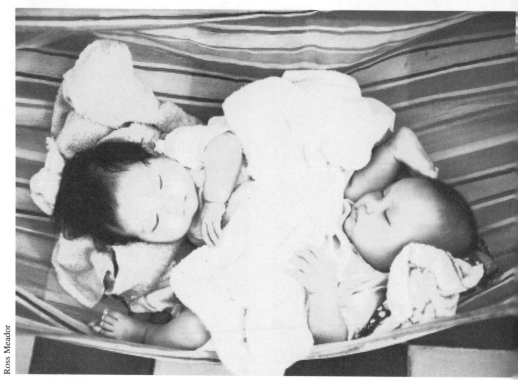

Ross Meador

Babies in foster care.

Ross Meador

Staff members at FCVN Center in Saigon.
Tet 1975

Jason's birthday party, February, 1975, at the FCVN Center.

Cherie's children at nursery school with Laurie Stark (back row, second from left) who died in the C-5A crash. Beth is in front of Laurie; Brian, Joanna and Jenny are in the front row.

Mick Markson

Cherie at the gate of Tran Ky Xuong Center.

FCVN Center and van.

FCVN's Tran Ky Xuong Center.

From the balcony of the FCVN Center: the narrow lane and low wall provided virtually
no security.

Tom Clark and Mick Markson unloading shipment of incubators, January 1975.

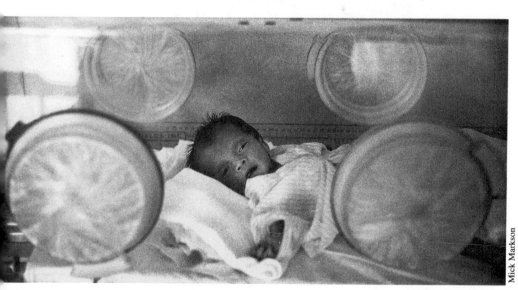

Nga a very special baby who did not survive despite all the love and care she was given.

Ross Meador

Sue and Cherie making some difficult decisions, March 1975.

Mick Markson

Mai Markson in Da Lat January 1975.

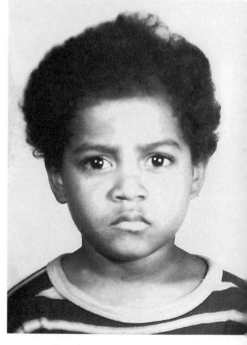

Nam just after his evacuation from Quang Ngai. March 29, 1975.

Chapter Eight

*N*ineteen seventy-five, the Year of the Cat, initially promised to be a good year for FCVN. We had expanded our programs again.

Two American Catholic sisters, Sister Therese Le Blanc and Sister Nancy Aycotte from the Immaculate Heart of Mary order in Michigan, joined us. They were teachers and, along with Ross and Sue, they ran the center for toddlers and older children in Thu Duc. By then the children at Thu Duc were all thriving in the rural location. The sisters replaced the Supers, who, along with their newly adopted son, Luke, had returned to America.

With the help of the Georgia FCVN chapter and their president, Lya Engleken, we were finally able to purchase a newer van we so desperately needed. The van was a blessing; from that time on our weekly forays to the Mekong Delta were much easier. The van also allowed us to take all the children on occasional trips to the coastal town of Vung Tau, about three hours east of Saigon, where they played on the beaches and swam.

We painted the sides of the van with large blue crosses, supposedly to protect us from being attacked while we drove around. The new van also made it easier to transport sick children to the hospital at night. Seeing our blue crosses, the police and soldiers allowed us to pass, and we could travel in violation of Saigon's strictly enforced nighttime curfew.

In mid-January Cheryl and Mick Markson came from the United States to visit us and escort children from Saigon to the States. During their visit the Marksons also traveled to Da Lat to visit a child they had long wanted to adopt. They felt that at last they were making progress and perhaps some-day she would be able to come home to them in America.

Previously Mick had been an officer in the U.S. Army, stationed in Da Lat, where he was captivated by a young orphan girl named Mai. Mick and Cheryl desperately wanted to adopt little Mai, and for five years they had been sending money to the orphanage for her support and education.

Within days of Mick and Cheryl's arrival, we learned that a much-needed shipment of incubators and medical supplies had arrived from the States. The incubators would allow us to save many premature babies who other-wise may not have survived.

Finally, after months of struggling, our adoption programs started progressing smoothly again. Taking into account the state of the country and government, we thought it was a miracle. Months of hard work were paying off, and Thuy and I had developed a great working rapport with the higher-in-rank South Vietnamese officials who oversaw the issuing of passports and adoption paperwork. In effect, we bypassed Madam Quoi. Children's passports started coming through within a reasonable amount of time, and each week, children left Vietnam and were sent off to their adoptive families in the United States, Australia, and Europe.

Our foster care program continued to prove a huge success. Now that word about our work had spread, we were receiving armloads of babies each week, sometimes even as many as twenty infants a day from our trips to the Delta. Some came from the provinces, from hospitals, and others were just abandoned in the street. Too frequently they arrived with no paperwork, and we named them after our friends and family members.

In the FCVN Center we provided plenty of fresh milk and much-needed vitamins for the malnourished babies. None were ever turned away from our doors. Every day we took them outside for sunshine baths; we hugged them and made eye contact with them, played with them and picked them up whenever we had a spare moment—they were all our children.

Most of the babies just needed love, attention and good food. They thrived with all this contact and sustenance, quickly gaining weight and health. As soon as a baby was stable, we would place it in our foster mother program.

We were lucky—donations from FCVN chapters across America provided enough funding so that we could hire sufficient staff for our intensive care nursery. We had one trained worker for every baby. That level of one-on-one contact ensured that each baby received a daily dose of love as well as the essential milk and vitamins.

Steve continued to support our efforts, frequently traveling to the provinces to take supplies to the outlying orphanages and bring back weaker babies and children who needed the extra attention we could provide in the FCVN Center.

While he was still unmarried, Steve adopted twin toddlers, Anthony and Christopher, from Sister Angela in Da Nang. In early 1975 he married his fiancée, Carol Kim, who had a ten-year-old son of her own. Taking a well-earned break, from time to time we went with him to hear her sing in

Saigon's Baccara Club, where we met and became close friends with Jimmy Joseph, another well-known singer there.

In early February, the imminent arrival of Tet, the Vietnamese New Year, brought a great deal of joyful anticipation. This celebration of the lunar New Year is the Vietnamese equivalent of Christmas, New Year and birthdays—all rolled together into one giant celebration.

There is always a great deal of preparation for the coming of Tet. Houses are scrubbed spotless, and almost every surface is decorated with a blaze of colorful blossoms. The whole city takes on a vibrant atmosphere, with even the poorest homes looking bright and cheerful.

Besides decorating their homes, Vietnamese people prepare delicacies for their dead ancestors. It is a time when good and evil spirits are appeased. Families gather and remember their lost loved ones, perform rituals, swap stories and reminisce, and at a designated time they eat the elaborate meals.

We prepared for Tet at the Center in a similar manner. We scrubbed the place from top to bottom and decorated it with narcissus, mums and roses. Like almost every other employer, we gave each of our staff a customary Tet gift, equivalent to one month's pay. Workers used that money to settle bills and to prepare for their own Tet celebrations.

It is important to the Vietnamese that they enter Tet with a clean slate. To be seen without new clothes on the first day of Tet would be considered a disgrace. Debts are paid off and differences and squabbles settled. Tet is a time of friendship, remembering, and looking forward; the whole country is charged with a friendly, benevolent attitude.

At midnight on the tenth of February that year, a massive celebration erupted in fireworks and gunshots as bullets were sprayed into the air. The people went wild in the streets, and after several hours of fireworks, the air in the city was laden with sulfurous smog that brought tears to our eyes. The celebrations lasted for days with people partying in the streets; work was forgotten and normal city activities ground to a halt, leaving only emergency services available. Our staff carefully divided their time to be certain that the babies were cared for but that everyone had time with their families as well.

Despite the ominous gathering of war clouds on the horizon, most people went on with their lives as if the potential for war was only a media-generated story, another empty political threat, and had no real meaning. Life continued as normal in Saigon: people married, made plans, and looked to their futures. Builders and architects carried on with the business of constructing new homes and factories.

On the other hand, it wasn't difficult to find others with widely differing viewpoints. There were those who looked at the bigger picture and perhaps saw through the government's propaganda—they thought that the bubble would soon burst and that communist troops would pour down from the North.

ಳ

By the time March arrived, it became obvious that the South Vietnamese military was struggling to contain the communist forces. For the first time, we thought that perhaps we would have to change our long-term plans.

The Centers were still exceedingly busy as more babies and older children kept piling in by the day. All the staff were exhausted by the long hours and the never-ending stream of children who badly needed care.

We were aware that the war wasn't going well. The Vietnamese staff were worried about the military reversals, and an undercurrent of tension pervaded the atmosphere in the Center. Laughter and jokes among the staff became less frequent as people contemplated the uncertainty of their futures.

The undercurrents and rumors came to a head on March fourteenth when, without any warning, South Vietnam's President Nguyen Van Thieu surrendered the Central Highlands to the advancing enemy forces. Everybody, including Americans and other foreigners in Saigon, was stunned by the shattering news.

The war had been fought between the North and the South for more than two decades; hundreds of thousands of soldiers and civilians on both sides had already died in the bitter ideological struggle. Then, with a sweep of his pen, the President gave it away. Had all the lost lives been given in vain? The people of Pleiku, Kontum, and the rest of the Central Highlands were given only hours to leave their homes and head for refuge in the South, or ready themselves for the communist victors.

The South Vietnamese population had been fed propaganda for years—newspapers, radio and television telling them that the American and South

Vietnamese armies were better trained and equipped than the communist guerrillas they were fighting. Many had believed that the South could ultimately overcome the communist forces, which after all were only foot soldiers without any supporting navy or air force.

To learn that the President had simply given up the struggle, withdrawn his forces and left hundreds of thousands of his people to fend for themselves was a terrible blow to the country's morale.

That day changed things forever. Suddenly the newspapers and television were full of images of a country in flight and panic. More than half a million South Vietnamese fled south into Saigon to escape the communist forces. People abandoned homes, farms, and their belongings in a headlong rush for the security of the country's capital. They came on foot, bicycles, water buffalo carts, in buses, trucks and private cars, all seeking sanctuary. Nobody dreamed that the South Vietnamese government, or their American allies, would let the capital fall to the enemy.

Almost immediately communications with the Highlands were lost. Families were split, and our staff were deeply worried about the fate of their family members, last heard of in the now communist-controlled areas. Everyone was stressed, and laughter became a thing of the past.

As the atmosphere of panic increased, so did our work in the centers. We were flooded with a new influx of half-American children. Mothers who had kept their children in the hope that their American boyfriends would someday return thought that the child would be under a death sentence if it fell into communist hands. These children weren't unwanted—their mothers loved them dearly but thought that now there was no way they could protect them and bring them up as their own. Their world was turning upside down.

Soldiers deserted by the thousands and mingled with the civilian refugees streaming into Saigon, many bringing horror stories of what they had seen. From our protected position in Saigon, we heard terrible accounts of carnage and death. We heard of people being crushed underfoot on the road and people drowning as they tried to escape south by sea on makeshift rafts and boats.

The Marksons' seven-year-old daughter, Mai, was in the orphanage at Da Lat that had been overrun by the communists. I prayed she would survive. I knew Cheryl would be terrified when she heard about Thieu's surrender of the Highlands.

As the war progressed, American officials in Saigon started holding regular briefings. We attended some of them to be as informed as possible about the war effort. From the start, straight-faced officials offered a great deal more hope than our friends. Just about any situation could be colored as a "good news" day. They were always optimistic and talked about the stability of the South Vietnamese forces, yet the truth was there for all to see on the charts that they showed us. The provinces that had "fallen" were red and the secured area's were blue. Red was increasing rapidly.

It is difficult to know what prompted the officials to lend such a positive stance to what looked to many like a lost cause. Some said it was to prevent panic, others that it was an effort to get more money from Congress. Maybe some of the officials also loved Vietnam and didn't want to believe that it could soon be lost forever.

We planned what would be our last trip into the Mekong Delta. The sisters from the orphanages there had sent cables, urgently asking us to visit them and collect as many abandoned babies as possible, before they were overrun.

Thuy and I made the journey in mid-March, after the provinces in the Central Highlands had already fallen. Sy, our young Vietnamese driver, who also helped around the Center, drove us. It would be our most dangerous trip yet to the Delta, and we planned to make it a quick run down and back.

As we drove slowly down to Vinh Long, we could see the war closing in around us. Soldiers, military transports, tanks, self-propelled guns and jeeps were everywhere.

When we arrived at Vinh Long, we visited the military hospital to search for a dear friend who was a soldier; it was rumored that he was wounded and might be there. Inside, the conditions were appalling—it was more a charnel house than a hospital. The entire building was crammed with cots, each holding at least two soldiers who lay side by side, one's feet alongside the other's head. A few soldiers were connected to IVs, but I saw several empty bottles and blood was backing up into the clear plastic tubing.

Flies were everywhere, crawling over open wounds. These poor men weren't being treated; they were waiting in the anteroom of death. The stench was terrible—the reek of blood, dirt, feces and death cloyed the air. Some men lay quietly weeping, awaiting the inevitable, while others moaned in pain, longing in vain for someone to come to their aid.

There was no control evident. Nobody seemed to be in charge, and we were allowed to wander around the place at will. We searched each room, looking for our friend, but it was a waste of time. Many of the soldiers were badly injured or unconscious and they couldn't talk to us.

There was nothing we could do for the men and, feeling like interlopers, we quietly backed out of the building, shocked by the stark reality of the war that was being fought around us. We were seeing the results of the shootings and bombings that had become our nightly serenade, so commonplace that we almost ignored it—now we were looking at what happened when the bullets and bombs found their mark.

We continued driving south, stopping at makeshift field hospitals where we saw some ARVN medics ministering to the wounded soldiers. These "hospitals" were nothing more than a few small camouflaged tents gathered around a truck or jeep, where the injured and the dying lay on stretchers or propped against trees and truck wheels.

As we searched again for our friend, I came across a young dying soldier, leaning against a tree. Instinctively I leaned towards him and saw that his abdomen was ripped apart, his stomach a red, gory mess. He was bleeding freely as he pressed his hands into the wound, trying vainly to staunch the flow. He looked up at me and reached out a blood-smeared hand. I knelt down and grasped it in mine.

The soldier tried to speak to me but no words came, just a trickle of blood from his mouth. He stared at me, his face questioning as he tried to come to terms with his own imminent death and his eyes begged me to stop the pain from his massive wound. I could do nothing for this young teenager, and I felt devastated at this senseless waste of life.

Thuy motioned me to join the others quickly, but the young soldier wouldn't let go of my hand. Despite the horrific wound, his grip was strong, as if the hand he held were life itself. In tears I pulled away, wiped the tears from his face and left him. As I joined the others in the van, I knew with a sickening certainty that he would soon be dead, released from his unbearable pain. I cleaned the blood from my hands, but I couldn't wipe off the feel of his grip on my hand.

When we arrived at the orphanage in Can Tho, night was falling. The sounds of battles being fought in the jungle around us were loud, and close, as we settled down to spend the night in the orphanage. The sisters told us that their orphanage in Bac Lieu was in desperate straits. We hadn't planned to venture any further south into the war zone, but we knew we had no alternative—we had to help the children. The sisters refused to take any of our supplies, preferring that we save all the medicine for Bac Lieu.

The following morning we set off early—we needed to make the unplanned trip as fast as we could and be out of the battle zone by evening. The journey to Bac Lieu was about fifty miles along a narrow, bumpy Delta road. That far in the Delta there was no front line and the roadway was not heavily defended. As we traveled in grim silence, we knew that we might be attacked at any moment.

At the Bac Lieu Orphanage, we were met by the frightened sisters. Quickly we off-loaded all of our supplies and they pressed ten babies on us, anxious that we take them back to Saigon. We didn't hang around for the offered cups of tea or make any pleasantries. We knew we were in a dangerous situation and we had to get back to relative safety before nightfall.

On the return trip we were stopped by some soldiers, who warned us that there was a firefight ahead of us; we couldn't drive any further. We sat by the roadside, nervously listening to the roar of low-flying planes as a battle raged a few miles ahead.

By the time we were allowed to continue toward Can Tho we were running out of daylight—we wouldn't be able to reach Vinh Long before dark. At Can Tho the sisters brought our babies into their center, and we stayed there for the second night, listening again to the horrific noise of battles being fought just miles away in the surrounding Delta. The orphanage telephone wasn't working, so we had no way to contact our Center and let them know we were all right; we knew they were worrying about us.

The next morning we wept as we said goodbye to the sisters. We all knew there would be no more trips to the Delta until the military situation had eased, and we had no way of knowing when that would be. They promised to tell the sisters in the Providence orphanages in Soc Trang, Sadec, and Rac Gia, whom we had come to love so much, that we would return as soon as it was possible. Even as we made that promise, we had no idea what fate had in store, or if we would ever see them again.

Saying good-bye to Sister Eugenia was one of the hardest things I had to do. Her sister, Dau, was working with us in Saigon, and I promised Sister Eugenia that somehow I would take care of Dau and do all that I could to stay in touch with Can Tho. The thought that we would be cut off from them was unbearable. We loaded the van with our precious cargo of babies, now thirty in number, and set off for Vinh Long, the first leg on our dash for Saigon.

We reached the ferry by mid-morning and crossed without too much difficulty. The lack of civilian traffic reduced our waiting time considerably and we crossed the muddy, brown river in near record time.

A few miles beyond Vinh Long we were stopped by soldiers manning a barricade strung across the road. They told us that there was heavy fighting ahead, and that the road had been badly damaged by enemy mortar and rocket attack. Frustrated and frightened, we had no option but to wait by the roadside again, the hot sun broiling us in the van.

The heat was unbearable and the babies started to dehydrate. One of the weakest babies, a premature infant girl who we had thought had little chance of survival, died in my arms. I wrapped the tiny body in a blanket and laid her on the seat beside me.

Tanks rumbled past, followed by squads of heavily armed, tired-looking soldiers, all heading toward the battle. Our route to Saigon was effectively cut off by the fighting.

Suddenly a loud whistling noise ripped the air and a rocket smashed into the ground behind us, missing our van by just a few feet, spattering us with mud and soil. We were all too scared to talk—we just looked at one another, then continued tending the hot, sick babies while we waited nervously for some word that we could travel on.

A few minutes later a jeep screamed to a halt beside us. A Vietnamese officer jumped out, and I saw three dead soldiers in the back without even a blanket covering their bloody bodies. He said that the ferry further behind us had been attacked and sunk, and that many of the passengers were dead. Before leaving, he promised to return and tell us when it would be safe for us to continue to Saigon.

By now we were all very frightened, and when another group of soldiers stopped and told us to try to make it to Saigon, because the fighting was drawing closer, we didn't hesitate. We knew that if we were on the road when darkness fell we would be trapped and caught in the battle raging around us.

Driving carefully, Sy dodged fresh craters on the road as we aimed for the outskirts of Saigon and relative safety. We finally made it there just before curfew. In the city we picked up speed and ended up racing against the clock as we headed for the safety of the Center. Once we were inside, our friends and the staff wept with relief—they had feared we had pushed our luck too far this time.

We knew that the situation in Qui Nhon and Da Nang was worsening rapidly. Thuy and I made one of our last visits up there to bring back as many of the half-American children as we could. One was a small boy named Chau that Thuy hoped to adopt herself.

We spent a restless night at St. Paul's. In the early morning what we assumed to be a stray rocket hit the side of the orphanage and cracked the wall. We were jolted awake as the babies and children all began to scream. Thankfully, no one was injured. Only the week before, Thuy and I had a similar experience in the Da Nang orphanage when it too was hit by a rocket. The war was too close.

Ross and Tom spent days at the Air America offices, trying to get seats to fly up to evacuate our other orphanage children who had already been assigned to adoptive families.

Air America adamantly refused to transport us because the situation was so dangerous. We couldn't risk flying on Air Vietnam. Their flights going up were empty, but coming back, they were so overbooked that there was no chance of getting seats for the children we wanted to evacuate. Tickets were being sold on the black market for two hundred to a thousand dollars in gold.

We were effectively cut off from the northern orphanages; there was no way we could get back up there with medicine and supplies. As predicted, the enemy moved in quickly, and many of the sisters left their centers to try to make their way to Saigon, with their babies, on their own.

On March twenty-four the ancient city of Hue, the religious and cultural capital of Vietnam, surrendered to the communist forces without a fight. We learned from the radio that fifty thousand vehicles were gridlocked bumper-to-bumper on the two-lane highway between Hue and Da Nang.

At Hue's port on the South China Sea, forty thousand refugees waited desperately for boats to carry them south to safety. Others streamed into Da Nang on foot, struggling to stay ahead of the encroaching communist armies. The enemy was only a few military steps behind them, and sanctuary in Da Nang was nothing more than a temporary illusion. The war was quickly turning into a rout.

I had always spent a lot of time in the Passport Office, dragging around the files of the orphans in our care and begging officials to provide the necessary papers and passports. As the situation worsened after the collapse of the Central Highlands, the bureaucrats became more reluctant to help.

We heard that many Vietnamese were trading their life savings, paying thousands of dollars for exit visas. This made it even less likely that the harried officials would help us—we had nothing to offer. I persevered, sometimes waiting frustrated and anxious at a desk for three or four hours, while officials who had helped us before did their best to ignore me. Occasionally my perseverance paid off and I left the building triumphantly with a fistful of passports.

The war was advancing toward us daily. Rocket fire could now be heard day and night, planes and choppers wheeled continually overhead, and soldiers and police roamed the streets, trying to keep some sort of order in the ever-escalating population.

As the days clicked away in March we heard of more provinces falling and being abandoned to the oncoming forces. The tension increased. Everyone was now nervous and looking to find some way to escape from what was quickly becoming the siege of Saigon.

The nights were growing hotter, and the continual sound of rockets combined with the heat made sleep difficult. I tossed and turned in my bed, exhausted but unable to sleep, worrying about my own adopted children.

All three were still Vietnamese citizens, and I feared that something might happen to stop us from getting them out if the situation got worse. I had listened to the horror stories of the refugees, and I had to get them to safety.

I knew it would be traumatic for Jenny, Joanna and Thanh to return to America without us, but finally Tom and I decided that they had to leave. I called Cheryl in Colorado and asked if we could send them to her. Then I voiced the fear that was foremost in my mind.

"Cheryl, if the rest of us don't make it out, can you and Mick keep them—or if you can't, will you please, please promise me that they won't be separated?"

Cheryl tearfully agreed.

We reserved seats for them on March twenty-sixth, the next Pan Am flight to the States. It was agreed that Sue should take them back. At least with her nearby, their adjustment wouldn't be so difficult.

I had continued to suffer with bouts of illness caused by a mixture of hepatitis and stress. Now, looking at Sue as she prepared for her trip, I saw for the first time how ill she looked. Pale, fatigued, far too thin, she needed to see a doctor, and soon.

Jodie Darragh, a person well known for her work with orphans, was leaving on the same flight. She and Sue would share the responsibility for my children and a group of orphans on the long flight home.

My children already had passports, but those were worthless without the essential exit visas. After waiting impatiently for days, Tom finally lost his temper at the Passport Office. His persistence paid off, and at last we held three passports stamped with the precious exit visas.

For the first time, I was voluntarily letting my family be split. It grieved me, but we were doing what we knew was best for the children. There was a great deal of crying as we packed the children and Sue into the van and left for the short drive to the airport.

I feared that I might never see my children again. Now I could empathize with the Vietnamese who wailed hysterically about their lost family members—I understood the pain and torment that they continually endured.

We crossed the hot tarmac to the aluminum steps leading up to the doorway in the 747's side. As we had done with every other flight with orphans, we planned to escort the children onto the plane and have a last-minute good-bye after we settled them in their seats.

But as we started to climb the steps, we were forcibly stopped by the Pan Am staff. They told us they had received a bomb threat, and only passengers were allowed to board.

I was devastated—my hopes of a loving farewell with my children were dashed. My last vision of them, perhaps to be my final vision, was watching them being dragged into the plane as they screamed "Mommy! Daddy!" as if their lives were ending.

Heartbroken, I was sobbing as Tom guided me back to the terminal. A huge truck roared past us, laden with wooden coffins, each draped in the yellow and red striped flag of South Vietnam. The nauseating odor of rotting corpses assailed my senses, the smell overpowering despite the stench of diesel fumes belching from the overloaded truck.

The sight of the coffins brought home the horrors of war to me. I was in the middle of a war zone in a country that was rapidly collapsing, and I wondered if I would ever see my beloved children again.

On March twenty-ninth, Tom, and I received word that an orphanage in Quang Ngai, a coastal town north of Da Nang, had been rocketed during heavy fighting in the city. This was the third orphanage that, to our knowledge, had been bombed in March. More than one hundred children and workers had died in the attack.

Surviving nuns and children had been flown by the South Vietnamese army to a field near the coastal city of Vung Tau. They had fled empty-handed; all their supplies and provisions had been left behind.

Soldiers were patrolling the city streets; concertina rolls of barbed wire were strung across roads. The noise was deafening. Planes and helicopters were arriving and departing continually at the nearby Tan Son Nhut airport. The war machine was kicking into top gear all around us as the fighting drew ever closer.

I decided we had to go and help the stricken sisters and children. Despite the obvious danger and against the advice of our astonished friends and coworkers, we crammed the van with clothing, milk, and other supplies, and set off in the early morning light with Tom at the wheel. There was a very real risk that we would be attacked, but our concern for the victims won over our own fears, and our friends watched silently at the gate as we pulled away.

Along the way, we were frequently stopped by South Vietnamese soldiers manning makeshift roadblocks. The soldiers were hostile and surly as they checked our papers and examined our supplies at each stop. We finally completed the journey after a grueling five hours; we were all hot, sweaty, dusty, tired—and scared.

We found the children housed temporarily in an open-sided, dilapidated corrugated building that might once have been a storage warehouse. There was no running water or electricity and the floor was just packed dirt. There was a stench of raw sewage, and we saw an open pipe dripping filth into a small pond; the area was filled with millions of buzzing mosquitoes and big black flies.

Inside the warehouse, babies and children were sleeping on the floor—there were no beds to be seen. The scene inside the building was atrocious, dirt and filth everywhere. Older children were trying to comfort the crying babies. Having escaped from their bombed-out orphanage in the middle of the night, the children and nuns possessed only what clothes they wore. They had no towels, bedding, or even the most basic necessities.

It was obvious that many of the babies were very sick. Without boiled water or fresh milk they would dehydrate and ultimately die. The metal roof seemed to concentrate the sun's heat, and the temperature inside was overwhelming. The smell of vomit and diarrhea added to the foulness in the air. Flies crawled over every baby, landing on their eyes and mouths; many babies didn't have the strength to push them away.

Tom helped the older children clear an area of trash so they could have a place to sleep. Working under the appalling conditions, I began examining babies and giving out medicine as well as I could.

Amongst the desolate group was a four-year-old black child whose father had obviously been an African American. The sisters told us that they feared for his safety if the communists arrived; they too had heard rumors of half-American children being killed by the Viet Cong throughout the country-side. They wanted this boy to be taken to the city and hopefully adopted by an American family.

They told us his name was Nam.

I thought I had never seen such a beautiful child. In the midst of this terrible situation, with so much desperation, suffering and loss, I was amazed that this one small child could offer me such a trusting look. When the sisters asked him if he wanted to go to Saigon with Tom and me, he immediately nodded yes.

One sister, in the middle of all that suffering, teased him, telling him we were his new American parents. I looked into his huge black eyes and saw the sadness there, and wondered if her words would come true.

We spent several hours helping out, but we knew that if we didn't make it back into the city before the curfew we would be in serious trouble. We had to leave.

Nam readily left with us, without even a backward glance to the nuns. The trip back to Saigon was as tedious as when we came. We were stopped at roadblocks every few miles and subjected to a barrage of questions, repeated mindlessly at each stop.

While we were driving Tom asked me if we would be taking Nam to Thu Duc, our center for orphaned children. Not just yet, I said. Let him stay with us for a while.

Finally, after another five-hour, mind-numbing journey, we arrived back at our Center. The staff rushed to embrace us. Exhausted after a long and emotional day, we simply fell into our beds and slept the sleep of the just.

While we had been working to save the lives of the orphans in Vung Tau, and tussling with petty-minded soldiers throughout the lengthy and dangerous journey, we were ignorant of other important events taking place that would soon affect all our lives.

Several hundred miles north of where we had been that day, the coastal city of Da Nang—the second largest city remaining under South Vietnamese control, and one of the largest military bases—fell to the communists without a fight. A week earlier President Thieu had announced that the city would be defended to the last man.

The doorway was now open to Saigon.

Chapter Nine

*T*he pressure was mounting; we all felt that something was going to break. The government machinery carried on, apparently indifferent to the masses of tense, angry people streaming by their doors and the sounds of warfare echoing down the corridors. But it was only a facade—the infrastructure was beginning to break down.

Our paramount concern was for the safety of our forty-plus children and three American staff members in the Thu Duc center, which was located outside the city limits, too far away for us to guarantee their safety. The children were age two and over; many of them were half-American and had adoptive families waiting for them in the States.

We had already obtained Vietnamese passports, complete with exit visas, for the babies and children who had been cleared for adoption by the Vietnamese government, including the children in Thu Duc. All that was required to complete the adoption process were U.S. immigration visas—which usually took months to obtain.

I knew that in the past the U.S. had granted humanitarian parole visas; that was how Jenny had bypassed the immigration process. I went to the U.S. Embassy and met with a Consular Officer, Mary Lee Garrison, in an attempt to get the INS visas we needed. She dismissed my desperate pleas and imperiously told me that she would telex Washington and try to get the visas expedited; that was the best offer of help she would make.

We had heard through our Vietnamese contacts and from FCVN directors in the States that there was a strong possibility the American government might evacuate our children. We all hoped that the rumors were founded in fact and not simply another fabricated story. When I mentioned the rumors to Garrison, she flatly denied them; she was adamant that there were no official plans for an evacuation. Dejected and upset, I left the passports in her care, hoping against hope that the U.S. visas would be stamped in them soon.

Despite the Consul's emphatic denial, events had been moving on the international scene. On the first of April the South Vietnamese Ambassador to the United Nations made a plea for the urgent evacuation of orphans from Saigon to the safety of the United States or other friendly countries.

In Saigon, we were unaware of the Ambassador's pleas, but we would soon learn of his impassioned speech from friends who telephoned us from the States. They told us that the two governments were considering mounting an evacuation of the orphans.

Closer to home on the first of April, Qui Nhon fell to the communists. We were frightened. We knew there was little time to get our children to safety.

At the same time, afraid that children already approved for adoption would be trapped in Saigon as the North Vietnamese advanced, agencies and prospective parents in the States were pleading with both the Vietnamese and American governments to cut through the red tape and urgently expedite the evacuation of the orphans.

Eventually, the mounting pressure on the two governments proved to be enough, and they formally agreed that the orphans could be evacuated. The agreement was not only a humanitarian gesture, but was also part of a greater strategy. The governments thought that the publicity derived from such an airlift would win sympathy for the plight of Vietnam in the U.S. Congress and encourage the passing of a bill to provide yet more millions of dollars to help the besieged South Vietnamese government.

Unknown to us in FCVN, USAID charged the U.S. Military Airlift Command(MAC) with overall responsibility for the airlift and provided funding for them to evacuate the orphans and set up reception and processing centers at military bases in the Pacific and on the American West Coast.

We did not find out about the proposed airlift until Wednesday, the second of April.

On the morning of April second, Tom and I had been on another fruitless visa-begging trip to the U.S. Embassy, more frustrated than usual because of Garrison's emphatic "No" when we asked if there would be an evacuation. We arrived back at the Center hot, tired and frustrated, to be met with a great surprise.

A delighted Thuy waved a note and a letter in our faces. The communications had been hand-delivered in our absence. The letter was addressed to the Prime Minister from the Minister of Social Welfare. The contents of the letter were extraordinary.

Minister Phan Quang Dan's letter to the Prime Minister read:

April 2, 1975
Dear Mr. Prime Minister:

At the present time, approximately 1400 orphans have been brought to Saigon, and are being cared for by international welfare agencies prior to being taken to foreign countries where they will be placed with permanent adoptive parents. At present, operations of the Ministry of Social Welfare and Hamlet Building and the Inter-ministerial War Victims Relief Committee have been severely hampered by some complicated situations, among which requiring immediate resolution are the problems. The orphans cited above which must be handled in conjunction with many other important difficulties that we are faced with. Moreover, the whole question of collective emigration of this number of orphans mentioned above is further exciting world opinion, particularly in the United States, much to the benefit of the Republic of Vietnam.

Right now, there are two 727's belonging to World Airways that have been waiting all night at the Tan Son Nhut airport, prepared to transport free of charge the emigrating orphans. Mr. Daly, the President of the above mentioned airlines, is an international figure. The American Ambassador has also interceded with me to permit the orphans to leave the country together. He stressed, in addition to this emigration issue, how a million refugees and war victims fleeing the areas taken over by the communists would help to turn American public opinion regarding Vietnam, particularly the orphans arriving in the United States, given extensive TV and press coverage with narrated reports from witnesses of the situation, would have considerable influence.

If you agree, Mr. Prime Minister, to approve the emigration of the orphans mentioned above, the Ministry of Social Welfare and Hamlet Building will coordinate with USAID to carefully monitor and control the international welfare agencies' implementation of this operation.

Respectfully,
Signed and sealed
Phan Quang Dan
Approved
Prime Minister Signature

National Police should be
Aware of the Prime Minister's
Decision and to allow departure
Of the children
Signed/Sealed
Chat
Translated by, and Distributed through USAID

The note from Dr. An's office accompanying the letter from the Director of Social Welfare asked that we urgently bring to his office a list of all the children under our care.

We were so ecstatic about the letter and note that we all laughed with joy, and despite our tiredness we danced and hugged in the driveway. We hadn't the time for more celebrations; if we were to get the children out quickly, we had a lot of work to complete in a short space of time.

Clutching the note and letter, I ran indoors to the telephone to call USAID, but once again the telephone lines were down.

Tom and I drove through the crowds to the USAID offices, located near the U.S. Embassy, where Juanita Nofflet, a friendly USAID officer, was conversing with one of her colleagues, Robert King. They looked at the letter and confirmed its authenticity. I asked for further instructions and advice and was told by Bob King that everything had been approved and that the next step was to prepare the children for departure and to arrange air transportation to the United States.

"Just like that?" I said. "Nothing else?"

They assured me everything was all set. There was one caveat; we would have to locate and organize our own transportation.

Initially I thought that would be no problem, I was holding a letter confirming that World Airways had two planes on the ground at Tan Son Nhut and they were ready, willing and able to move children immediately.

Everyone had heard of Ed Daly. Only a few days earlier he had dramatically flown several of his World Airways planes into Da Nang as the city was falling to the communists.

The American Consulate had promised to evacuate all of their Vietnamese staff to safety. In the last moments of the evacuation the planes were mobbed, and rifles and fists held back the Vietnamese as the Americans boarded the flights.

In the process they made lots of promises but ended up leaving behind their loyal and trusted staff. The situation became critical, and apparently Daly went back to Da Nang and tried to rescue as many women and children as possible. Unfortunately, the planes were stormed again. Pictures were shown of men hanging on the landing gear and falling to their deaths as the planes took off. A full media crew was on board so the flight was well documented and controversial.

The USAID officer quickly killed the idea that we could use one of the Daly planes. He told us that the planes had already been designated to transport Rosemary Taylor's children later that day.

We learned from the USAID officer that some of the other adoption agencies had already arranged evacuation flights. Despite my happiness at the imminent evacuation of the children, a nagging question hammered at the back of my mind. How had other agencies had the time to organize the evacuation of their charges, yet we had been consistently told—even earlier the same day—that there was no planned airlift?

It was obvious that FCVN had been kept out of the information loop. We had never enjoyed a cozy relationship with the U.S. Embassy and USAID, and while we were still struggling to pin down hard information, some of the other agencies had already been preparing to evacuate their children to the United States. Once again petty politics had intervened, and our children were being used as pawns in a game they didn't understand.

I put my anger away—I had to deal with the here and now. Where could we get a plane on such short notice? Where could we find a company willing to charter us a passenger airplane, and how could we pay for an international charter of a jet plane?

Despondent again, we trailed back to the FCVN Center. Luckily, our telephone was now working, and we began calling everyone we knew who might be able to help us organize a relief flight at such short notice. We had no idea how much it would cost to charter a plane or where we could raise the necessary funds. I heard that one Saigon agency had agreed to pay half a million dollars for a charter.

I tried to call Cheryl to ask for help but the international operator told me it would take four days to get the call through. Despite my pleas, she remained unimpressed and I banged the receiver down in frustration.

In between calls, the telephone rang. It was an American nurse I knew from another relief organization. Excitedly she told me that Ed Daly, the president of the charter airline World Airways, had empty airplanes sitting on the runway at Tan Son Nhut airport and was preparing to depart for the United States soon.

I told her that we already knew about the planes and that Rosemary's children would be leaving on them. The nurse told me that at the last moment Rosemary had refused Ed Daly's offer of transportation. Immediately our spirits picked up. Tom, Ross and I piled in the van and drove to the airport. If Rosemary didn't want to take advantage of Daly's offer of a free flight to freedom for the children, then we would.

One way or another, surely, our children would soon be leaving Saigon. Meanwhile, thousands of displaced refugees were still piling into the overcrowded city—they had nowhere else to run. By then there wasn't a spare bed to be found anywhere, and whole families were reduced to sleeping in the streets. The constant noise of war in the distance was a steady reminder that the days of Saigon were numbered.

At Tan Son Nhut we cleared the security checkpoints and made our way to a cafeteria, where Ed Daly was holding court.

The air in the small room was blue with cigarette smoke. The room was packed with journalists and airline staff, all listening as Daly ranted about the government and FFAC, who, he had just learned, had refused his offer to evacuate their children.

Apparently, the American government was furious at Daly about the Da Nang fiasco, perhaps because he brought so much public attention to their betrayal and their empty promises. Perhaps they had influenced Rosemary not to take his flight.

As we walked through the door Daly looked over and stopped in midsentence. In the silent lull, the three of us walked towards him. My first impression of him was not good. He was wearing some sort of soft hat that lay askew on his head; his face was flushed, and he clutched a bottle of Johnnie Walker in one hand and a gun in the other. He was banging the table with the silver-colored handgun, emphasizing his anger. He looked like an enraged bear—definitely not a man to tangle with.

He paused in his shouting and looked at us questioningly; we quickly introduced ourselves and told him of our plight. Angry and dismissive, he cut me short and said, "I'm not talking to any fucking women!"

Shocked, I backed off and Tom and Ross stepped forward and tried to reason with him. They told him that we had two hundred children in our nearby Center that we desperately needed to evacuate out of Saigon. Tom showed him the Ministry letter and an aide translated it for him. Daly thought about the situation. He quickly made up his mind. Assured that we weren't involved with the FFAC, he told us that he would evacuate our children and that we had two hours to prepare everything and get them loaded on the plane.

We shook our heads; it just wasn't possible to prepare so many children in such a short time. Some of the babies were critically ill and some were in foster care; we would have to collect them from their foster homes around the city. Two hours was an impossible deadline for us to meet.

The situation seemed hopeless. Besides the short time frame, we had little faith in Daly, who seemed out of control. Regretfully, we realized we would have to try again on our own to find a suitable plane for the evacuation.

Disappointed again, we tailed back to the FCVN Center, where I tried the telephone but still had no luck in placing an international call. Instead, I composed a cable to send to Cheryl and Carol, asking for their help. By now it was dark outside and I started the mammoth job of typing a list of names of all the children in our care.

The routine of the Center carried on as normal around me. While we had been pleading with Daly, one of our sick babies had died. The eternal dance of life and death continued while our meager attempts to shape destiny seemed to go unheeded.

But somewhere God smiled on us. At about quarter to eight that night, several jeeps raced into our driveway, disgorging men as they screeched to a halt. Rushing inside, boots stomping noisily on the tiled floor, they introduced themselves, and they all seemed hyped and raring to go. Two of them were officials from the airport immigration staff; they were accompanied by a few police officers and a couple of World Airways staff. The immigration officials told me that they had received clearance from Minister Dan's office and the Ministry of the Interior that our children could leave immediately. The World Airways men told us that we had one hour to ready the children for evacuation.

Tom and I quickly discussed the situation. We agreed it would be impossible to ready the babies in time, so we decided to send the older children. The only trouble with that plan was that they were located outside the city at Thu Duc, a thirty-minute drive away.

Tom rushed out and drove our van to Thu Duc, where he arrived unannounced, to tell the shocked staff that the children were going to be evacuated immediately. The children had heard the evacuation rumors and there was already an excited undercurrent in the villa. Many of the older children already knew their new families, who had traveled from America to meet them. They were ecstatic at Tom's news that they were going to leave that very night; their laughter rang around the compound.

While Tom and Ross hustled and squeezed the orphans into the vans and drove back to Gia Dinh, I spent time organizing and hurriedly preparing boxes of food and supplies to sustain the children on their flight to freedom. As I frantically rushed around, filling boxes and bags, I was unaware that Ed Daly had already stocked his plane with goodies: Coke, milk, baby food and the ubiquitous diapers.

When Tom and Ross arrived with the Thu Duc children we decided at the last minute to also evacuate Jason, Jeff, Jeremy and Thanh, as well as Nam, the child we had fallen in love with on our trip to help the bombed-out orphans. Thuy asked me if we could also send Chau, the lovely, four-year-old, half-white orphaned boy who had recently been brought down from Qui Nhon, and whom she had hoped to formally adopt. It was a hard, tearful decision to send these precious children away, but we wanted to do the best for them, and this might be their only chance at getting out of the hell that Vietnam was becoming.

My children, Ron, Dan, Beth and Brian, were crying as their friends made ready to leave, but they wanted to stay with Tom and me. They seemed to be the abandoned ones now—all the friends they loved were leaving them behind. My heart went out to my kids, and I would have loved to send them along on the Daly flight, but they weren't orphans, and the permission we had was definitely for orphans only.

When we left the Center, the two vans were crammed beyond capacity with fifty-two children and four adults. I traveled in one of the accompanying police jeeps, loaded up with fresh bread, drinks, and some clothing for the children.

A convoy of Saigon police and immigration officials escorted the vans on the drive to Tan Son Nhut. We made an impressive sight as we drove along the dark streets, lights flashing and horns blaring as the crowds parted before us. The rotating beacons flashing from the police jeeps threw surreal shadows on the buildings that lined the road.

At the airport, we were waved through the security checkpoints by saluting soldiers, without even pausing to show any identification. The convoy lurched to a halt at the side of a small, well-lit building. Ed Daly rushed out and suddenly the darkness was split by flash bulbs. Reporters appeared, jostling each other and shouting questions, mobbing us—surely they didn't expect us to be interviewed now?

Ed Daly seemed to thrive on the attention. He was larger than life, and his magnetism drew the reporters around him. He took charge, climbing onto the running board of the lead jeep and shouting for us to head out to his plane.

Our convoy raced across the darkened runway to Daly's plane. On its tail I could clearly see the red and white World Airways logo, picked out by the jeep's headlights.

The children poured from the vans, by now confused by the bustle of their imminent departure. Daly ran up the steps, frantically urging us to load the children as quickly as possible.

Soon the plane was ready to go. The flight crew was already on board and the engines were whining in preparation for takeoff.

I bounded up the steps into the plane. There were no seats inside; the cavernous passenger area was covered with blankets and pillows. It seemed tragic that we only had time to get so few of our children ready for the rushed departure; the plane could easily have swallowed every one of our charges.

I looked around at the sea of small familiar faces, saying a mental goodbye to each and every one of them. Immigration officers boarded the plane and walked up and down, performing a last-minute inspection of their small countrymen who were leaving their homeland.

We realized that we didn't know where the plane was headed. I didn't even know how long it would take for the children to reach their final destination in America. There was nobody to look after them; nobody even knew their names.

Quickly I called out to Tom and the others; we had a hurried two-minute conference. We decided that someone had to stay with the children to support and comfort them during this very stressful time. Daly, noisy as ever, was trying to rush us off the plane even as I explained to him that someone whom the children knew had to accompany them.

It was an instant decision. Tom and Sister Nancy were chosen to join the evacuation. Neither of them was prepared—they had no luggage, passports or exit visas, just the knowledge that they had to make this final effort to help the children whom we all loved so dearly.

Tom, my husband and the father of my children, was leaving, and I was staying behind in Saigon. When I returned from the airport alone I would have to explain to my own children that their father had just left the country and we didn't know when, or if, he would return.

As soon as all the children were on board, the immigration officers told us to leave the plane. Finally it was over and we had finished our task; our children were on the way to their new lives. As I walked off the plane Ed Daly was standing in the doorway. Impulsively I hugged him and kissed him on both his cheeks, thanking him profusely.

His whole demeanor altered in that short instant. The swaggering ebullience was gone and he looked like an overgrown schoolboy. He brushed me off with a shy grin, but as I looked in his eyes, I could see that he was truly happy to be helping the children and us. I thanked him again and pushed past him. Without a backward glance, I almost ran down the aluminum stairs, accompanied by Ross, Thuy and Sister Theresa.

On the tarmac we looked at each other, still in shock at the speed of the day's events. The day had been bizarre. Halfway through, it had seemed just like any other day in the struggle to get a few of the adoptees their U.S. immigration visas. Now here we were, ten hours later, waving goodbye to fifty-two of our charges, my husband, and Sister Nancy, a dear coworker.

As we looked up at the bright cabin windows, the older children were crammed against the Plexiglas, waving their last good-byes to us. They were excited and ready to go.

Suddenly there was a commotion at the plane doorway and Tom appeared, looking agitated and yelling for me to come back. As I started back up the steps, all the elation drained from me—surely nothing could go wrong at this late stage.

As I reached the doorway one of the senior immigration officials appeared, dressed in a military-style uniform. He was angrily dragging two of the young teenagers, Jason and Thanh, in a rough headlock, one under each arm.

He shouted, "These boys aren't leaving. They are old enough to be fighting for their country and they shouldn't be running off to America."

Daly appeared as if by magic and tried to intervene on the boys' behalf. He thrust a wad of hundred dollar bills at the officer, who I recognized as Major Tan—a man we had worked with for months. We had seen him almost every week as he processed orphans who were flying off to America.

Angrily he shook his head at Daly and his money; he wasn't going to be bribed. We all pleaded with him to let the boys go, explaining that Jason's younger brothers were on the flight and he should be with them. Tan was adamant—the boys were staying in Vietnam.

He started down the steps, dragging the scared boys with him. For a moment, I thought he was going to throw them down the stairway.

Without warning Daly slammed the door shut, and that was it—the two boys were staying and everybody else was leaving. A couple of ground staff pulled the steps away from the plane.

Tan was still holding the boys as he made his way over to one of the jeeps. I feared he was going to arrest them. Suddenly he released his hold and the boys rushed to me for safety. Having made his point Tan ignored them; he climbed into his jeep and angrily told us to follow him.

The jeeps headed away from the airplane and we followed quietly behind. As we headed back to the lights of the airport, we heard the roar of the plane's engines spooling up to full power. I stopped the van and we all watched the plane lumber down the runway. It gathered speed quickly and lifted off into the night sky, bound for freedom. We were so happy that we had managed to get so many of our children to safety.

Ross, Thuy, Sister Theresa and I returned to the Center where, in high spirits, we immediately went back to work on creating lists of the names of the remaining orphans. We were required to submit them in triplicate, and all we had for the job was an old mechanical typewriter.

By now it was very late and we were all tired but happy, exhausted by the ups and downs of the long day. Thanh and Jason went to their beds after explaining to my children why they hadn't left. My kids looked happy to see their friends again, and I thought Jason and Thanh had accepted Major Tan's decision really well. Despite the fear that they could be conscripted into the army at a moment's notice, they maintained a cheerful disposition and continued to help where they could.

In the dead of night, as we doggedly compiled the lists, the phone suddenly rang loudly. It was Cheryl. The phone gods had smiled on us for once and we had a connection. As usual, the line was terrible and we could barely hear each other.

"Cheryl, our kids are on the way! Fifty kids in Japan. Thu Duc kids," I screamed into the old fashioned receiver.

A wave of static and interference blocked the conversation. When it cleared for a moment I could faintly make out Cheryl's shouting, "Fifty FCVN kids in Japan?"

"Yes, the Thu Duc kids," I confirmed.

Suddenly the line went dead; the conversation was over and wouldn't be renewed that night. It didn't matter though—the news was out, and I knew Cheryl would pick up the ball and take control from that end.

While we were typing the lists I switched on our old radio and we listened to the boring music, interspersed with English-language news bulletins. It seemed like hours before there was any mention of the evacuation. Finally, the newscaster announced that fifty-three orphans had left Saigon, destined for the United States.

As we continued working and listening throughout the long night, the radio broadcast regular updates. We heard that the flight had made a refueling stop in Tokyo, and then a short time later there was another announcement. The radio reported that the airport control tower had warned the pilot, Ken Healy, not to take off, as there was a risk the plane might be attacked by the NVA, but the plane had left anyway. That was the first hint that somebody was putting a different spin on the facts.

Later, as dawn was breaking in Saigon, the radio announced that Daly's flight had left Tan Son Nhut without authorization. It was obvious that the spin-doctors were now writing the news bulletins and somebody somewhere had decided that Daly's humanitarian actions were to be painted a different color. It looked like he was going to be thrown to the wolves.

As the Center came to life and another day started, I could hear babies crying out for their morning bottles. I realized that we had been working all night again—small wonder we all looked so tired.

Taking a five-minute break, we heard yet another radio announcement about the evacuation flight. In a dry, sterile monotone the announcer told us that a spokesman for the U.S. Department of Immigration and Naturalization had confirmed that World Airways was going to be fined $218,000 for each child that landed in America—apparently because some faceless, petty bureaucrat had decided that the baby flight was illegal and the authorities had not granted their prior approval for the children's entry into the country.

We stared at each other in disbelief. I knew that both governments had approved the flight the day before. I snatched up the letter and waved it around as I ranted futilely against the bureaucrats that seemed intent on destroying Daly.

The ringing of the phone interrupted my tirade. Quickly I grabbed it. It was United States Ambassador Martin's secretary wanting to speak with me. She was scathing and demanded my immediate presence at the U.S. Embassy. Taken aback by her imperious tone, I responded in kind and confirmed I would be there as soon as possible.

I looked down at myself; I hadn't slept in twenty-four hours. I was still wearing the same clothes I'd worn the previous morning to the Embassy, when they had denied any knowledge of an airlift evacuation. Since then, I hadn't had time to shower or wash; I felt dirty and my hair was a mess. I looked like one of the street kids who hung around every corner.

Before I had the time to even contemplate a quick shower, the compound gates opened and a shiny black limo pulled up in the drive. The driver walked into the Center and demanded to see Cherie Clark. I greeted him, and he told me I was required at the USAID offices immediately.

I laughed. From being an outsider all this time, it suddenly seemed that everybody now wanted a piece of me. Two urgent summonses, two urgent demands upon my time, delivered within seconds of each other—something unpleasant was in the air. Ross and Sister Theresa offered to deal with the Embassy meeting and I elected to meet with the USAID officials.

The driver wanted me to go with him in his fancy limo, but I rejected his offer, determined to maintain my independence. I drove myself to the USAID offices, expecting to get straight on with the urgent meeting, but instead I found myself waiting around for more than an hour, cooling my heels. Finally, an aide told me that I should return to attend a meeting at three o'clock in the afternoon, when all the adoption agencies would be present. And that was all—I was dismissed.

Incensed by the indifferent arrogance of the aide and the ridiculous waste of my time, I stormed out to my van and threw it into gear. Heading back towards the FCVN Center, I cursed the bureaucrats who seemed to run Saigon.

Alone in the van I crept along in the crush of traffic. For the first time in days I looked around, and the drastic changes in the city shocked me.

The streets were packed; crowds were scurrying along, overflowing the sidewalks and spilling into the road. I could see that many of the people were not city dwellers but refugees from the provinces. They looked unhappy, lost and utterly out of place in the bustle of the streets. Children still played on street corners and in the gutters, oblivious of the war raging just a few miles away, but adults only too familiar with the coming horrors looked haunted and afraid.

The street noise was tremendous. People shouted, horns blared and kids cried. Bicycles and small motorbikes wove in and out of the stalled traffic, dicing with death as they sped across intersections without slowing. I noticed a significantly increased military presence on the streets; trucks and jeeps filled with soldiers were everywhere. The signs of approaching war were all around and ominous—Saigon was becoming scary.

Back in the Center I took a much-needed shower and lay down for a rest on the rattan sofa in my office—but I couldn't sleep. Images of the children and fear for the future of my Vietnamese friends pressed down on me like a heavy weight.

Finally I gave up trying to sleep and sat down with Ross and Sister Theresa, ready to discuss their Embassy meeting. They told me that the meeting had been awful and that I had too much going on right now to hear all the details.

They left to return to the now childless Thu Duc center to explain the situation to the staff and start packing up some of the supplies. We intended to close that facility and bring all the staff into Gia Dinh to help with the evacuation process.

After they left I drove to the airport to meet two FCVN members, LeAnn Thieman and Carol Dey, who were due to arrive on an incoming Pan Am flight that afternoon.

When they cleared Customs and Immigration we drove back to the Center, and on the way I explained the preceding day's unreal events.

LeAnn and Carol were both registered nurses from a small town in Iowa. They had never traveled abroad before, and for their first trip they had landed in the middle of a city that was in a state of war.

The culture shock for them was profound. These two brave ladies, who had been planning for months what should have been a routine orphan escort trip, were totally unprepared for the chaos and fear that greeted them in Saigon. By now even hardened residents were worried about the situation, and thousands of people were planning a hasty departure.

They brought with them ten thousand dollars that LeAnn had hidden about her body, with the bulk of it stuffed in her bra. There was at last something to bring laughter to all of us. The money was a godsend. By this time the banks had closed their doors and nobody could get any cash. Like everybody else in Saigon, we were lost without hard cash. We still had to buy food, pay our staff and buy incidentals and essentials needed to keep the centers running and the children fed.

The closing of the banks was another critical turning point in the final collapse of Vietnam. Everyone desperately needed dollars or gold in order to procure food for their families, bribe officials for exit visas, or fund their last-minute escape bids. With the closing of the banks, it was terrible to watch their reactions. People panicked and started rioting. The fabric of society was breaking down, and the government was powerless to prevent anarchy from taking hold in the city. Anger and fear quickly escalated into a tangible, brooding presence that pervaded the last days of Saigon.

After delivering LeAnn and Carol to the FCVN Center I was finally ready to attend the afternoon USAID meeting, and I returned to their offices. I was late—the meeting had already started. When I walked into the conference room a great silence fell over those assembled, and all eyes were on me as I took a seat. It wasn't going to be a good meeting.

As soon as I sat down, the immaculately attired USAID officer in charge, Jay Ruoff, criticized in no uncertain terms the evacuation of our Thu Duc children. He berated me at length, like a schoolteacher chastising a naughty pupil. I sat silently, watching him and listening as he pulled me and Ed Daly to pieces.

We were worlds apart. I lived down at street level while he prowled around neat, air-conditioned offices, cushioned from the reality we lived in. We had never seen eye-to-eye; we each saw the problems in Saigon from opposite viewpoints.

I clutched the letter of authority, given me by the South Vietnamese government, in my hands. I knew Ruoff's arguments were specious. He blamed me for risking the children's lives by sending them out on Daly's unauthorized and unsafe plane. But the letter I was holding put the lie to his high-sounding, self-righteous sermon.

Meanwhile his aide, who only twenty-four hours before had agreed that the impromptu evacuation could go ahead if we could locate a plane willing to take us, sat there refusing to look at me. The hypocrisy was disgusting.

The lambasting continued for nearly an hour. I was told we had endangered the entire orphan evacuation effort and the lives of our children. Ruoff's harangue was becoming ridiculous; at any moment, I expected him to blame me for the fall of Saigon. Whatever he said, the fact remained that the FCVN orphans were safe. We had done our best and knew that we had sent them out of Saigon legally.

The real problem, in my estimation, was that by seizing the moment we had interfered with their planned timetable. President Ford was lined up to meet the first planeload of orphans, but the early arrival of the FCVN orphans diluted their publicity opportunity and stymied their plans to make political gains from the evacuations.

So, from being humanitarians and helping save lives and uniting families, we were suddenly painted as loose cannons, dangerous and risking lives without cause.

Ruoff was interrupted by an explosion nearby that made everyone jump. The war was knocking at the door. He resumed his long-winded castigation, saying that he personally expected Vietnam to be around for a long, long time. The incongruity of his statement, made as bombs exploded in downtown Saigon, seemed lost on him.

Finally he ran out of steam and there was silence in the room. I asked the only question I was interested in: When would the rest of the FCVN orphans be evacuated?

My question set him off again. He waved a sheet of paper across the polished table, telling me that this was the manifest for "Operation Babylift," the name given to the evacuation of the orphans. He said that because of last night's fiasco, he couldn't tell me when the FCVN orphans would be sent to the United States. He also made it clear that in the future, all our evacuation flights would be handled by USAID, and all we had to do was to get the children ready to leave.

The meeting drew to a close. It had achieved nothing of substance, except that the USAID officer had given vent to his feelings about Daly and me. Well done—now we could get back to work.

❦

By now our Center was packed to capacity. The communists were outside the city and it was no longer safe for Ross or Sister Theresa to return to Thu Duc, so they moved in with us. The Center was so overcrowded that Ross slept in one of the vans. I moved my four children into my bedroom; I wanted to keep them as close to me as possible.

Late that night, we were taking turns catching some well-deserved rest. Suddenly the house shook as an explosion reverberated outside. The noise woke everybody. I was sure that we had been hit by a rocket. The entire house shook and the wall in the bedroom where my children were sleeping, near LeAnn and Carol, cracked. Plaster dust and fragments filled the air and covered my children as they lay in their bunk beds.

They all screamed in fear. Shocked myself, I jumped up from the sofa where I had been resting and rushed to the bedroom, stepping carefully over babies sleeping on mats in the hallways. Seeing that my children were safe and being comforted by LeAnn and Carol had a calming effect on me. I gathered them to me and brushed the plaster from their hair and bodies.

Everyone in the Center was awake and asking nervous questions. We all rushed onto the balcony to assess the damage. There was nothing to see, except for a few of our neighbors walking about, also looking for damage. We could hear machine gun fire in the streets, but there were no soldiers in view from our balcony. After a few strained laughs and with a sense of anticlimax, we returned to comfort the hundreds of crying babies. No more sleep for us that night; even my young children were comforting shocked babies.

The next morning we learned that the Bien Hoa ammunition dump had been blown up. The dump was located twenty miles outside the city, yet its destruction was so powerful that buildings within Saigon were damaged. The massive base where the dump was located had been heralded as a symbol of the invincible power of the South Vietnamese government. A suicide group of communist guerrillas had penetrated the much-vaunted base defenses and destroyed the power symbol in one immense explosion.

To most of us there was no longer any doubt that the end was near—yet daily briefings held by the Americans at Tan Son Nhut airport continued to be positive. It was hard to believe they were describing the same war that we were living through. We desperately hoped that things would reverse and our friends and loved ones would be safe. But none of us could see any reason why the communists would stop their advance when things seemed to be going very smoothly for them so far.

On the third of April, Sister Theresa and I worked the entire night getting the babies ready for evacuation. For days we had been bringing in our children from the provinces and from our foster homes. We were told that our babies would leave sometime on the fourth but we were not certain what time. We had to be ready at a moment's notice.

General panic was setting in among the population, and everyone was seeking a way out of the country. People we knew began approaching us for help in getting themselves or their relatives to safety.

Steve Johnson was one of that number. We simply had to help him, we were so indebted to him. Steve wanted to send his twin boys and his wife's ten-year-old son to his parents in Illinois. He couldn't leave because he was still trying to get the necessary papers to evacuate his wife. We agreed to somehow find a space for his children.

Thuy's family was particularly worrisome for me. We all knew the family well. Thuy's nephew, Phuong, his wife, Hung, and their four children had suffered through the horrors of war. They had fled from Pleiku and Da Nang, always moving a few steps ahead of the enemy forces. At one point the family was separated and two of the children were lost; the parents were shoved onto one flight and the two small children on another. A friend of the family recognized the children and helped them rejoin their family in Nha Trang.

The family had then fled again, south to Saigon by boat. In the process their newborn son had become so ill they didn't expect him to survive. The parents didn't want their children to suffer anymore, and begged me now to take the children out and give them to a good family for adoption.

I was torn. The FCVN policy was to accept only true orphans; we didn't believe in splitting families or accepting children with living relatives. The only general exception was that we would take half-American babies or children, for it was a well-known fact that these children were not accepted in Vietnam.

After hearing Phuong and Hung's pleas, and after much soul-searching, I finally agreed to take the children out, provided that the parents signed legal relinquishments, confirming that they wanted their children to be adopted.

LeAnn, one of the FCVN escorts, had long wanted to adopt a child. She and her husband had previously prepared the adoption paperwork, and she had brought it with her to Saigon. Her visit made it possible for us to bypass the selection process; there would be no photographs in the mail for them or months of agonized waiting.

I told her it would be best to choose her new son herself. The adjoining nursery was filled with babies of all ages and sexes, waiting to be assigned to new families. All she had to do was pick one for her family.

She walked slowly through the nursery and finally settled on a little boy who had not yet been named. In time to come she often related the story, saying that the son she picked, and later called Mitchell, had chosen her as she walked through the room.

It was a time of hope and a time of sadness. We would soon be sending our children off to their new homes around the world. Many of them had families waiting anxiously for their arrival, and we all felt that it couldn't happen soon enough.

Chapter Ten

By Friday, the fourth of April, we were all jumpy and tense from lack of sleep and the daunting administrative tasks of preparing the babies who would leave on the next evacuation flights. We had been notified that the first "officially sanctioned" orphan airlift would leave sometime that afternoon. I had called to alert FCVN to be prepared for our babies, and we were working nonstop to be ready. By late morning we still hadn't received word as to what time buses would arrive to pick us up.

We were contacted by the Australian Embassy, who informed us that twenty-one of our children who had adoptive families waiting for them in Australia had been authorized to leave Saigon on that same day. The Embassy kept us informed throughout the day, finally telling us that the flight would depart Saigon at four p.m., and that we should be ready to leave the Center with the children at two o'clock. We still had no word from USAID about the time of the departure to America.

After another spurt of furious effort, we finally had all the children divided into the Australia group and the children leaving for America. With over two hundred infants and staff in a fairly small compound, it was difficult to keep people from wandering around with babies who were destined to go to two separate countries.

LeAnn and Carol were turning out to be a real godsend. Although they had only been in town twenty-four hours, they were proving quite useful. They shepherded the children destined for Australia to the airport with Ross, while I stayed behind at the Center to wait for news as to what time we would leave for America.

I said another tearful good-bye to young Thanh, from Qui Nhon. After our abortive attempt to send him on the Daly flight, I was more worried than ever about getting him out, and determined to keep trying. He already had a family waiting in Australia. Had he made it on the Daly flight to America I would have arranged to have friends send him on to Australia. I had no idea that the Australian government would provide planes to airlift their children out as well.

Time passed quickly, as I answered one telephone call after another and dealt with the steady stream of visitors pleading with me to take their babies and children to America. I still had no word from the American Embassy or USAID as to when our children would depart.

Our Vietnamese staff of course could not leave the country, and we knew that the evacuation flights were going to be short-handed. USAID had asked us to provide one escort for each five babies. We had to juggle that requirement with the need to keep enough adults around to cope with the ever-mounting work in the Center. I called everybody I knew, asking for volunteers who could accompany our children during the evacuations.

The telephone calls and stream of visitors were incessant. It seemed that everybody in Saigon wanted FCVN to provide them or their families with some sort of escape route from the besieged city. The problem was that no one wanted to leave without their entire families, and we had no way to evacuate Vietnamese citizens. By now, my head was pounding and I needed a break, but I knew that wasn't going to happen.

Sometime after four o'clock in the afternoon, the telephone rang yet again. My first thought was that it would be news as to what time our flight would depart for America. It was getting late. The babies were sick and screaming and we were all hot and tired. I only hoped we would be on our way soon.

"Cherie, are you alone?" Steve Johnson asked. He sounded as if he were struggling to breathe.

"Alone?" I asked. "Alone in a crowd!"

Steve didn't pick up on my weak attempt at banter. "Cherie, I've got some really bad news. A plane carrying orphans just crashed on takeoff from Tan Son Nhut."

I was stunned. I stared at the clock. It was almost five. Our children were due to depart for Australia at four.

"My God, what plane?" I finally managed to say.

"I'm not sure," Steve said. "I'm here at the airport. You'd better come now."

I put the telephone down and stumbled from my office, too stunned to think properly. I couldn't drive—Ross had taken the van to the airport. One of the nurses volunteered a friend of hers to take me on his motorbike.

Steve's office was at the airport and I wanted to find him, but when we arrived, the place was in absolute chaos. We couldn't get inside. There were people, trucks and jeeps racing around madly. We saw helicopters hovering over the far end of the runway. That had to be the site of the crash because thick black smoke was rolling upwards—smoke so dense, it looked like a solid black pillar rising into the sky.

We found a perimeter road and followed it toward the smoke. We approached as near to the crash site as we could. A fence separated us from the actual area and we couldn't get any closer. Soldiers were running everywhere; one came up to us and told us not to go any further. If we wanted to help, he said, we should go to the Seventh Day Adventist Hospital. I asked if the flight had been headed for Australia. He told me he had no idea. I looked into his face and saw that he was crying, his tears cutting through clods of mud on his cheeks. He was obviously on the point of nervous collapse himself.

The huge military plane had crashed just short of the main runway. It seemed to have pancaked into the ground, and wreckage was scattered everywhere. We saw helicopters powering straight up into the air, heading for the hospital.

Other soldiers were wading around in water-filled ditches, frantically looking for survivors and bodies. Some of the bodies had been stripped of clothing by the impact. Clothes fluttered in the muddy waters of the rice paddy; suitcases and bags had burst and scattered the passengers' belongings everywhere.

We were silent, too stunned to talk.

We hurriedly drove to the hospital while I sat, numb, watching. Roads were jammed with mud-spattered vehicles, all with lights flashing, delivering bodies to the hospital. Large military helicopters carrying the dead, dying, and injured were landing at the military base; soldiers and others were ferrying bodies from the choppers into the stream of waiting vehicles.

Ambulances from other hospitals were arriving, along with Embassy cars. There was no way to drive close to the hospital, so I thanked my driver, then trekked towards a side entrance.

As I approached, making my way through the crowds, I saw a stack of body bags piled high, lying in a haphazard fashion. They were unattended, just waiting for God knows what. A makeshift morgue was being set up.

As I walked closer I saw that the pavement was covered with thick brown mud from the paddy field. I had to walk past the body bags to pass into the hospital. There were people outside on the steps. I saw a young Vietnamese nurse that I knew, sitting on the steps near the entrance. She was always good with the babies that we admitted to the IRC unit here. Her white uniform was covered with mud and blood, and her head hung low as she sobbed uncontrollably.

She looked up to see me and our eyes met. As we looked at each other we exchanged a silent message of loss, pain and unquenchable sorrow. Slowly she stood up and came to me. No words were exchanged—we just silently hugged each other and sobbed as if it were the end of the world. Then I asked her if she knew whose plane had crashed. She couldn't answer—she just shook her head.

After a moment I left her and walked through the open door. It was a scene of pandemonium. The room was jammed with people, many crying or screaming as they recognized dead loved ones and friends among the bodies. Some of the bodies weren't even covered and they lay, naked and dead, on tables or on the dirty floor. I couldn't find anyone that I recognized, and I still didn't know who had been on the flight or what kind of plane it was. I tried to ask others for information but I couldn't even speak.

There were bodies on every available surface—women, children and babies, some with limbs missing, others ripped apart, heads bashed in—and others looked as if they were sleeping quietly, with no apparent signs of injury.

People were rushing to take as many of the babies up the stairs to the children's ward as possible. At that point, it was just a matter of separating the dead from the living. I finally found Dr. Cuong, a close friend who was on staff at the Adventist Hospital. He came to me and shook his head. He had been a military doctor but looked shaken. He told me he had never seen anything like this.

He told me FFAC's flight had crashed. In a voice broken with emotion, he said the sight of the dead and dismembered children was making work virtually impossible, even for the experienced staff. It was a scene straight from hell. Nothing could have prepared anyone for the terrible carnage we were witnessing.

I wanted to help. He guided me to a makeshift entry room where I saw they were hosing off babies, their pathetic bodies completely covered with mud. Dr Cuong told me that minutes before, one child, mud-covered, whom they thought was dead, had opened his eyes when the mud had been washed off. They were not leaving anything to chance, and so they cleaned off all the bodies.

People were rushing around, doctors and nurses, soldiers and civilians, all intent on their tasks. The floors and walls were covered in the thick brown mud and blood, and more of it was being tracked in by the stream of men carrying stretchers from the emergency vehicles outside.

People were unzipping the body bags that lay all around, frantically searching for their friends or relatives. It was still more of a sorting process than a medical operation; doctors and nurses placed the dead on one side and the living on another.

The noise was unbearable. Above the cries, screams and wails, panic-stricken men were shouting orders, and I kept hearing the words "bomb," "sabotage" and "rockets." I couldn't believe that anybody would shoot down a plane full of innocent children and volunteers.

Dr. Cuong asked me to help him move a lady, who looked as if she were sleeping, off a stretcher. She was dead. As more staff appeared from hospitals all around the city I felt useless. My legs were like rubber and the entire room was spinning; I knew I was about to vomit or faint—I didn't know which. It seemed that half of Saigon's medical personnel had descended upon the hospital. The last thing they needed was to have to take care of me. I went outside for fresh air.

I saw some of Rosemary's staff, but there was nothing I could say to them. Naomi and Christie were huddled together in a corner. I had no idea who was dead or alive. I wanted to ask about Rosemary and Margaret but I couldn't.

I stumbled out of the hospital. A Mission Warden car was standing outside, almost in the middle of the road. The driver stood next to the car as he had no place to park. I must have looked totally in shock. I asked him if he could give me a ride back to our Center. He kindly helped me inside the car; I apologized because my shoes and clothes were covered with mud. He reached out and gripped my shoulder, then patted my arm as we drove through the traffic. We rode silently.

At the Center I walked through the nursery and upstairs to my dusty room. It was the first time I'd set foot in my own quarters since the ammunition dump had been blown up—it seemed weeks ago. I shut the door and sat on the bed, my head in my hands, wishing that I could cry.

Ross and the others came back and we all cried together. Sister Theresa did everything to comfort me. LeAnn and Carol gathered Jason and my kids together and reassured them that their dear friend Thanh had not been on the plane that had crashed.

In fact, to try to bring some relief to the gloom that encompassed us, they told us that Thanh was now safely on his way to Australia. Although we had permission from the Australian government to send Thanh, we feared that immigration would again decide he was too old. While carrying the babies onto the Australia-bound plane, with the help of the Australian crew Ross had hidden Thanh under a seat when the immigration officers boarded to check the passengers.

Some time later I was called back to work in the nursery. I moved around like an automaton, my emotions too wrung out to allow me to think. I was working in a dream state. Time passed in a blur as I moved from mat to mat, carefully stepping around the babies covering the floor. By now our nursery, which was equipped to accommodate thirty, was jammed with hundreds of babies and staff.

We were all working in the nursery—me, LeAnn and Carol, Sister Theresa and all the Vietnamese staff—discussing the tragedy and its cause, when suddenly, looking around the room, it hit me like a bolt from the blue that everyone in America had expected us to leave Saigon that day.

I had to get a call through to America. As always I booked it through the operator. I told her it was an emergency. She understood and said she knew what had happened and would do her best.

As I waited for the telephone call, I went back to the nursery. Dr. Cong was struggling to keep a small baby alive. Through my tears, I realized that it was Hung and Phuong's son. Dr. Cong refused to give up hope, but he shook his head. I looked down at the little baby boy. He was hanging on, but just barely.

I hadn't seen Thuy since early morning. Her relatives were coming in from the provinces and some were ill, after living through hell trying to get to Saigon by boat. If the baby wasn't going to make it then he should be with Hung and Phuong. I sent someone with a note to Thuy's house to tell her the baby was in critical condition and to bring the parents. I no longer had any questions about accepting their children for the flight; one of the children was dying already.

We filled in the time talking and tending to the babies as I waited for the telephone call. I had to get a message to Tom and Cheryl. The day before, Cheryl had managed to call me and had confirmed what USAID in Washington, D.C., had told her. It was the same information that I had: that the FCVN orphans and staff would be leaving Saigon on the fourth of April. The news was bad enough that I didn't want to cause them any more grief worrying about us.

As dusk was falling and the lights went on, friends arrived from the airport with more news. We gathered around, desperate for information. The news was bleak. They were saying that there had been two hundred and forty-three children on board, and they thought half of them were dead. Miraculously there were some survivors.

Steve confirmed that Rosemary was alive—she hadn't been on the flight. And it was still just a sorting-out process. The only way that they were able to tell who was dead and who was alive was by seeing someone still walking around.

Ross told me that Christie was a survivor. I had already known that she was alive because I had seen her and Naomi in the hospital, but I hadn't known that she had actually been on the plane. Christie survived because she had been on the upper passenger deck, whereas many of those killed had been in the lower cargo area of the plane.

They also told me that Dr. Stark had survived because he too was on the upper deck, whereas his daughter Laurie, my kids' teacher, had been killed with the babies below. We knew the Starks well. Mrs. Stark taught Ron and Dan at the American school, and Laurie had taught my younger children at the Montessori School. Dr. Stark had a close friend who had adopted one of our children and was a frequent visitor at FCVN.

They told us that the plane had been a C-5A Galaxy, the largest military plane in existence. The lower cargo deck was almost half the length of a football field and two stories high, with an upper deck that could seat upwards of ninety passengers. It seemed inconceivable that such an invincible military machine could crash. It was also unbelievable that anybody could attack a plane filled with civilian passengers. This was still the general assumption, although now some people were beginning to say that perhaps it was a technical problem. But it seemed unlikely that in the middle of a war zone a plane would suddenly have a mechanical failure of this proportion.

We started to hear the news on the radio. They didn't identify which organization had been in the crash, only that there were about one hundred and fifty fatalities. The radio said that the pilot of the plane had done a tremendous job in getting the large crippled plane back to the ground. Though the loss of life was huge, without his expertise the semi-controlled crash landing would have had an even higher death tally. They repeated every few minutes that the cause of the crash was unknown.

I suddenly remembered hearing on the radio that there had been a threat to the Daly flight; they had been warned that the plane could be attacked as it took off. Perhaps they had been right all along. Fate had taken a hand yet again in Saigon.

Finally the telephone rang; I snatched it up and heard Cheryl's voice from America. They had been tormented for hours. She had learned of the crash at half past three in the morning on Friday, their time. An FCVN member in Georgia who was a ham radio operator had heard news that the FCVN plane had gone down. The member immediately telephoned Cheryl and broke the terrible news.

Cheryl had been frantic. She sat with Sue and Mick, agonized as they watched the unfolding news of the plane crash playing on the television and radio.

As the magnitude of the crash became apparent and word spread that FCVN members had been killed, news reporters started calling them at the house, asking if they had any further information. She couldn't help them; she had received no word from Saigon. Other chapters scattered across America met informally at members' homes to comfort each other and wait for some word from the government or Saigon. The Illinois newspapers carried banner headlines that morning that the FCVN plane had crashed and that the "fate of the Clark family was unknown."

At six o'clock in the morning Denver time, Cheryl had called the State Department in Washington and spoken with Bernie Salvo. Bernie was a friend who had served with Mick in Da Lat and was in charge of the Vietnam desk. If anyone knew what had happened, it would be him. Bernie confirmed that there had been a crash and told Cheryl that they had a board posted with planned departures—the flight listed was FCVN's.

Cheryl had continued to call Saigon every few minutes, hour after hour, to no avail. To add to her pain, a woman called anonymously and said, "I hope all those little bastards die."

Meanwhile Mick called Tom and Nancy in California, where they had finally arrived on the Daly flight just hours before. Exhausted after their long flight looking after the children, they were sleeping in a nearby motel. Mick's call awoke Tom. He broke the news that a flight carrying babies had crashed in Saigon, that there were some survivors and that they were seeking more news. He couldn't confirm or deny where the kids and I were.

On the telephone at last, Cheryl was hysterical when she heard my voice. I couldn't understand a word she was saying.

"Cheryl, Rosemary's flight crashed," I told her.

"We thought you were dead! The news reports are saying that it was the FCVN flight that went down," was all I could manage to make out.

"It is so tragic, hundreds of the kids and women are dead—it's so terrible." I started sobbing again. "Please tell Tom and Sue that me and the kids are safe."

Cheryl confirmed that Tom and Sister Nancy had arrived safely in California, and that arrangements were being made to get them back to Saigon as soon as possible. The State Department was issuing both of them emergency passports, as they had left on the Daly flight without theirs.

We continued talking, on that bleak and terrible day, and I was able to give Cheryl news that she and Mick had waited so long for. Mai was safe—she had made it down from Da Lat. It was a very long story, but she was at the FCVN Center that very moment.

The next day more information started to trickle in to the Center. We learned the names of some of the victims. They included friends as well as those we had come to know and admire.

Compassionate Margaret Moses, the woman who had placed Jenny in my arms and had introduced me to the real work that needed to be done for the children of Vietnam, had been killed. Birgit Blank, the young German nurse from whom I had learned so much when I worked in Rosemary's nurseries, was another victim.

We were greatly shocked to hear that Sister Ursula, our dear friend from the Good Shepherd Orphanage in Vinh Long, who had worked with us as we prepared our children for departure, was also dead. She had offered to go with our babies, and then left us to visit and say good-bye to Rosemary and others, with a promise to return soon. She must have been enlisted to help with the large number of Rosemary's babies that were being evacuated. She was a kind soul and would have volunteered to help wherever she could.

My last sight of her is forever etched in my memory. She had held Brian in her arms, teasing him one last time and promising to return soon. She loved my little boy and had even come rushing from Vinh Long when she heard of his fall. She had bought him a dark blue silk *ao dai,* done in a traditional style for males, and he loved to wear it around the compound. He was her special little person.

The list went on—names, faces of those we knew and those we didn't continued to emerge from the confusion. We learned that many of the dead adults included women working for the DAO in Saigon who were being sent out of Vietnam as "non-essential" personnel. Thirty-seven of them were now dead.

The traumatic losses from the Babylift crash pressed heavily on each of us, at a time when we were already stretched beyond endurance. Exhausted, under great emotional pressure, we were worried about our babies, our friends and family, and trying to work efficiently with a crumbling government that would soon be overrun by communist forces.

It was a terrible, tragic day in all our lives. Many lost friends or relatives in the crash, and nobody in the child welfare community remained untouched. But pressure of limited time and the advancing war forced us to put our emotions on hold and turn back to face the realities of the ongoing struggle to save the remaining babies, our families, and ourselves.

Chapter Eleven

*O*n the day following the crash, Saturday, April fifth, we were told that our children would leave on two MAC flights. We all worked feverishly to make the last-minute preparations necessary to get two hundred and seventeen orphans ready for departure. We boiled water to fill the feeding bottles, made a list of medications and dosages for the sick babies, packed diapers, and carried out a myriad of similar tasks.

It was perhaps for the best that we were so busy we barely had time to think too much about the Babylift crash. Despite the tragic loss of so many lives, we had to look ahead to the departure of our own children and babies. We had to keep going.

The most time consuming and exhausting of all the work we had to do was what should have been the easiest. We had been instructed to compile lists of the babies' names. Children in our care were given an English or Vietnamese "nursery name" on the day that we brought them into the Center. Because so many of them came to us without any identification papers, that was the best we could do for them. We had already made a master list and placed identification tags on the arms and legs of each child. These had the child's nursery name, a number that coincided with the list, and the letters FCVN.

Following the C-5A crash, we received new instructions to submit in triplicate the full Vietnamese name of each child. Each child's name would be checked off at the time of departure, and the name on the list would have to match the name on the baby. We supposed that this new requirement was prompted by the confusion of trying to identify babies after the crash.

But most of our babies had no formal Vietnamese name. Now we had only hours to come up with first, last and middle names. We had no alternative but to simply pick names at random. Once each baby was given a Vietnamese name, we had to compile a new list of names and produce matching identification tags.

Sister Theresa and I, ready to drop from exhaustion, sat down to retype the list of names and make the new armbands on our old portable typewriter.

Each baby was given two tags bearing the letters FCVN, the child's new name and a number coinciding with the FCVN master list, held by me. We put a tag on an arm and a leg of each baby. Then, for the babies who were already assigned to families in America, we added one more tag. This had the name of their adoptive parents and again the letters of FCVN. The nursery names by which we knew our babies so well were not on the tags.

❦

Cheryl finally got another telephone call through, and for the second day in a row I told her we were scheduled to depart. Fate had intervened and spared us from yesterday's flight. We were concerned, exhausted, and hoped our babies would depart safely today on schedule. Everyone was still shaken by the crash and no one yet was certain what caused it. It was no longer just a matter of "getting out"—it was getting out alive.

As Cheryl and I spoke, Mai stood in front of me. I told Cheryl some of the extraordinary events that had brought her to us.

The day before, when I was certain that we were leaving, I had decided that I couldn't leave Vietnam without doing my best to find some news about Mai.

In the early morning, Ross, Thuy and I had driven across Saigon to visit the St. Vincent de Paul Polio Center for orphans, run by the Sisters of Charity. They were of the same order as the sisters in Da Lat and we hoped they might have some news of the orphanage.

As we entered the compound, a small girl stood watching us. I immediately recognized her from the photos that I had seen over the years; the little girl was Mai. I couldn't believe that we had found her so easily. Despite the chaos throughout the country and the millions of displaced people running to the South, this one little girl had suddenly materialized on the day I thought we were due to leave Vietnam.

Sister Katrina, who knew that the Marksons wanted to adopt Mai and had supported her for years, related the story of their escape from the advancing enemy.

When the communists invaded Da Lat, the nuns evacuated the orphanage and headed for the coast, joining in with the exodus of refugees. Sister Katrina wanted to get Mai to us, where she knew the child would have a chance of getting out of the country. She and about a dozen other people floated in a small, crude boat down the Vietnam coast to the inlet at Saigon.

The boat was overcrowded and Sister Katrina had to stay awake through-out the five-day journey, fearful that Mai might fall overboard. Finally arriving in Saigon, Sister Katrina took Mai to the Polio Center, which was also the mother house of her order. Their journey down the coast had been a nightmare, and they were one of the few fortunate groups that made it successfully. My heart went out to the faithful and loyal sister.

She added that all along the beaches of Vietnam, the sand had been littered with dead bodies of people who had tried to escape.

Finding Mai was a remarkable, blessed event, although the good fortune that brought her to us was overshadowed at the time by the crash. The sisters had agreed to bring her to our Center later in the afternoon. Despite my joy in finding Mai I had barely remembered to tell Cheryl that she was at long last safe and with us.

Now the critical time was upon us. After so much time and uncertainty, the babies would soon be on their way to America.

We were departing in two groups. I had already made up my mind to send the first flight out with most of the babies and all of the American staff. I would follow on the next flight with my children and the remaining babies.

My most pressing concern was Jason. I couldn't fly out of Vietnam and leave him—that would be like leaving one of my own sons behind. He was relieved that his younger brothers Jeff and Jeremy were safe in Wisconsin with the Johnson family, but also afraid that he might never see them again. I would attempt to get him on the flight with the first group of babies. If that was not successful, I would try again with the second flight.

The USAID buses were too large to drive down the narrow lane leading to the FCVN Center, so we shuttled out to the main road in our van and transferred the children into the buses. It was hot, and the babies were dehydrating right in front of us. We were all sweating with the hard physical labor of carrying so many children and their supplies.

I rounded up Ron, Dan and Jason to help take the crying babies into the vans. I told the boys to wait for me at the Center, that we wouldn't be leaving just yet, and that they should look after Brian and Beth.

The small convoy of buses with DAO escorts headed into the airport. The bureaucratic machinery took hold again and we waited for three hours until the paperwork caught up with us. We sat outside in the vans until we could no longer bear the heat. Finally we were taken to some old deserted Quonset huts. They were filthy but at least they were not nearly as hot as the buses.

We were the first military flight to depart after the crash. We feared the delay more than anything and wondered what was holding things up.

During the long wait, we attended to the babies as well as we could, frightened as they dehydrated in the sweltering heat. LeAnn was taking care of babies and keeping a close watch on her new son, Mitchell. She and Carol were relieved to be leaving the madness of Saigon behind. They had done all that had been asked of them and more, helping us through what at that time was our greatest hour of need.

Finally, the long wait was over and we headed out to the flight line. We began to embark as instructed onto the waiting USAF C-141 planes. The babies lay two or three together in cardboard boxes that served as makeshift cribs. Then they were secured by straps to the cargo area floor.

Jason helped board the babies but was stoically resigned to the fact that he might have to stay in Vietnam. I did not want to raise his hopes. Ross had successfully hidden Thanh on the Australian flight the day before, and I wanted to try the same method with Jason on this flight. Jason was older than Thanh, and if the immigration police were looking they would of course see that he was way above the cutoff age of ten.

Thuy tearfully kissed her daughter Kiki good-bye on the tarmac. Hung and Phuong had already said good-bye to their children at the Center, and the cousins were ready to board the plane after saying goodbye to Thuy.

Steve Johnson's twins, Christopher and Anthony, had already been taken aboard and were even now being strapped into one of the cardboard boxes by the U.S. Air Force staff on hand to help with the evacuation. They were bound for Illinois to Steve's parents' home, where they would wait for their father to join them after he had arranged his wife's exit.

We all walked up the loading ramp, and the children sat down in canvas jump seats lining the fuselage walls. Jason sat next to Jackie, Steve's stepson. I feared at any time that the immigration police would board and pull Jason off the plane. I held the evacuation roster in my hand, ready to check each baby and child off against the carefully prepared lists. I had added Jason's name.

Nobody arrived to even look at it. Despite all the urgent requirements to rename the babies and prepare complete lists, nobody looked at our manifest or checked the babies' identification. No one even glanced at Jason.

Sister Theresa, Ross, LeAnn and Carol were seated for departure. After a few tearful good-byes, those who were remaining behind, including me, walked off the plane. We knew the babies were in safe hands; we just prayed the plane would take off without incident. Twenty-four hours had not yet passed from the hour of the crash. We were fearful.

We climbed into one of the buses as the plane's door closed with a final thump, and drove a safe distance away as it readied for departure.

Slowly the plane trundled onto the main runway and then, with a massive roar, lifted into the shimmering sky. We watched the plane climb, accelerating rapidly out of our view, willing them onwards and praying that nobody was aiming a rocket at our babies.

When the plane disappeared from sight and the last sounds had died away completely, we cheered with relief. Even the Vietnamese USAID driver was smiling as we boarded the bus.

Back in the Center, we told everyone that the evacuation had been successful. Jason had gone to America to join his brothers, and Steve's kids were on their way too. Hung and Phuong, Thuy's relatives, thanked me yet again for giving their children the chance of a better life.

It was a good-news day for a change. In my absence, they had learned that Tom and Nancy were on their way back from the States. Knowing that the Center would be in good hands when they arrived, and now that Jason and the others had left, I could look to my own family.

The next buses were due in just a few minutes. I only now realized that Dan was a very sick eight-year-old boy. Dr. Cong, the FCVN pediatrician, told me Dan had been vomiting for hours. I went to see him—he was lying on my bed, pale and shaking. He started to cry when he saw me.

"Mom, I want to go home, to see Dad and to leave the war—but I don't want to say good-bye to my friends. Mom, can we ever come back?"

Ron and Dan and the other children had so many friends in the neighborhood and the Center that it almost seemed cruel to take them away. Naturally, they were scared by the accelerating events. Death, a plane crash, an explosion, nightly machine gun fire, street riots, and the absence of their father all conspired to make the children nervous and insecure. Before the events of the last week they had considered Vietnam their home and had been happy here. But now, as many of their friends left and as the war moved closer, they wanted to leave.

Aware of their insecurity and sadness at losing so many friends who had been evacuated, I still hadn't told them of our friends killed in the Babylift crash, such as Sister Ursula and their warm and gentle teacher, Laurie Stark.

USAID had informed me that for this second flight, military personnel would help look after the infants. I was the only adult traveling from our Center and I had my own four children. They were aware that it was impossible for us to find volunteers with the proper papers to go out with every flight. I filled a carry-on bag with a change of clothes for the kids and me. The buses had arrived to take us with the remaining babies.

Just before we left for the airport I called all the remaining staff together and explained that I had to take my children to safety. Having taken a mother role to so many orphans over the past year, I now had to return to being a mother to my own. The staff supported my going, albeit tearfully. Chau, our dear child care worker, had loved my children as her own and was particularly upset at their leaving, but she wanted them to be safe.

Neighbors gathered in the lane and driveway to say what they felt were the final good-byes. I assured them that I would soon return and that the kids would come back to Vietnam when it was safe to do so. They heard all the words, but they also knew that many foreigners had made similar empty promises—some on a governmental scale. There was nothing I could do to prove my intentions; too many lies had already been spoken by others. In my heart, I knew I would return, but the truth of my words would only be believed when they saw me again in the flesh.

Time was now pressing; we were loaded into the buses with the babies and taken to the airport.

After boarding another MAC flight carrying crying infants in yet more cardboard boxes, again without any paperwork checks, we set off. There were many Americans on board to help with the babies. Some of those who assisted me were husbands of women who had been killed on the previous day's flight.

The noise was deafening as we powered down the runway. The military transports were not insulated against noise like civilian planes are, and it was impossible to hear anything other than the almighty roaring of the multiple jet engines.

Lifting off the runway into the air, the plane climbed steeply to avoid the possibility of ground fire, and maintained maximum speed for a long time. My children were terrified by the noise and the fear of being shot down. I hugged them and tried to comfort them as well as I could, although I was anxious too.

Eventually an Air Force officer made his way past the screaming babies and leaned over to me. Shouting in my ear, he told that we were now out of enemy rocket range, and we were safe.

For the first time since boarding the plane I relaxed a little, and felt some of the tension ease from my body. We settled down in the uncomfortable canvas seats and waited for the flight to end. There seemed to be plenty of people to help with the babies, and I suddenly had only my four children to care for.

Dan vomited almost the entire way and had a high fever. I looked at my kids and felt sad. The last weeks had extracted a heavy toll. They had lost weight. All of the new children coming into the Center had skin rashes, and the rashes had been passed on to my children. I was thankful to have this time just to be with them.

Three hours later, after a deafening flight, we eased onto the brightly lit runway at Clark Air Force base in the Philippines. At last we were safe and felt protected by America's military force.

On the ground, we received the red-carpet treatment. The base commander came aboard and welcomed me, as the director of the organization, to the Philippines. We posed for a few photographs among the babies.

Once off the airplane, we could see and hear the Air Force going about its business. Planes flew overhead, their lights winking in the dark blue sky, but the flickering lights were no longer symbols of danger to us. Vietnam was, for the time being, behind us. There was no backdrop of rockets, mortars or gunfire; we were on friendly ground. Despite the surrounding military activity, I felt safe. At that moment, the thought of going back into the hell of Saigon seemed like a nightmare, and I suddenly dreaded returning to Vietnam—but I knew I would have to, and soon.

The kids were relieved also. Dan perked up and said, "Hey Mom, we must be really famous—our name is on signs everywhere." He was referring to the "Clark AFB" signs. This drew a great laugh from all around us as I explained that this was the name of the base.

Ron's cautious question was not as reassuring. He asked, "Mom, are there any Viet Cong around here?"

I shook my head and tried to comfort them all. They were still not convinced that they were safe; such was the trauma of Saigon that it had imprinted itself in their minds and hearts. They would suffer nightmares for a long time to come.

The base commander assigned a Sergeant O'Brien and another man to help me with the children. It was a windfall, for now the weariness and relief were kicking in and I felt ready to drop. The two military men were great; nothing was too much trouble for them.

We were escorted to officers' quarters on the base, and the kids immediately hopped on the beds and switched on the color TV, something they hadn't seen for quite some time. Everything, from the wall-to-wall carpeting and air-conditioning to running hot and cold water, was a great novelty to them.

To me it felt like being in a real home. I suffered a pang of guilt, realizing what material things my kids had been missing while living in Vietnam. Now the normalcy of a motel room was like a palace to them.

Sergeant O'Brien took charge, bringing hamburgers for the children and, even at that late hour, a doctor, who examined Dan and prescribed some strong antibiotics. The sergeant also offered to baby-sit my children while I went off in search of our friends from the first flight out.

A friendly driver took me in an open jeep to the base gymnasium to see the babies. An airman in a smartly creased uniform stood guard at the entrance. He asked if there was anybody inside who could vouch for me.

Peering past him, I saw Ross and Sister Theresa. I heard Jason before I saw him. He yelled with joy and ran into my arms. I caught up on events with Ross and Sister Theresa. We were all so happy and relieved. For the first time in days, there was no tension, and for the first time in as long as I could remember, there was no pressing work to do.

The transformation was amazing. Only a few short hours before, the babies had been crammed into our small villa, tended by our harried and worried staff. Now the children were housed in the base gymnasium, each baby on its own mattress. The mattresses were covered with clean white sheets. The babies had been bathed and dressed in new clothes, and smiling volunteers were looking after their every need. I was so grateful at this moment to my country and to these people for receiving and caring for our babies in such a fashion. The little ones all looked so peaceful, as if they didn't have a care in the world.

On the other hand, having commented on how well our babies were being cared for, we looked at each other. We were dirty, bedraggled and tired—more like a bunch of refugees ourselves than the FCVN professionals we were supposed to be. We all laughed aloud, happy to be safe and free.

After a few minutes' conversation, another Air Force officer found us and confirmed that the babies would fly to America the following morning.

Relief turned to tiredness. We said our goodnights and I walked outside into the balmy night air. The silence was impressive. For the first time in weeks there was an absence of noise. I had forgotten how peaceful silence could be.

Returning to the motel, I checked on my kids. Beth and Brian were sound asleep and the boys were watching a television show with their "babysitters." These men had outdone themselves. In my brief absence they had surveyed my children's wardrobe, which consisted of dingy, tattered clothing that was worn out from hand-washing and harsh detergents in Vietnam. One of them had herded the kids into the shower while the other had quickly run to the gym to pick up clothing that had been donated for the orphans.

I thanked these men for their kindness to my children and said goodnight.

Beth and Brian looked like angels, lying on the soft pillows, fresh, clean, and sleeping safely and relaxed. I leaned over and kissed each one goodnight and thought of my other three children, so far away from me. I was eager to unite my family again.

In the bathroom I took a long, hot shower. It was luxurious to feel the hot, soapy water pounding my skin for endless minutes. As the dirt sluiced down the drain, I finally felt free from all my responsibilities. It was great just to be a woman again and to take pleasure in knowing that I had done my work to the best of my ability.

Curled up in bed, I lay quietly, listening to the regular breathing of my babies. Now we were safe and in the midst of plenty, but millions of others, just a short plane ride away, were still living in hell. Fear, death and destruction would be their only bedmates tonight. While they tried to sleep in open fields and city streets, we slept in clean sheets, comfortable in air-conditioned luxury.

I also thought of the FCVN staff, holding the fort at Gia Dinh, scared and lonely. Tom and Sister Nancy would be arriving there tomorrow. I hoped they would remain safe and well in Saigon's mean streets.

I knew as I drifted off to sleep that though at this moment, I feared the thought of going back to Vietnam, I would do so, and nothing would stop me.

Chapter Twelve

*T*he next day we prepared to leave with our babies on preassigned flights to America, after a brief stopover in Hawaii. My children and I went on a flight with many of the orphans but not with the others of our group.

All of the babies were taken off the plane in Hawaii, and Dan was seen by military doctors again. They suggested keeping him behind for a few days, until I explained that he was *my* son, not one of the orphans. He was responding well to the antibiotics, and the absence of stress had helped. We flew on another MAC flight into Oakland International Airport, California.

Cheryl and Carol met us when we landed in California. We had all been through so much; we hugged and wept as we were reunited. Our contacts had been limited to scratchy telephone lines for months, and it was a pleasure just to hear each other speaking, without fearing we would lose the connection.

We were all bussed to an army base called the Presidio of San Francisco. Following a request from Ed Daly's daughter, Charlotte Behrendt, it had been agreed that USAID and the Department of Defense would arrange accommodation and facilities for the reception and temporary care of the orphans as they arrived from Vietnam. The Presidio was subsequently designated as the accommodation center.

Cheryl and Carol were both delighted and relieved to see the kids and me, but concerned that we looked so tired and had lost so much weight. Looking at my two friends, I thought they both seemed in as poor shape as those of us who had just left Vietnam. They had not had a full night's sleep since the Daly plane had arrived, almost unannounced, several days before. They had left their own families and responsibilities in Colorado, including my three children, and rushed to California to care for the hundreds of incoming FCVN orphans.

We were taken to our rooms, and after I had made sure my children were safe and being looked after, I set off with Cheryl and Carol to see the other children.

We had a problem. Since their arrival at Clark Air Force Base in the Philippines, each baby had been bathed numerous times. After all this immersion in soapy water, the identifying information on the arm and ankle bands had started to fade; the light green ink was leaching into the paper, and some names were already barely legible. Fortunately, the green ink from my typewriter back in Saigon was permanent. We could spot our children with just a glance by seeing on their arms and legs the green stain that would not wash away.

To make matters worse, the Presidio had received eight hundred and nineteen orphans from Vietnam in a seventy-two-hour period and had more on the way. The babies were all housed together in Harmon Hall, a massive gymnasium building with several large rooms. The one hundred and sixty-one FCVN babies that had arrived so far were mixed in with babies from eight other organizations. Locating and identifying our babies was a colossal task for Cheryl and Carol, who had already spent hours walking from mattress to mattress, peering at the faded green labels and trying to identify the children.

When I arrived it was easier. I knew my babies by sight; they were a part of my extended family. Together with Cheryl, I checked every baby, identifying those belonging to FCVN. I knew most of them by the nicknames that we had given them many months ago when they first arrived at the FCVN Center. When Cheryl and Mick had visited Saigon in January and traveled to the provinces with me, they had experienced the unique pleasure that comes from naming babies. Many of those babies were now in Harmon Hall.

As I walked around the makeshift room, the name of every FCVN baby I saw was recorded on a yellow legal pad. Referring to my master list that I'd sweated over in Saigon, I wrote down the Vietnamese name and the American name, as well as noting the adoptive parents' family name.

Many of the FCVN babies evacuated in the first flights had been our longer-term residents who had already been legally processed by the Vietnamese for adoption in the United States. Many had passports and had only been waiting for their U.S. visas. Prospective families were already waiting for them across America, having seen photographs and made their own applications to adopt an overseas child as an immediate relative. Prior to the emergency evacuation, the children had only been waiting for U.S. immigration visas.

Now the prospective families knew that the orphans, their new family members, were in the United States, and they were anxious to have their children. Some of the families had arrived at the Presidio to collect their new babies themselves. At the same time, we were eager to get our babies out to their new families as soon as possible.

I spotted one of Steve's twins almost immediately but couldn't find the other one. Finally, with Jackie and Jason's help, we soon had the two brothers sleeping near each other.

We played with Kiki and with Hung and Phuong's children. They had small dolls, which someone had brought them, and were making up a game which looked very much like a child's version of an evacuation. The dolls were lined up and the children asked Jason to bring them small boxes for the babies to sleep in. The children seemed comfortable and happy.

After several hours of walking around and making copious notes, I was exhausted and returned to my assigned sleeping quarters, where my own kids were by now fast asleep. I had brought Jason out with me so he could have a look at America, and he stayed with us in the rooms we were given. The night was so quiet, almost eerie. The few vehicles that we saw seemed to be gliding by with none of the jerks and fits of the traffic in Vietnam. It was a totally different world.

A few hours later I was awakened from a dead sleep by the loud ringing of a bedside telephone. It took me a few seconds to realize where I was. It was Cheryl. Panic-stricken, she was barely coherent. Shaking my head to clear the fog of sleep I listened carefully as she shouted through the phone, telling me to rush to Harmon Hall immediately—somebody was stealing our babies!

Throwing on some clothes, I ran to the building as fast as my tired legs could carry me. Inside there was a lot of activity as volunteers and doctors tended babies who were now nearly one thousand in number.

Cheryl met me at the door. She was in controlled hysteria as she told me what had just happened.

She had been working all night, preparing some of the babies for their departure the following morning to their new families. Crossing between two rooms, she had seen a woman that she didn't know carrying a baby. Cheryl recognized the baby; it was a boy whom I had named Duy Bien after a friend. She stopped the woman and demanded to know who she was and where was she taking Duy Bien.

The woman pushed Cheryl aside. Then she saw other women carrying out more babies; she recognized all of them. She could also see that the babies' arms and legs were stained with green ink. These women were stealing our babies, right from under her nose!

The women rushed through the door and disappeared. Cheryl was stunned. After all that the babies had already suffered in their short lives, now they were being kidnapped.

She rushed to call me and then went to talk with an army doctor, Doctor Lieutenant Colonel Stark, who was on duty at that time. The doctor brushed her off, telling her the babies belonged to a Christian organization based in Washington State and they were leaving for families in the Seattle area.

Cheryl was enraged and started arguing with him.

She ran to let me inside the hall and tried to fill me in on the events. We rushed back to speak to the doctor. Cheryl was shouting, demanding that someone listen to her. I explained to the doctor that I had just arrived with babies from Saigon. They had been in my care, most of them for months, and now they were gone. The doctor didn't seem to understand the urgency of our plea for help.

Cheryl led me back to the area where the babies had been lying asleep. Volunteers were curious and wanted to help as we tearfully explained what had happened. A nurse came over and told us that she had been very busy but was curious when she saw a woman cutting arm bands off and throwing them in a nearby trash can. The nurse had assumed that the woman had some authority, never dreaming that she was watching a kidnap in process.

We all ran to the trashcan. There inside lay the cut armbands. I reached in and grabbed a fistful of the familiar FCVN green-inked bands from the can.

Clutching the cut-off armbands, I ran back to Dr. Stark, who was supposed to be the man in charge. Cheryl headed off to make a telephone call to Mick, a Denver Deputy District Attorney.

Faced with the armband evidence, Dr. Stark relented a little. He finally admitted that the women who had taken the babies had not shown any identification or authorization. They told him they were in a hurry to catch a flight. I couldn't believe that he was so calm about this. Those were babies that we had loved, named, nursed and brought back from hell through every conceivable medical problem—real babies with real identities. I told him that I couldn't believe these women could just walk into a supposedly secure military facility and steal several babies—babies that were already legally assigned to families for adoption.

The doctor seemed out of his depth. When I asked him to call security, seal off the base, or do something to help get the babies back, he seem more puzzled as to how to go about doing that than disinterested. I was distraught with fear for the babies' safety.

Cheryl was just slightly calmer. Mick would handle this. The only real information we had was that the women had told Dr. Stark that they were from Washington State and had to catch a flight to Seattle. They had lied to him about everything else, but we hoped at least this much was true. Although it was late at night, Mick told Cheryl he would raise the matter immediately with the Denver District Attorney, Dale Tooley. Tooley immediately took charge and called in the FBI, and wheels quickly started turning.

We learned that the women had indeed taken the babies on a flight bound for Seattle. The FBI boarded the plane at the terminal before any of the passengers deplaned. On the plane they found the eight FCVN babies that had been stolen from the Presidio.

The babies would be taken care of by Seattle Social Services. FCVN volunteers would fly from Denver to take the babies to their legal adoptive families.

Back at the Presidio, Cheryl and I discussed the situation. A group of women without any paperwork had calmly walked into a military facility and stolen eight babies, after first removing their identification in front of a host of volunteers. We wondered who was responsible for security and where were the military police.

Those important questions, and the answers, would be left to others. We had to turn our attention to other pressing matters. We knew the babies were safe, but there were a hundred other details we still had to work out. I had to make arrangements for the care of my own children and to get myself back to Saigon.

In the morning I learned that Ross and Sister Theresa were as determined as I was to return to Vietnam. This was a courageous decision—they knew the situation was deteriorating in Saigon, and they would certainly be putting their lives at risk by going back. We all knew that despite the risks we had to return and do what we could for our staff and friends.

I was relieved that they had decided to return too. We were a tightly knit group, bonded together by the experiences we had all shared.

Decision made, we decided to take up the promise of a free flight into Saigon, made by one of the senior Air Force men we had met at Clark Air Force base when we first arrived in the Philippines. But first I had to arrange for my own children's care.

I wanted all my children together, but Sue, in Denver, was too ill to look after Joanna, Jenny and Thanh as well as helping care for Cheryl's children. It was impossible to have them all in one place, so I had to accept that my children would remain divided for the time being. I called on the McGees in Iowa to help me again, and they graciously agreed to keep my children. I was relieved that they were going somewhere familiar.

Nam, who had been one of the first orphans to arrive, on the Daly flight, still had an uncertain future. Tom and I hadn't had five minutes together to discuss our feelings about adopting Nam. We both loved him and wanted to keep him with us, but we hadn't made any formal arrangements. Dr. Richard Flannigan and his family in Denver, who were awaiting the arrival of Danny, their own adopted baby who was still lying on a mattress in the Presidio, agreed to take care of Nam until his future was confirmed.

After I said good-bye to my children and waved them off for the airport, Ross's father, who lived nearby, took us for something to eat. Over the meal, we explained that Ross, Sister Theresa and I simply had to go back to Vietnam to help with the remaining babies.

The newspapers in the airport were already announcing the imminent fall of Saigon. Ross's announcement that he would return to Vietnam didn't make his father very happy. Although he understood Ross's chivalrous personality, he believed that this time Ross was risking his life. However, he was resigned to the fact that Ross, although a young man, was determined to shape his own destiny.

We reserved seats on a commercial flight from San Francisco into Manila, in the Philippines. We must have looked a very strange trio: a sprightly forty-year-old nun, a longhaired youth, and a skinny housewife from the Midwest. On the plane, we sat amongst professionals who were dressed conservatively and flying to their important meetings. Nobody would have dreamed that we were on the first leg of a trip into a war zone. We had been in the United States for just over a day.

Before we left, I had managed to call through to the Gia Dinh center in Saigon and had spoken with Tom. He described a bleak picture. The Center was being flooded with new arrivals daily from other orphanages that were moving south from the provinces. The enemy was advancing inexorably towards Saigon, and the situation in the city was rapidly going from bad to worse.

They were trying to send out more orphans to the States, and Sister Nancy was going to escort them. The call only intensified our desire to get back to Vietnam as soon as possible, before it was too late.

Arriving in Manila after a half-day's flight, we didn't take any time to rest. The constant changing of time zones added to our weariness, but we were determined to make a speedy return. We traveled by bus, an old, smelly contraption filled with people carrying live animals to market, and were happy to finally reach Clark Air Force Base.

There we met with a major problem. The base was humming with activity as the pace of the evacuations increased. Despite the earlier promises of a return flight, we were told in no uncertain terms that the U.S. Air Force was busy evacuating Saigon, and they would not contemplate flying civilians back into that area.

The base personnel were firm but friendly. While refusing to fly us to Saigon, they did let us use their communications office to place a call to Tom. On a surprisingly clear, static-free line, I told him we were currently in the Philippines and would soon be home, one way or another. Dejected but not defeated, we trudged back to the bus station and awaited the next bus to Manila.

Back at the Manila airport, we explored our options. There were no direct flights from the Philippines, but we knew that if we could get to Hong Kong there was a chance we could pick up a flight to Saigon from there. We spent most of our quickly dwindling reserves of cash and booked three one-way tickets to Hong Kong.

We arrived in Hong Kong late at night, weary but excited—we were nearly home. The following morning we bought our way onto a private Air Vietnam transport that was carrying Vietnamese Embassy personnel back to Vietnam to their families.

The plane was nearly empty. During the flight, I struck up a conversation with a woman named Helke Ferrie who had also managed to get a ticket on the flight. She was the head of the Kuan Yin Foundation, a Canadaian based organization that had been working in Vietnam.

Helke and I got along well. She had led an interesting life; of German descent, she now lived in Canada, but had been raised in a small town in India by her scholarly parents. We didn't know it at the time, but our paths would cross again.

We worried endlessly throughout the flight; we had no visas for Vietnam and feared we would be denied entry. We were traveling with no baggage, and by now we all looked bedraggled. We would surely have a tough time if the immigration department decided not to let us into the country.

As the plane made its final approach and we heard the thump of the landing gear locking into place, we crowded around the windows for a first glimpse of Saigon. We were surprised to see that the airport and surrounding roads looked deserted.

Out on the tarmac, we realized that there were no other planes arriving or taking off. The whole airport seemed eerily quiet. Gone was the usual hustle and bustle; it was as if everyone had decided to stay at home. As usual, it was hot and sunny, though not yet noon.

In the terminal, all our fears about the lack of entry visas proved superfluous—there was not a customs or immigration officer in sight. This was an unscheduled, private, official flight, and no one was checking identification.

Tom met us in the arrival lounge. It seemed like an eternity since we had been together—so much had happened in only a few days. It was just over a week since the Daly flight.

Tom told us that the Presidential Palace had been bombed, and the authorities had immediately declared a curfew in the city. A pilot who had defected from the South Vietnamese army had bombed the palace and fled to the North.

We were used to riots, machine guns and rockets, but bombs were something we had never dealt with. I thought about the city, now packed to capacity with refugees, and wondered how much damage had been done. Tom assured me that the bomb had only hit the Palace, sparing the people on the street.

It was becoming obvious that Saigon was not going to be our home for much longer.

Tom had fixed a white cloth bearing a red cross to the van antenna, hoping that, coupled with the blue crosses on the sides and roof, it would ensure our safe passage through the streets and from any roving military patrols.

En route to the center, he told me that Sister Nancy had already left on an evacuation flight with another thirty-eight children. Some of them were the sick babies who had not been able to travel on the earlier flights.

Tom had assumed responsibility for some other babies and children from a British male nurse, Doug Grey, who had worked long and hard in Vietnam for many years with handicapped and orphaned children. Doug had been instructed by the British Embassy to leave Vietnam, as they could no longer guarantee his continued safety. He couldn't simply abandon those in his care, so he returned non-orphaned children to their families and entrusted the orphans to FCVN. Still more had come from Reverend Phat, of the Vung Tau Christian Children's Home, who could no longer care for the orphans in his home. Those extra children and babies comprised some of Sister Nancy's latest group of evacuees.

Tom had one piece of really bad news to impart. Sy, our trusted co-worker, had been arrested and imprisoned by the Saigon police.

Tom and Sister Nancy had tried to hide Sy on Nancy's flight, just as we had managed to smuggle out Thanh and Jason earlier. The ruse had backfired; Sy was spotted by a Vietnamese immigration official and hauled off to jail. This was awful news. We all knew that the Vietnamese prisons were hellholes. Bad treatment, bad food and frequent beatings were the normal order of the day. God knows what the conditions were like as panic grew in the city. Prisoners would be a low priority on any official agenda.

As we drove down the narrow lane to the center, I commented on how quiet it was compared to the day I had left. Tom told me that before the curfew had been imposed, the area had been jammed with people. I looked at the Center from a new perspective. Physical security was nonexistent. We had a brick wall, about four or five feet high, topped with a few strands of rusty barbed wire; the fencing wouldn't keep out any determined intruder. We had already seen street riots and knew that looting was becoming a problem. Suddenly I realized how exposed we were in the Center.

As we pulled into the driveway, people rushed out to greet us. Thuy, Hong and all the other staff were so thrilled that I had kept my promise and returned. I had come back.

Inside, the place had been transformed. My last memories were of a Center trashed by the passage of so many in such a short time. The floors had been littered with diapers, mats and abandoned clothing. The air had been fetid. We hadn't had time to clean; we were all too busy preparing for the departures.

Now the place smelled fresh and clean again. I walked through the rooms, which had all been thoroughly scrubbed and disinfected; my office was spick-and-span and once again looked like a place of work. The whole interior looked like an FCVN Center again and not some refugee post.

The intensive care nursery was quiet, but babies were starting to come in again, I was told. The Saigon maternity hospitals were calling daily. Refugee mothers were giving birth and walking off without their infants. They had nothing to give them—they had come with only the clothes on their backs. Many had seen their other children die as they fled to Saigon. They left the babies with the hope that somehow the newborns would be cared for as the mothers went back on the streets to simply exist.

I picked up a little baby boy. He was only a few days old. He smelled clean and fresh, with that unique new-baby scent. I hadn't held a baby for a few days, and I badly needed a baby fix! The nurse told me that he had been delivered to them just the day before from a local maternity home. Hong giggled and told me they had named the baby Tom.

There seemed to be more adults than children in the Center. Two medical students from America had arrived in my absence to help out with the children. They had been sent by the Emergency Committee to Save the Children, a Washington, D.C., organization. The students, Bill Holles and Steve Weinstein, were great guys and we soon called them "Dr. Bill" and "Dr. Steve."

Steve Johnson and his wife, Carol Kim, had also moved into the Center while Steve continued to try to get permission for Carol to leave. Many Americans married to Vietnamese naturally refused to leave Saigon until they could take their partners with them. MAC planes sat on the runway at Tan Son Nhut airport, waiting to evacuate the American nationals, but they wouldn't leave without their Vietnamese families.

We all gathered in the nursery and sat around on the floor. We talked for hours and hours, swapping stories of our escapades and the orphans. Nobody could believe that some of babies had been stolen from the Presidio and that the FBI had intervened to rescue them.

Later that night we received a call from Cheryl, who was still organizing the transport of babies to their new adoptive families across the United States.

Cheryl was distraught—she had terrible news. Operation Babylift had been suspended. A class action lawsuit was in the works against Henry

Kissinger, as the Secretary of State, claiming that the babies and children taken into America were not all orphans and that some of them had been kidnapped from their parents. The rumors were strong enough to convince the skittish State Department to suspend Operation Babylift.

I was devastated by the news. How could anyone believe that we had taken the children without their parents' permission?

Even as I was attempting to understand, the hospital called. They were terribly short-staffed and had several abandoned babies. They asked if I could send someone immediately, as there was no one even to feed the babies. How could I refuse?

In the airplane, Sister Nancy (far left) and Tom Clark (center in plaid shirt) look after the tired children upon their arrival in Tokyo.

Nam, just arriving in Denver, with Barbara Flannigan who cared for him until Tom and Cherie left Vietnam.

The first U.S. military plane to depart with orphans, a C-5A Galaxy, crashed just after take off.

We are greatful to Dennis "Bud" Traynor, Pilot of the aircraft for the use of these photos.

Preparing for evacuation flight.

FCVN evacuation flight (Cherie is in red shirt).

Carol Dey and Sister Theresa and others caring for babies at evacuation holding center.

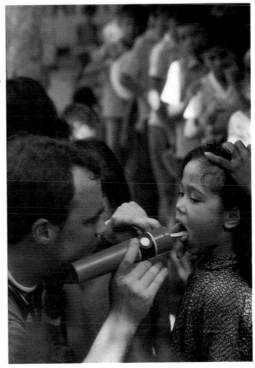

Ross Meador

Lining up for final evacuation flight at FCVN
Center, April 26.

Dr. William Holles examining children at
FCVN Center before evacuation flight.

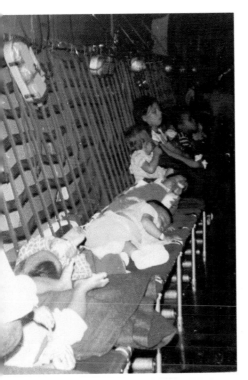

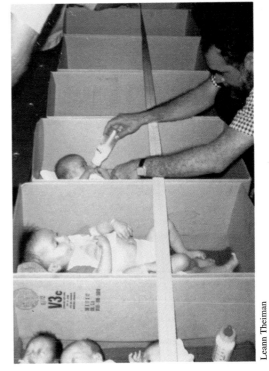

Leann Theiman

On board evacuation flight, April 5.

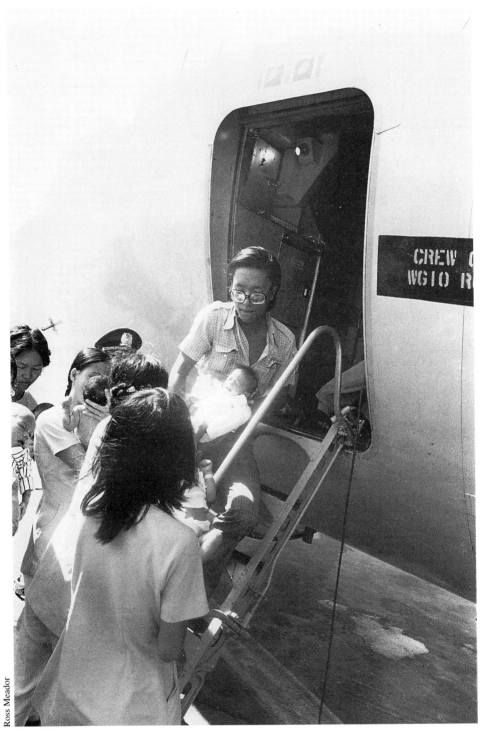

Ross Meador

Dr. Cong and FCVN staff loading babies onto evacuation flight.

Chaos erupts as people frantically try to board an evacuation flight.

Chapter Thirteen

*T*he day after we arrived back in Saigon we woke to find ourselves under siege.

Gone was the calm of the curfew from the day before. Outside the Center, people packed the narrow lane, many of them with babies or children.

From the balcony, which stretched along the front of our center, I could see the desperate refugees jamming our short, narrow lane and pressing against our fence. I'm sure they thought that because we were Americans we somehow had the power to save them or, in many cases, at least to save their young children from the war that was now just around the corner.

We were told the end could be days, even hours, away. The areas surrounding Saigon were under North Vietnamese control and the city was heavily infiltrated with communist agents who mingled with the flood of refugees.

The phone rang almost ceaselessly, all day and all night long. The niceties of polite society had evaporated. People we didn't know called us at all times, even in the middle of the night. Each time it rang, I rushed to answer, hoping it would be a call with some news about my own kids. But no, nearly every call was someone pleading for help.

I answered the telephone once with only the slightest bit of patience left. I listened as a woman asked if I could possibly help with some children who were in an orphanage and destined for already assigned families. To my surprise, in a polite and respectful voice, she introduced herself as Princess Grace of Monaco. I was taken aback but assured her, as I had everyone else who called, that we would do whatever we could to help—and we did.

Our Vietnamese mailman, whom we tipped substantially, arrived several times daily with handfuls of telegrams, after fighting his way through the crowds that packed the lane outside the Center. The calls and the telegrams had one thing in common, wherever they originated from across the world: Every one sought to enlist our help in saving family members still in Vietnam.

What could we say to these people? How could we answer them and give them any hope?

We didn't know how long Saigon would survive. We didn't know if Operation Babylift would ever resume after the legal problems in the States. We were in limbo ourselves. Staff members were concerned about their own families; some were outside the city, in areas probably already overrun by the communist forces. How could we comfort them?

Everybody in Saigon was looking for a way to get out. Crowds were waiting in lines outside the American Embassy, other Embassies or the Vietnamese Passport Office, everybody wanting the piece of paper that would grant them and their families freedom from the hell that was Saigon. Many of the people that were calling us were American or other nationalities, who told us they had already stood in line for days.

Many of the Americans had Vietnamese wives or long-term girlfriends and children. The Americans were guaranteed safe passage by the Embassy, but that guarantee was not extended at that time to their families. After waiting to plead and bargain with officialdom they called us, asking if we could look after their families and get their babies and children out.

Vietnamese who worked for American organizations believed the communists would target them when they entered the city. The deaths in Hue in previous years had given them cause to fear for their lives. Many of those people begged us to take their children away.

The phone calls and telegrams were a strain, even more so because we couldn't offer any concrete help to these desperate people. But the throng demanding attention outside our gates was a more pressing issue.

Members of the staff mounted a guard near the fence and gate, trying to keep people from rushing the compound. The low wall and fence made any sort of real attempt at security an impossibility.

The quiet lane where my children used to play marbles and soccer with their young Vietnamese friends had been transformed into a scene of bedlam. The narrow lane was literally packed wall-to-wall with bodies, all trying to get into our compound. The temperature was oppressive and the hot sun beat down on the gathered masses. The clamor was incredible, a primal, throbbing din that continued without letup—babies and children crying, women screaming and sobbing and men shouting towards the Center. It was a living nightmare.

Every day we had to descend into the mob to get supplies and to attend briefings at the DAO, now set up at Tan Son Nhut airport. We drove slowly through the crowds with doors and windows shut tight. The van wasn't air-conditioned, and the heat and press of people seemed to force the temperature to unbearable levels. Mothers held babies to windows, banging on the glass and demanding our attention. The horn added a constant blare of noise, but it hardly phased the panicking throng.

Sometimes we simply couldn't get the van through the mass of people. One day Tom and I abandoned it at the end of lane and tried to make it back on foot to the compound. The mad press of the crowd made me faint, and Tom saved me from being shoved to the ground as people reached out to grab at me. The situation in the lane was becoming impossible.

Meanwhile we were trying to make sense of Cheryl's terrible news that Operation Babylift was suspended indefinitely. The authorities were obviously reacting to the rumors that some of the Vietnamese babies and children taken into America had not been orphans but had only been lost, separated or even kidnapped from their parents. At the same time, the North Vietnamese were using the controversy for their own propaganda purposes, claiming that the Americans were kidnapping and killing Vietnamese babies. Attacked from both sides, the South Vietnamese and American governments halted evacuation of the babies.

Back in America, the first thing Cheryl and Carol had to do was to get all the babies out of California and into another state before any legal actions commenced. Within hours, an FCVN task force staff and volunteers proposed a plan to evacuate the children again. A new nursing home in Denver was donated temporarily for FCVN use. It was complete with staff and a full range of medical equipment, and was ready to handle the needs of hundreds of orphaned babies. Arrangements were hurriedly made and the children and babies were flown to Stapleton Airport in Denver.

Public response to the Babylift had been mixed. The Babylift headquarters in Washington, D.C., was flooded with calls from people wanting to adopt the children, but there was also intense criticism that the United States was removing Vietnamese children from their own culture for political reasons.

Friends and colleagues started turning up outside the compound entrance, people who had worked in other orphanages and centers in the provinces. They had abandoned their centers to the advancing enemy and made their way to Saigon, along with a million other refugees. Many had traveled for days, risking their lives to reach us, knowing we wouldn't turn them away.

In their headlong flight, these people—nuns, nurses, volunteers and priests—had lost everything but the clothes on their backs. It broke my heart to see them in such pitiful states: tired to death, hungry, unwashed, clothes ripped—and yet each of them carried one or two babies, starving to death after the long, hot, frightening journey.

We looked after them as well as we were able. Without a moment's pause, we broke into our emergency stocks of kerosene, rice and some supplies donated from the American USAID stores. We gave them food and a place to wash; we relieved them of their precious bundles of life and cared for them as well.

Everybody that arrived had a terrible tale to tell. One nun, Sister Emelienne, had traveled for days with twelve young girls from her own center in Qui Nhon. Each of the girls had started out carrying an abandoned infant in her arms. The arduous trail had proved too much for the infants. One by one the babies were lost as exhaustion and dehydration claimed their lives. When they arrived at our door, only one of the twelve babies was still alive, a little girl named Kim Cuc. She had become a symbol of hope for them all, and they were determined that she would survive.

There was little we could do in the face of such tragedy. We just managed the best we could.

Only days before, the Center had been nearly empty. Now it was rapidly filling with the orphaned and abandoned. Babies in the nursery cried and adults worked endlessly. Much of the time we sought relief from the stress of the situation outside by immersing ourselves in hard, mind-numbing work.

Doctors from the Saigon maternity hospitals were also in a quandary. They continued to call us daily, asking us to come and pick up the newest abandoned babies. Heavily pregnant women with nothing but the clothes on their backs continued to come, deliver their babies and then quietly disappear, leaving the lives of their newborns in the hands of the staff.

The hospitals couldn't cope with the influx of small babies, and once again we said yes—and the numbers in the Center swelled yet more. Suddenly we again had more than one hundred orphaned and abandoned babies to care for. This time the babies were accompanied by a rapidly growing number of stressed and tired adults to manage as well.

The crowds in the street contained many mothers with their children, many of whom were half-American. These mothers were especially pathetic. The war was forcing them to relinquish children they had been raising alone, long after the GI fathers had returned home. Some of them obviously deeply loved their Amerasian offspring, but having already lived with prejudice against their children, they believed the problems would only intensify when the enemy conquered Saigon.

Other half-American children hadn't fared so well. Unwanted products of illicit relationships, the children had been farmed out by mothers who seemed to have little interest in their welfare. Now that the end was near, the women no longer wanted the stigma of being seen as the mother of a half-foreign child. They feared their motherhood would become a death sentence, and they too chose to relinquish their offspring.

In desperation, having waited so long to plead with us to take their children, some mothers literally threw their babies over our compound fence, and we would find them lying in the courtyard. One of these babies, a little boy, didn't survive being pushed through the barbed wire and dropping to the concrete below.

In the midst of all the panic, we never forgot our young friend Sy, still locked in Saigon's jail after his abortive evacuation attempt. Tom and Sy's father made frequent trips to the jail, trying to negotiate his release. Finally, frustrated by the lack of any progress, they offered to exchange Sy's new motorbike for his freedom. To their surprise, their none-too-subtle bribe was accepted. Sy walked free that same day, as a cop polished his new motorbike.

On the sixteenth of April, elements of the Khmer Rouge, communist followers of Pol Pot, overran the Cambodian capital of Phnom Penh.

The news was a bitter blow. Saigon was only a hundred miles away from Phnom Penh, and less than fifty miles from the border between the two countries. The end was getting closer.

Now the situation in the whole of the city gravitated overnight from desperate to ugly. The Vietnamese became angry with all Americans, who, they felt, had deserted and abandoned them to their fate at the hands of the communists.

Whenever we went out—which we had to do, to get updates on the latest developments and news about Operation Babylift—people in the streets became angry. They banged on the sides of our van, jeering at us. After one trip to the DAO, Tom and I drove our van into the lane outside the Center. As usual, the drive to our compound gates was accompanied by a great deal of shouting, jeering and rocking of the van. The crowds parted grudgingly as we edged up to the gates. Steve, Bill and the guard carefully opened them just enough to let us drive in.

Suddenly a great body of people pressed forward and rushed into the courtyard. Our men fought off more of them as they closed the gate. Now the compound was filled with almost a hundred screaming men and women rushing around, some running into the Center itself.

I finally made it inside and grabbed the phone. Quickly I called the Mission Warden of the USAID police and the Saigon police for help. When the authorities arrived they started violently clearing the intruders out. Using batons and rifle butts, they beat both men and women, some with children in their arms, forcing them off the property.

Poor, frightened people were found in every nook and cranny—we even found some underneath my bed. It took more than three hours, even with the help of the police, to clear the building and compound of all the terrified people.

The trespassers were not intent on looting or robbing; rather they were panic-stricken and hysterical. Somehow they believed that if they gained entry to the Center, we would be able to whisk them out of the jaws of the war. Nothing was further from the truth. We were now scared about how we could get ourselves out with the ever-growing number of babies in our care.

The Vietnamese people had heard rumors of atrocities that followed in the wake of Khmer Rouge victories, and many were certain a similar fate awaited them when the communists took Saigon. Words can't describe the intense feelings of panic that gripped the city.

On the political front we learned from the constant radio bulletins that the Vietnamese government had confirmed that Operation Babylift was suspended. The arguments raged as Americans debated the pros and cons of Vietnamese children being raised in America. They argued that the youngsters would be better off in their own culture, brought up by their own countrymen. As we fought the battle for life in our nursery we wondered just what culture they were speaking of.

Our staff told us that Radio Hanoi, the communist state radio station, was broadcasting information about the adoption groups in South Vietnam. The broadcasts claimed that anybody who worked with the adoption agencies would be considered war criminals. The broadcasts struck fear into our staff, but their loyalty to us and to the needs of the children was greater than their fear of reprisals. It was evident to everyone in our Center that the children had no hope of survival in Vietnam. If not evacuated soon, many of them would die.

We managed to visit other orphanages in Saigon and asked the sisters if they would look after our babies and youngsters if we, as American citizens, were ordered out. We offered money, milk and food supplies if we suddenly had to leave and they would take the children. Every single place we visited rejected our plea. They too were struggling under insufferable difficulties; they had no staff left, no resources and little hope for their own futures. We usually came back from those trips with a few more half-American children that the sisters convinced us to take.

With the fall of Cambodia, the politicians and military finally realized that the end was very, very near. The two enemy forces were now pushing the South Vietnamese military into a stranglehold, with Saigon lying in the center—the last bastion of democracy in Vietnam. Saigon was the only real pocket of resistance left in the country, and even there the social and economic infrastructure was near the breaking point.

Suddenly there was an even greater push to evacuate the remaining Americans in Saigon. Many had steadfastly refused to leave until the politicians relented and granted their relatives exit visas. Miraculously a door opened, and the American and Vietnamese governments agreed to let relatives of American citizens leave. That momentous decision started an exodus.

Steve managed to get permission for his wife, Carol Kim, to leave. They made arrangements to go as soon as possible, along with Ray Ebbets and his wife, Nguyet. Before they left, Steve and Ray explained the procedure to us. All that was required was that an American citizen sign a form confirming that they were married to, or intending to marry, the person they wanted to be evacuated with them. The Vietnamese person named would then be able to evacuate his or her extended family also.

After months of carefully tiptoeing through a maze of paperwork and interminable delays, we now saw a loophole in this latest quickly devised piece of bureaucracy. We decided to use the loophole to try to get our faithful staff out of the country. Thuy was one of the first to be able to leave, utilizing the new relaxed evacuation procedures, and accompanied Steve and Carol on their flight.

We went to the American officials at Tan Son Nhut airport and asked how we could start to evacuate our staff. They told us to claim they were members of our family and bring them through slowly, two or three at a time.

Tom and Sister Theresa volunteered to stay at the airport and facilitate the evacuation of male and female staff. In the next few days each of them "married" many of our staff members and watched them leave for America. Using the marriage ploy, we were able to evacuate Doctor Cong and his family, Chau and her family, and many of our nurses and child care workers. Steve Weinstein also left, accompanied by several of our staff members.

We knew that evacuating Sy was going to be the most difficult task, for he was of military age and could be conscripted into the army at any time. But we would have to take the chance anyway.

Sister Theresa arrived in the MACV movie theatre where the sham weddings were taking place. She went up to the American official who sanctioned the Vietnamese evacuees and told him that Sy was her husband. They made a strange couple. Sister Theresa, a mature woman in her forties, stood there, straight-faced, presenting herself with a nervous young Vietnamese man just past twenty. Both she and the official ignored the fact that the day before, she had made several similar claims of marriage to other men.

Looking at the obvious difference in ages the official commented, "Maybe, in this case, this man should be your adopted son, and not your husband."

And so with a grin and a lighthearted comment, Sy had the freedom he desired.

Back in the FCVN Center things weren't going too well. We were very happy that our friends and staff were escaping the war, but each departure made life harder for those remaining. The number of sick and dying babies still rose daily, yet we had fewer and fewer personnel to cope with them. Our medical staff now consisted of three Vietnamese nurses, Bill Holles and me, to care for the very ill babies and children.

❧

It was at this time that Iowa-based FCVN volunteers arranged for us to meet with their relatives living in Saigon. It was to be a great quid pro quo for all of us.

Vu Trung Thanh and his wife, Lan, had lived in America for several years and returned with their four sons to Vietnam, where Thanh had taken up a post as a university professor. Like many other ordinary people, the war had overtaken them.

Thanh came to plead with us to evacuate his wife and children and send them on to their relatives in Iowa. He himself didn't intend to leave, but he was fearful for the rest of his family. We told him that we couldn't evacuate any children at that time, but we could probably send out his wife, using the new marriage technique. But Lan refused to leave her children behind, and so elected to stay in Saigon.

Thanh had fought his way through the crowds to reach the FCVN Center, and had been amazed at the mob scene outside our gate. Inside, the situation was desperate. By now we were very understaffed, we were nearly broke, we had little food, and on top of all those problems we had to somehow cope with nearly two hundred babies and children. Thanh and his family offered to stay in the Center and help out where they could. Their arrival was a windfall and we put them to work immediately.

Thanh joined the Americans who were trying to calm the crowd at the gate, where his added authority helped keep the peace. Acting as a translator, he told the press of people that there was nothing we could do to help them—we had no resources and we couldn't take any more babies. Despite his pleas for reason, the crowd continued to clamor for help. Inside, Lan worked tirelessly, helping to care for our babies as well as her own four small children.

It was so hot. The sporadic electricity gave us the comfort of a twirling fan from time to time, while the loud static blast of the radio brought news confirming our fears that the situation was worsening. Music was interspersed with the news, and the happy upbeat rhythms seemed inane as we fought life-and-death struggles in the nursery.

By now the compound was jammed with vehicles. Not that long ago, we had longed for transport, and thought ourselves in paradise when the Volkswagen van was donated to us. Now all our friends gave us their vehicles as they left the country, and suddenly we had to start turning away the vans, cars and jeeps—we had no place to put them any longer.

Rumors were flying that the Ministry of Social Welfare wasn't going to allow any further evacuations of orphans. We had no alternative but to tell dear friends that we simply couldn't take any more children into the Center. We worried constantly what would happen when the enemy arrived.

By now we were all extremely despondent. Lack of sleep and food, constant shellfire and the sound of rockets, plus uncertainty about our own safety, combined in a debilitating mix to push us all into deep depression.

The situation was becoming more critical by the day. The North Vietnamese army had just captured Xuan Loc, only thirty-eight miles northeast of Saigon. We stood on the balcony, watching planes leave Tan Son Nhut. Now that the enemy forces were so close, all the planes climbed steeply after takeoff to avoid enemy fire.

In a last-ditch attempt to get clearance to evacuate our children, Thanh took Tom and me to meet some of his influential friends at the Ministry of Social Welfare in downtown Saigon. The ride was a waking nightmare.

Saigon was prepared for a street battle. Soldiers in battle dress manned concertina-wire blockades. Tanks stood silent and resolute at intersections. Sandbag barricades had appeared almost overnight at every corner. Military trucks raced around the streets, packed with soldiers and ordnance. The materiel of war was all around us. Saigon residents and refugees crammed together with the soldiers to make an unbelievable assemblage in the main thoroughfares. We had to detour through mean narrow backstreets to reach the Ministry building.

Thanh's friends in the Ministry were sympathetic to our needs but were unable to help. In their opinion there would be no further evacuations. Their country was falling apart; there were thousands of displaced people, families split, lost children and deaths to contend with. The fate of a few hundred orphans did not rate highly on anybody's agenda, except ours. They suggested that we go back to the department that normally handled adoptions. Dispirited, we trudged along packed corridors to try one last time.

Stepping into the Adoption Office was like going back in time. The whole demeanor of the place was surreal. The Adoption Officer, Madam Quoi, and I had never seen eye-to-eye. Now she sat at her desk, carrying out her assigned duties by the book. She seemed completely oblivious that the fall of Saigon was only days or hours away.

We pleaded with her to help us process the children for evacuation. Her reaction was bizarre. According to her we had to follow the full bureaucratic procedure that required us to supply a Birth Judgment for each child—a document that was only available after a Court hearing—and multiple passport photographs, as well as lengthy medical and social reports on each child.

Her instructions were meaningless. She didn't grasp the reality of the situation we were living in. Babies were arriving almost hourly in the Center, often with nothing more than the rags they were wearing. We had no idea, and no way of finding out, which city they came from or who their parents were.

The woman knew she had presented an insurmountable block. There was no way we could even begin to attack the mountains of paperwork that would be required to satisfy her.

Looking over her shoulder, we could see other office workers. They were emptying file cabinets and shelves of documents, sweeping them all into large blue plastic bags. Thanh called over to the women and asked what they were doing. They told him that the documents had to be destroyed because the communists were coming any day.

I looked back to Madam Quoi. She had heard the exchange, but she remained as stone-faced as ever. Stubbornly wielding her petty power, she had just condemned our babies to death. Without another word we about-faced and left the office. Now totally depressed and unable to see a way forward, we fought our way back to the FCVN Center.

In the early evening, Tom and I drove to Tan Son Nhut to help some friends leave. The airport was so close, but without permission to take the orphans, whose lives were completely dependent upon us, out of Vietnam, it might as well have been a million miles away.

The airport was a mess. When it was controlled by elements of the United States government, the place had been run like a military base and had always been pristine, with trimmed hedges, neat lawns and white-painted curbs. Now it was trashed. The parking lots were full, and abandoned vehicles were parked haphazardly in the streets and on the grass. Litter, Coke bottles, cans and diapers lay everywhere, a grim reminder of the panic-stricken flight of those who had already left.

The activity was frenzied. Civilians and military, refugees and officers were swarming together, all intent on their own problems. Public address speakers blared constantly, reminding people to leave their keys in vehicles and not to board planes with keys in their pockets.

For the first time I noticed that the ratio of Vietnamese to Americans was increasing. Most of the Americans with Vietnamese families had left, and now we were surrounded by nearly all-Vietnamese families.

We noticed some barracks full of Vietnamese men, with their families, obviously awaiting evacuation. We were told that they were all high-ranking South Vietnamese army officers who worked for Military Intelligence.

For weeks the leadership had told the nation that anyone who left the country was a traitor. Suddenly they were all fleeing themselves. What chance did the rest of us have if all the Military Intelligence were leaving Saigon? The end could be only hours away.

At quarter to eight an American voice came over the loudspeakers, announcing that an emergency curfew had been imposed, starting at eight o'clock. A shoot-on-sight order would enforce the curfew. The disembodied voice instructed everybody not scheduled for evacuation to get off the base and return to their homes as fast as possible. Tom and I raced to the van to try to reach the Center before the curfew began.

Normally it would have been a fifteen-minute trip, but the streets were packed and the journey seemed to take forever.

On Vo Tanh Street the traffic and pedestrians collided in a kind of crazy death-defying race. Loudspeakers on poles were blasting messages in Vietnamese. The people were panicked and running frantically to reach their families and safety.

We drove as fast as we could towards the Center. Further down Vo Tanh Street the roadway was lined with soldiers. We could see in the light cast from the streetlights that all of them were dressed in full combat gear, hand grenades swinging from their jackets, machine guns clutched tightly in their arms. It was a frightening spectacle.

Barrels had been strung across the road, with just enough space for one vehicle to pass at a time; it was like a massive chicane. Tom swung the van this way and that to drive through the blockades. Soldiers stared impassively at us from the roadsides as we sped past them in a crazy race to beat the clock.

Reaching the top of our lane, we saw a line of soldiers blocking the entrance. The van ground to an abrupt halt and the soldiers advanced towards us. They didn't look friendly. By now it was a quarter past eight and the curfew had been in place for fifteen minutes—they could have shot or arrested us on sight. After a couple of minutes arguing with them, the officer in charge relented and allowed us to pass down the lane and into the Center.

When we got inside the compound, all the lights were on. Our staff rushed to the van and shouted that the President had resigned. We jumped from the van and ran to the home of our neighbors, who had a television. They were watching the President's resignation speech. He was blasting the American government who, he claimed, had deserted the people of South Vietnam in their hour of need.

It was official: President Nguyen Van Thieu and his entire cabinet resigned, live on TV. The date was the twenty-first of April.

Dejected and frightened, we returned to the Center. Ross, Sister Theresa, Bill, Tom and I sat on the balcony with our new Vietnamese friends and talked into the long night hours.

We were all so depressed—we had just seen the army officers leaving, and now the government had resigned. The telephone wasn't working again; we had no money, and no contact with the outside world. We joked that soon we would be scrubbing floors for the Viet Cong.

Somehow we had to leave—but to leave without the children was not a possibility that any of us would consider. One of our allies, Dr. Phan Quang Dan, the former Minister of Social Welfare, had resigned along with Thieu. It seemed that we were on our own to find a way to save the ever-increasing numbers of babies—and adults—in our care.

Chapter Fourteen

*I*t was soon well known around Saigon that many senior South Vietnamese Army officers had fled the country. Within hours the army started to fall apart as the soldiers' morale hit rock bottom. The men felt abandoned, deserted by their leaders—and much of their anger was directed at the few remaining Americans. Undisciplined soldiers roamed the streets, looking to vent their anger on anyone who crossed their paths.

For the past year the South Vietnamese Army had been dragging teens off the streets to fill its manpower needs. We feared those untrained, armed teenagers and the angry, frustrated mob outside our gates almost more than we feared the communists.

It seemed that everyone was leaving the country but us. From April twenty-second onwards, C-141's and C-130's were departing around the clock. Every half-hour at least two hundred people were leaving on these flights. Between the twenty-first and the twenty-fourth, fifteen thousand people were evacuated.

The officials who had assisted with the "marriages" had moved from the movie theater to the gymnasium because they needed more space. Ken Moorefield, who was helping with the screening, told us that he could get anyone out at this point—except our orphans. At one point, he had up to ten thousand people waiting to be processed out. One American would show up with as many as thirty immediate relatives.

We knew how it felt to have crowds of people pleading to be taken to safety. I felt like my office was the back door of the American Embassy. We would listen to cases of people who stood before us with tears running down their faces. They would tell stories of how they had escaped down the country, and how many of their relatives had died in the flight to safety.

The next three days passed in a blur as we waited to be evacuated.

We listened to the radio whenever we had electricity. The American Embassy had made it known that when the final evacuations were started, they would signal everyone by playing the famous Bing Crosby tune "White Christmas" over the radio. As we listened for the evacuation alert, we heard bulletins stating the latest military situation. By now eleven battalions of North Vietnamese soldiers were ranged around Saigon. The city was under siege from the outside, and Viet Cong soldiers intermingled unobtrusively with civilians inside the city.

DAO officials issued automatic handguns to American citizens for our personal protection. I placed the gun in a desk drawer. I wasn't about to start shooting people, even if I had known how to use it.

The weather was hot and my clothes were sticking to me. Despite the heat and the anger in the streets, we had to fight through the ever-increasing crowds and roadblocks to make our regular rounds to the American Embassy and the USAID offices, trying and hoping to get news about the restart of the evacuations of orphans. After another unsuccessful trip, I was walking dejectedly back to the van when my path was blocked by a large group of drunken Vietnamese soldiers. They jeered, and one raised his gun and pointed it at me.

I didn't think he would shoot me, but I was alarmed to be looking down the business end of an automatic rifle held by an angry, drunken teenager. My fear turned to shock when, without warning, he spat in my face. His friends all laughed and gesticulated menacingly. I felt his spittle running down my cheek; silently I pushed my way through the group and climbed into the van. Safe from further attack, I sank low in the seat and we drove off. My sadness at the unfairness of the situation was almost unbearable.

The situation was intolerable—even the once friendly Vietnamese were turning against us. We had made the decision not to leave, even if we heard the last evacuation alert. We simply could not leave one hundred and eighty infants and children alone to die.

Many of our Vietnamese staff were being pressed by their families to leave the Center and not return. They feared that their family members would be punished if the communists found them working alongside Americans.

Finally, Tom took Thanh's family to the airport where he "married" Thanh's pregnant sister-in-law and so was able to send her, Thanh's wife and other relatives out. However, at the last moment, the children were refused permission to leave, and Tom had no choice but to return them to the Center. We imagined it was because they believed we were trying to take out orphans who did not have permission to leave.

Thanh, who had remained at the Center, had known there was a possibility that his wife and children could leave at any time, and they had already said their good-byes. When Tom returned from the airport with the children but no wife, Thanh was shocked. We did our best to assure him that we wouldn't leave without taking his children. Somehow this had to work out.

On the twenty-fourth of April, it was announced on the radio that the evacuations had been a success and that almost all "non-essential" Americans had been safely evacuated. Inside our Center things looked grim. We were afraid that we had been forgotten.

Thanh talked with his brother Ngoc and asked for assistance. Ngoc moved into the Center to help with crowd control at the gate. Heavily armed, they patrolled our compound to keep the hysterical mob outside the wire fence. I, the ultimate peace warrior, who had vigorously protested against war, was now living in an armed camp.

On April twenty-five, Thanh proved to be far more useful than just as a guard and translator. He had influential contacts in the new cabinet, sworn in only hours before, following the hasty departure of President Thieu.

Thanh took Tom and me to meet Dr. Dan's successor, Minister Tran Van Mai, and to plead with him to let us take the children to safety. But Minister Mai told us that Operation Babylift was finished and that he couldn't authorize a further evacuation of babies without a meeting of the entire cabinet. With the country collapsing around us, that wasn't going to happen.

Minister Mai did offer us a ray of light: he agreed to talk with others in power and ask that they simply turn their heads and allow us to pass through the gates of Tan Son Nhut with the children, if we were willing to try it.

In a way Minister Mai put the onus onto the American government for the safe evacuations of the remaining children. His government would turn a blind eye, and it was up the Americans to allow or refuse the evacuation.

Finally I was able to tell USAID that we had loose permission to evacuate the children. After consulting with their superiors, it was decided that they would send buses to pick us up at half past seven the following morning.

And so our last hours in Vietnam began. Back in the Center we made our final preparations. We were leaving, never to return.

Ross and Tom made a huge bonfire in the sandbox, where so many children had played in happier times. They burned all the staff records and anything to do with names or details of the foster parents or anybody who had any contact with us. The sight of the bonfire told the crowd outside that our departure was now imminent and drove them to new heights of frenzied panic.

Before leaving I had to see Father Olivier one last time. I went to plead with the elderly Canadian priest to leave Vietnam with us. The Canadian government had already officially shut down their Embassy. Father Olivier held me near. He told me that I needed to understand that he had come to Vietnam in the summer of his youth, and he was now in the winter of his life. He preferred to die there rather than leave his adopted homeland.

Later in the afternoon Bill and I drove to the hospital to collect several of our sick babies whom we had hospitalized. We had a great relationship with some of the staff in the children's unit. These people now told us that the Americans they worked with had already left. Now they were alone and feared reprisals from the advancing enemy. They pleaded with us to help them get out of Saigon.

We explained that there was nothing we could do officially—but then I had an idea. If they were to dress up as patients we could try to take them out.

The staff set to work, helped by Bill and me, dressing up in bandages and slings. One doctor even applied a plaster cast to his leg. When they were suitably camouflaged as sick patients, I drove them to the airport. The soldiers merely looked at my ID card and the "patients" and waved us through. They were safe, and were evacuated the same day.

During the early evening more members of Thanh's family joined us in the Center to help guard the compound during our last night. By now the crowd had turned into a very angry mob; they were threatening us and could easily have taken over the Center. The fence was leaning under the weight of bodies as the crowds pushed against it, trying to force an entry. Though we could see and hear the crowd wherever we were in the Center, their ranting made no real sense to us.

Thanh and his remaining family patrolled the perimeters all night. Thanh's car, a white Ford Mustang, was parked inside the compound. He opened the trunk and handed out guns, grenades and all kinds of weaponry to his fellow guardsmen. He was a man of many hidden talents.

We packed formula, diapers and bottles filled with boiled water into boxes. I'd already experienced delays at the airport and watched babies dehydrate, unable to help them; this time I wanted to be as prepared as possible.

Our medical supplies were nearly gone. We had no new IV needles, so we had to boil used ones in a primitive attempt to sterilize them before pressing them back into service. Antibiotics were in short supply and we had to switch types constantly—we worked with what we had, rather than what we needed.

When the supplies were packed I took a walk around the Center. Stepping onto the balcony, I spotted the obligatory Vietnamese flag that every house in the country was required to fly. Impulsively I took it from its pole on the balcony and placed it inside one of the boxes packed with milk and diapers.

As the night of the twenty-fifth of April passed, we spent time making armbands for the babies. We also made up Vietnamese names for the ones who had come into the Center in recent days. Some of the names we fabricated made no sense at all. We were too tired to care; at that late stage it didn't matter if we had a boy named Sue.

I gathered the staff around me and gave instructions to the few that would remain after our departure. Someone had to take care of the bodies of the babies who had died that day, and the incubators and remaining supplies had to be sent to the sisters on Hai Ba Trung Street, in downtown Saigon.

I went next door and again pleaded with our neighbor to bring his five daughters and leave Vietnam with us. He explained that he had already run away once from the North Vietnamese. His sons had all died in the army, fighting the communists. If necessary, he would buy rat poison and kill himself and his remaining family, rather than run away again.

Our neighbor echoed the sentiments we had heard from many fearful Saigon residents. The rumors were that demand for rat poison had become so high that the price had tripled in the last few weeks. People told us that entire families preferred to poison themselves rather than face life under the communists. We had no idea if this was the truth, but it was told to us many times over.

I hadn't closed my eyes in the last thirty-six hours, and for weeks I hadn't slept for more than two hours at a stretch. I was exhausted and ill. It was impossible to tell if it was just lack of sleep and food or if the hepatitis had resurfaced again.

❦

As dawn broke on the twenty-sixth of April, Bill and I wrote up notes about each child—who they were, their medical condition, and whatever other information we had pertaining to them.

The USAID contingent arrived on time with four large buses, accompanied by the Mission Warden team and armed American personnel. Some Saigon police parked at the top of the lane.

We were ready to leave the Center and say our final good-byes to the staff who had been so loyal throughout. They had worked twenty-four hours a day, only stretching out on the floor with the babies when they were too exhausted to continue, and rising after a short nap to start all over again—a never-ending routine.

Three of our nurses, including Hong, elected to remain behind with their families to face the communist takeover. Hong was the oldest child in a large family and her father did not want her to leave. Sister Eugenia's sister Dau also stayed behind to support her family through the uncertain days to come. We realized that this good-bye was forever—we would not be coming back a second time. We had no money left, but Thanh gave us enough from his own pocket to help the nurses through what was yet to come for them.

We had one last job to complete before we boarded the buses. Some of the critically ill babies were on intravenous drips, delivering life-sustaining fluids and antibiotics. We wanted to keep them on the IVs until the last moment possible, and we couldn't leave any of them behind for further care. Our workers had made it clear that they would leave the alley as soon as we had departed the Center.

One baby was so near to death, I knew she wouldn't survive once the IV was removed, but there was no one else to take care of her. I couldn't leave her there unattended. I decided to keep her with me, IV and all.

At the gate, Nurse Hong held me and wept—we had supported each other through such demanding times. The leaving was tearing me apart. I didn't know if my good friends would even survive the collapse of Saigon.

We were ready to commence the last stage of our evacuation—but we were still uncertain if we would be able to leave. We had no exit papers for the babies and no formal permission. We needed representatives of two governments to look the other way.

After a heated discussion among themselves, Thanh, Ngoc and the other members of their family decided to leave with us. Thanh's children were leaving anyway, and he feared that somehow they would become separated before they found their mother; we had no idea where she had been evacuated to.

Altogether our group comprised seventeen adults, who would be caring for one hundred and eighty four infants and children.

Finally it was time to face the crowd and run the gauntlet to the parked buses. Vietnamese police in jeeps made their way down the lane. The crowd, seeing the police and noting their menacing weaponry, fell back a little. Reaching the compound gate, the policemen rushed out of their vehicles and formed a loose corridor through which we could proceed toward the buses.

We opened the gate and made our way between the policemen to the end of the lane. They were determined that our progress wouldn't be slowed, and they shouted at the crowd and pushed them back to keep the passage clear for us. Anybody that interfered too much received a stinging blow from a police baton.

Now that the gate was open, the crowd could have rushed the Center again. Thanh and his family stood guard inside the gate to keep the mob from overrunning the Center. The noise was deafening, and I recall fleeting images of people crying and begging us, to the last moment, to help them.

On board the buses were some armed DAO officials. They helped settle babies as we made repeated trips from the buses back to the Center to gather more. The babies were placed in cardboard boxes, three to a box, on laps, on seats, on mats on the floor—anywhere we could find a place to put them.

On my last trip from the Center, as I carried the dying baby and the glass IV bottle, an hysterical woman, clutching a child of about two, ran up and grabbed me by the arm. Her face and body were streaked with sweat and dirt, and her eyes were bright with fear. She grabbed my right forearm, and in her panic dug her long nails deeply into my flesh. I jerked backwards, but she held fast. No matter how hard I tried I couldn't pull free from her manic grip. She obviously believed that if she could just stay with me, she and her child would be taken to safety.

I saw blood spurt from my arm before I felt any pain. With the amazing strength of the terrified and demented, she twisted my arm, digging deeper and deeper. As her nails pierced my flesh and the blood flowed, a tremendous wave of pain hit me, and I screamed.

Tom heard my cries, and he and a nearby policeman rushed over to me. It took the strength of both of them to pull the woman away. In his anger the policeman struck out fiercely with his bamboo stick, clubbing the woman to the ground. One blow missed the intended target and instead hit me in the face. I felt a numbing whack just below my eye.

Tom pulled me onto the bus and grabbed the first thing at hand to staunch the flow of blood running down my arm: our faded yellow and red flag, lying on top of a box of supplies. Wrapping it tightly over the cuts, Tom made a makeshift bandage, then ran to the bus behind ours to summon Bill to come and check my wound.

Dr. Bill ran up and looked at me. I was still holding the baby while trying to favor my injured arm. He removed the blood-soaked flag and briefly examined the wound, pronouncing that I needed stitches immediately. We had no time for such niceties. I shook my head—we had to leave.

Ross drove the FCVN van, loaded with our supplies for the flight, which we had purchased on the black market. Following our prearranged plan, we made sure that each of us was assigned to a different bus, so that we could protect and comfort the children. I was in the lead bus. Even early in the morning, the heat and humidity inside was unbearable. The windows were sealed to prevent people from trying to shove their children inside, and the temperature was climbing rapidly. Outside, the mob was screaming, beating constantly on the sides of the buses, creating a deafening din that added to the confusion.

As we pulled away from the lane, I was in so much pain and so busy that I didn't even think to spare a glance backwards. We drove away from the Center that had been our home, and we abandoned it without so much as a thought. We had already said our good-bye.

Saigon, heart of the nation that I loved, had been transformed from a vibrating metropolis into Hell's reception center. The exciting city I had known was gone, replaced by teeming crowds of refugees and soldiers, all intent on saving themselves. Nobody who made that final journey will ever forget the noise, heat, panic and fear that surrounded every soul.

The barricades and barbed wire forced the buses to zigzag at walking pace through the crowded streets. Desperate refugees tried to force their way onto the buses, and only the presence of our armed American guards kept them from opening the doors and storming in.

Though the airport was only a few miles from the Center, the trip took us nearly two hours. By now it was late morning, and as we inched through the traffic on the airport approach road I looked out of the window for a moment. I could see the Tan Son Nhut airport perimeter fencing, topped with razor-sharp barbed wire. Bodies lay across the fence and on the ground nearby. One of the American guards told me that the Vietnamese army had been forced to shoot people who tried to scale the fence.

When we pulled up at the guardhouse in front of airport, masses of people pressed against the buses, obviously trying to enter the airport with us. The guards turned on powerful water hoses, jetting into the crowds and forcing them away from the barrier.

The barrier was raised for us. As we drove through, soldiers rushed out and forced the crowd back with threats, guns and bamboo sticks.

Once we were through the gate, several uniformed American officials boarded the bus. They asked me for written permission to move the children. More coolly than I felt, I brushed aside their query, saying that they had sent buses and an armed guard to escort us—obviously our movement was authorized.

One official noticed my bloodstained arm, and I could see he was concerned. After a quick discussion with his colleagues they agreed we could pass through—he even suggested that I get some medical attention.

My lead bus pulled forward, but as I looked back I saw that the other buses had not moved. Later I learned that one of the half-American boys had suffered a heatstroke. Tom took him off the bus, away from the sweltering heat, to get air. The officials who had just let my bus pass looked at the sick boy, and it took more than an hour of arguing back and forth before they finally agreed that the other buses could pass too.

Meanwhile my bus had been dispatched to a Quonset hut. From there I couldn't see the others and didn't know if they had been allowed to stay on the base or not. I was isolated, and by then my arm was throbbing intensely.

I was fearful that the Americans were not playing along with our hopes of them "looking the other way." If they stuck to the rules then everyone would be returned to the Center. If the Vietnamese became involved, Thanh and his brothers would be arrested as deserters.

The Americans had been airlifting Marines in from U.S. bases in nearby countries to help with the evacuation. Some of them were assigned to help load evacuees onto planes. A squad stationed nearby cautioned me not to venture outside the hut. The airport had been under constant threat of attack all day. It was dangerous to be out in the open.

The little baby girl that I was holding, still attached to the IV, had died minutes after leaving the Center. I pulled the needle from her tiny, wasted arm. I asked one of the young soldiers where to put the dead baby. He spotted my blood on the babies and assumed we had been injured, perhaps by enemy shrapnel. I assured him that all the blood he could see was from my injured arm—the baby had died of "natural causes."

Nonplussed, he ran for his officer in charge, as I set the dead baby down and turned back to help the living. Eventually the soldiers returned and took the little body away. One marine ran back and asked me her name. I simply shrugged and shook my head.

I needed more help; I was in too much pain to cope with so many dehydrating babies. I asked the Marines to help me find the rest of my group. Taking pity on the babies and me, the officer sent some of his men to find the others. At last they tracked them down in the empty base fire station, and they brought me and the babies there to join them. Everybody was together in a group, nursing the babies—except for Tom.

He hadn't been seen since leaving the bus with the sick boy, hours earlier. I knew he was on the base and felt certain that he would eventually find us.

After what seemed an eternity, a jeep arrived carrying Tom, the little boy and a medic. The medic examined my arm and bandaged the wound. I was determined to take the old flag with me, and I stuffed it into a nearby bag. Soon my new bandages were soaked with blood.

An officer visited us in our shelter. It was open to the outside air, and the heat was suffocating; we were as near to the runway as we could get. He told us that our departure would be delayed because the runways were damaged, and it was up to the pilots to make the call as to whether or not they could chance taking off. If the attacks resumed, then no planes would leave.

As the afternoon progressed, the relentless sun shone directly into the hangar. We moved the infants and toddlers into what little bit of shade we could find. We were all thirsty, and we sipped water from the babies' bottles.

We asked everyone with time to spare to help us tend the babies. Soon I saw a soldier feeding an infant in his arms, a look of bewilderment and kindness on his young face.

From time to time an officer came to report that the situation was unchanged. The longer we waited to be evacuated, the more our fears grew that somebody in authority would appear and tell us that we couldn't evacuate the babies or any other Vietnamese. At that time I feared the Americans even more than the possibility that enemy tanks would start rumbling across the runway.

We wanted to keep a very low profile, so I stopped asking any questions or making demands upon the obviously harassed soldiers. The hours dragged by and the sun crawled towards the horizon. There was little relief in the late afternoon shadows. We moved from one child to another, taking care of them, holding and feeding them.

At dusk some officers appeared and told us that the pilots had decided to leave now. They thought that if our plane wasn't airborne by dark then it would be too late. This was to be the last flight out.

Quickly we piled into the buses again and were driven to a C-141 transport plane. Ground staff told us to run to the aircraft and embark the children as fast as we could. We formed a human chain and passed the babies along as quickly as possible. Within minutes, they were all safely loaded onto the metal floor of the plane, some in cardboard boxes, but most on the straw mats we had brought from the Center.

As we returned for our precious cargo of milk, water, and diapers, the bus containing our supplies started pulling away. I screamed and the bus stopped. Two young Marines put down their rifles and helped load the three large boxes into the back of the plane.

At the last moment Ross decided that he was not going to leave with us. He insisted that he would go back to the Center and make certain all of the staff had left safely and give away what remaining supplies we had. I was frantic with worry for him and begged him to get on the plane, but he was adamant. My last view of him was as he turned to wave good-bye with a big smile on his face. I was in tears as I helped with the last of the loading.

There were no seats in the plane so Bill, Tom, Sister Theresa, and the other adults sat on the floor to tend the babies. The heat inside the plane was even worse than outside. The metal walls seemed to radiate heat, and it was suffocating.

Suddenly the pilot appeared, roaring and yelling like a madman as he rushed up the ramp into the back of the plane. He screamed that we couldn't take any luggage.

As I stood up to argue and explain that the boxes contained milk, formula and medicine, he kicked the supplies off the ramp and onto the runway. I watched in horror as the glass bottles shattered and milk splashed across the asphalt. Everything was gone. The few bottles we had in our hands were all we had left to care for our dehydrated babies.

The pilot glared at me and ordered the marines with rifles to close the rear doors before walking through the babies towards the cockpit. Within seconds the jet was moving.

After taking off, the plane tilted upwards sharply, in what seemed to be a forty-five-degree climb. None of us were secured, and we all slid towards the rear of the plane, forming a massive melee of bodies.

Once again the unbelievable noise of jet engines assailed my ears. I couldn't hear anything other than the incredible din. It was impossible to talk, impossible to even think. I could see the babies crying, the fear in their eyes plainly visible.

After climbing sharply for a few minutes the plane leveled out a little, the rate of ascent decreasing. As the altitude increased the temperature mercifully fell. As soon as we could stand we tried to restore some order. We arranged the babies around us, each within arm's length.

Bill leaned over to me, holding a dehydrated baby. I looked at the pathetic bundle. It was obvious that we had a major problem developing, and it was going to be exacerbated by the pilot's actions. Kicking out the only fluids we had available could become a death sentence for these babies. I knew that this lumbering aircraft would take at least three hours to reach Clark Air Force Base, the nearest friendly base where we could land. We needed to get more milk and water as fast as humanly possible.

I climbed to my feet and made my way unsteadily to the cockpit. Inside I saw the two pilots and a flight engineer, all concentrating intently on flying the plane. Ignoring the noise, I asked the first pilot where we were headed. He shook his head and brusquely told me to go back and sit down. I told him we didn't have any milk or water and that soon the screaming babies would all be dying. I needed to know how long it would be before we landed.

He looked up at me again and shouted above the noise that we were heading for Guam. My heart sank. I knew that Guam was a journey of at least eight hours and this man was not listening to me at all.

I pleaded with him to understand our dilemma. We had very little for the babies to drink and some of them were already dehydrating. If we didn't get some fluids soon, many of them would die.

The pilot barked that Clark was full, and no one else could land there.

Enraged, I told him that we would arrive in Guam with an airplane full of dead babies because *he* had shoved the medicine, the water and the milk off the back of the plane.

The crew ignored me and I stormed back to my place. When I told the others the problem, they were stunned. We were certain that most of the babies would die. Bill went up to the cockpit to talk to the crew.

A few minutes later a dejected Bill returned with the news that the crew were Air Force reservists, and they had been flying back-to-back missions under enemy fire; exhausted and tense, the pilot just wasn't getting the message. Bill told me to give it one more, gentler try.

Calming myself, I went back to the cockpit, holding a tiny blue infant in my arms who was breathing his last. Now that we were out of enemy gunfire range, the crew had calmed noticeably. One of them looked at me, fatigue and fear written all over his face.

I heard someone say, "Sir, that baby really is dead."

It was enough; the captain turned to me with his mouth wide open. He stared at the baby. His eyes were red and watery. He shook his head in disbelief, then looked back at the rest of the screaming babies. Immediately he radioed to Clark that we had to make an emergency landing.

After he received permission to land, the atmosphere in the cockpit settled down even more. He apologized profusely and told me that some evacuees had tried to take all sorts of personal effects out with them. The nearly vertical take-offs, designed to get the plane out of enemy range quickly, could prove fatal with too much unsecured weight in the cargo hold. In addition, he had been ordered by his commanders to bring out people only. Not a piece of luggage was supposed to be on board—they needed every available inch of space.

About three hours later we landed at Clark Air Force base—it was the second time I had been evacuated there in less than a month. Once again the friendship of the American Air Force enveloped us. Air Force wives were waiting and came to the plane, took the babies into their arms, and whisked them off to tend to their needs.

These babies were in much poorer condition than those on the previous flight into Clark. Many of the latest arrivals were in critical condition; they were rushed into medical care, but sadly many of them died. The evacuation from Vietnam had come too late for them.

Our flight at dusk on the twenty-sixth of April was the very last military plane to carry orphans out to safety. Memories of the infants who died in our arms when they were so close to medical care and a chance of survival will always be with me. Sometimes I remember, and I cry.

On the morning of the twenty-seventh, just over twelve hours after our departure the North Vietnamese Army launched a rocket attack on Saigon. This closed down all further evacuations by airplane. The reality of how close we came to being stranded with our babies through the chaos surrounding the fall of Saigon took weeks to penetrate. There was no milk, medicine, medical supplies or staff to care for the large number of infants through the communist takeover and no matter how gentle the turnover might have been the children's survival would have been impossible. We sheltered and cared for those children and they left their footprints in our lives. They were dearer to us than life itself.

With Saigon already smoldering in the wake of rocket attacks around the city the ever optimistic U.S. Ambassador Graham Martin cabled Henry Kissinger on the twenty-eighth of April to report: "It is the unanimous opinion of the senior personnel here that there will be no direct or serious attack on Saigon."

Ross left on the twenty-ninth of April, as helicopters evacuated the last of the Americans from the roof of the U.S. Embassy. The bewildered Ambassador and his senior personnel also departed. For the last time in this war they had underestimated their enemy and deserted their friends.

I watched the surrender of Saigon on television, from a hospital bed in Guam. On the thirtieth of April 1975, South Vietnam was a country consigned to history.

The End

Nik Wheeler / Black Star

Many young soldiers continued to lose their lives in the last days of the war, late April 1975.

Nik Wheeler / Black Star

Refugees attempting to enter Saigon late April, 1975.

Nik Wheeler / Black Star

Fighting to scale the wall of the U.S. Embassy.

Evacuation from the roof of the U.S. Embassy.

Boarding boat to escape.

Ross Meador photographing his arrival on
U.S. Navy ship.

Mobs of Vietnamese scale the 14 foot wall of the U.S. Embassy in Saigon trying to get to the
helicopter pickup zone.

Nik Wheeler / Black Star

Results of a rocket attack on downtown Saigon, April 27th, 1975.

Nik Wheeler / Black Star

I did not spring from the soil of Viet Nam.
I was not cradled in her womb and she did not
give birth to me. I was a child of another color
and I spoke another language and yet Viet Nam
received me as a mother receives an adopted
child from a far-off land. I went to Viet Nam to
give and I received. I went to teach and four
thousand years of history and wisdom enlightened me.
I went to a country ravaged by war and found peace.
I went expecting to find despair and sorrow and I found
hope and joy. I crossed an ocean and found a home.
There is a song in my heart called Viet Nam but it is
Wordless and I am incomplete. The words have gone
from my song and I am as a motherless child.

Cherie Clark
1975

Before They Had a Name

Book Two

*I*n September 1975 I met with Mother Teresa in Calcutta, India. It was a meeting that would have a profound impact on my life.

Our meeting was arranged by Helke Ferrie, whom I had met in April, after the first airlift, on the flight back into Saigon from Hong Kong. We had maintained contact since then, and when she invited me to travel to India with her and Jim Jones, a California photographer, I jumped at the opportunity.

The intervening months had been a whirlwind. After leaving Vietnam in April 1975 I had undergone surgery in Colorado, to correct ongoing medical problems that had first arisen in Vietnam. Nam, the young boy who went out on the first evacuation flight to America, came to live with us in Colorado. Tom and I loved him deeply, and despite all the hardships we were enduring at that time we began the adoption process; we wanted Nam as a member of our family.

After a very short convalescence I had traveled to Guam, intent on helping FCVN Vietnamese staff who had been evacuated from Saigon. The five hundred staff, family and friends were all detained in American refugee camps, awaiting processing of their applications to immigrate to America. Tom and I spent several weeks working in the camp and successfully sponsored all the families we had evacuated.

Meanwhile, the class action lawsuit that had been filed in California effectively aborting Operation Babylift because of allegations that children were being illegally removed from Vietnam, was moving into full swing. FCVN was not named in the lawsuit as a defendant, but they petitioned to be included as "friends of the court," in order to present a more balanced picture of the events of those last momentous weeks in Saigon.

FCVN was admitted to the lawsuit, partly because the action was brought in the name of Thuy's relatives, Hung and Phoung's children.

Despite numerous affidavits by family members, these children were portrayed as an example of children "lost" or "stolen" from Vietnam by the agencies working there in those last days—apparently because they had cried at the Presidio in California when they were evacuated, asking for their parents. The lawsuit never took into consideration the pain and hardship that the parents endured in voluntarily relinquishing their children. I was not alone in my belief that the lawsuit was politically motivated and had nothing to do with the children.

The costs of the lawsuit were astronomic. FCVN alone spent in excess of $150,000 attempting to show the true story of this humanitarian effort. The costs eventually mounted to such a high level that FCVN was forced to abandon humanitarian aid programs, spending much-needed time and cash on the lawsuit instead.

The lawsuit was dismissed on the thirteenth of February 1976 as a case without merit. (See Appendix)

During this time, an official inquiry into the Babylift crash concluded that the plane was not shot down and that there was no bomb on board the aircraft. It was determined that there was a mechanical failure of the rear cargo door, which caused an explosive decompression that damaged hydraulic lines, and thus control of the aircraft was lost. At the time we were all convinced it was sabotage or an act of the enemy, which put even more pressure on those of us who would make similar flights the following days.

With the court case rumbling in the background, I traveled to Colombia and Thailand for FCVN, visiting orphanages and talking with government agencies to see if FCVN could help with their orphans and handicapped. There was plenty of work to do in both countries, but by the time we were making definite plans it was too late; FCVN could no longer financially commit to any long-term programs.

Helke's invitation came when I was at a low point in my life. I was restless and without purpose and desperately needed a goal that I could work towards.

When the invitation arrived, Tom, who had by then returned to work at IBM in Denver, encouraged me to go. It was becoming clear that he did not share my restlessness; he was ready to settle down to a career. Our lives were taking different directions. So on the last day of August 1975, I flew to India alone.

❧

India affected me in ways that are hard to describe. It is a country unlike any other on Earth. The immense contrasts within the country overwhelm the senses of many visitors. Great wealth and poverty exist side by side; refined culture lives alongside illiteracy; mountain landscapes of sweeping beauty give way to harsh, barren deserts. The air is redolent with a unique blend of smells—wood smoke and cooking spices mingle in a cloying perfume that is the quintessential India.

Poverty abounds in the cities and in the countryside villages, with millions of people living their lives one step removed from the street. Poorer families actually live *in* the streets, sleeping on the ground and trying to keep their babies warm around small fires. They eke out meager existences, scraping for food to fill their families' bellies.

By that time I had seen a lot of destitution in my life, but never before had I seen the grinding poverty that was everywhere in India. In Vietnam the poorest people had had a shred of dignity; in India, even that most basic human right was denied to millions.

❦

In early September Helke, Jim and I traveled to Calcutta, to the Missionaries of Charities Mother House, a sprawling complex on a busy main road. We walked down a small alleyway and passed through wooden doors that opened into a courtyard.

A nun met us at the door. We introduced ourselves and told her we were there to see Mother Teresa. She led us to a sparsely furnished reception room, containing little but a table and a few wooden chairs, where we waited with eager anticipation to meet one of the world's most well-known women. Born in Albania in 1910, Mother Teresa had started the Missionaries of Charities Order in 1950 to comfort and aid India's "poorest of the poor," both young and old.

Mother Teresa entered the waiting room, wearing her trademark blue and white sari. She seemed tiny and frail, well under five feet tall, but her charisma filled the room. We jumped to our feet as she smiled and said hello. When we shook hands she held mine for a long time.

I noticed that when Mother Teresa spoke she gave the person she was talking with her full and undivided attention; her focus was phenomenal. Later I would discover that she had almost total recall of every conversation we had together.

Helke led the conversation from our side, and we talked about our work in Vietnam with the orphans and abandoned children. The conversation turned to the last days of Vietnam, and as the emotions of those traumatic days filled me I started to cry. Mother Teresa seemed to understand my sense of loss, and my resultant lack of direction.

I told her that I felt I'd lost everything.

Holding my hand and looking into my eyes, she told me that I was there for a very good reason. She said there were many people in the world who needed my help, and that we should go and visit her babies right away. It was an intensely personal moment for me. Helke and the photographer were in the same room, but I could have sworn that Mother and I were alone. Her words pierced my heart.

Mother Teresa led us out of the mother house and a few hundred feet down the road to their orphanage. She kept a tight grip on my hand as we walked. Many people, most of them poor and wearing ragged clothes, touched her feet as she passed by, and she touched their heads in blessing.

We passed through a set of tall metal gates that barred the entrance to the orphanage. Inside, I saw a small feeding center where nuns gave out milk and other supplies to mothers, many of whom held malnourished children in their arms.

Upstairs, in the main orphanage, Mother introduced me to the nuns in charge, who welcomed us warmly. The room was filled with more than one hundred babies, with as many as four babies sharing one crib. Some of them looked very sick, and it was obvious that there was a great need for more help and modern equipment. I asked if I could come back and help. Most certainly, the sisters assured me.

Later, Mother Teresa invited us to visit the Center for the Dying and Destitute in Kalighat, another area of Calcutta.

Kalighat is a Hindu temple devoted to the goddess Kali and located in the heart of Calcutta. The fierce black visage of Kali adorns the temple's altar, where the priests still offer her live sacrifices.

Many very ill people were taken to the temple in the hope that the powerful Kali would make them healthy again. As we walked around the Home for the Dying and Destitute, we saw nuns caring for and comforting more than a hundred very sick, dying people. The sisters helped as best they could, nursing, wiping brows and cooling the fevered bodies that lay around the center. Despite their tender care it was obvious that many of those who lay on the cheap wooden cots would never rise again.

❦

I returned to Denver a changed woman. I knew I had found a purpose in my life, and for the first time since leaving Vietnam I felt a sense of boundless energy. Almost immediately, I started making plans to return to India.

In March of 1976, less than a year after we had been evacuated from Vietnam, Sister Theresa, who had also been on that evacuation flight, flew to India with me to meet again with Mother Teresa. While we were there, Cheryl called us with the news that our dear friend Carol Westlake had died suddenly of a heart attack, at the age of thirty-seven. Cheryl and I were convinced that the strain of the lawsuit had intensified the stress our friend was under and contributed to her early death. Heartbroken, I simply wanted to return to America, but Cheryl and Sister Theresa convinced me that Carol would want me to stay. It was her great dream that I would start a program in India.

In November 1977 my wish was finally granted when Sue and I, with my eight children, left America and moved en masse to India. I had incorporated my own organization, International Mission of Hope, and was eager to begin. Tom wouldn't be traveling with us. Our marriage was unraveling and he was staying in Denver.

Once again, Ed Daly stepped in to help me out. He arranged free transport on one of his World Airways jets. The pilot was Ken Healy, the same man who had flown the first evacuation flight from Saigon, carrying our children.

We started our work in January 1978 in Calcutta. Both Sue and I volunteered in Mother Teresa's homes across the city, and at the Sealdah railway station, in one of her dispensaries. A man named Sunil Prakash joined us in the work. We handed out whatever medicines were available and helped the sick and the dying as well as we could, despite the almost total lack of medical care available.

We hired a social worker, Manidipa Halder, and by March 1978 we opened the first International Mission of Hope center, at 100 1/1 Alipore Road, a new building on a small, poor and crowded street. Young abandoned children soon started coming through our doors, and we knew that we were going to be able to help Calcutta's poor on a long-term basis. We were no longer mere visitors or voluntary workers—we were in India for the long haul.

On the twenty-sixth of April, Sunil and I returned to the center after a long, hot, tiring day of work. Sue and Mani greeted us expectantly. They had been standing in the door waiting. They pulled me forward and I saw four tiny babies lying on a cot.

Sue explained that they had visited a Calcutta nursing home earlier in the day. The poorest of the people used tiny back-alley nursing homes as a place simply to give birth. Sue and Mani had been talking with a doctor there, who explained that abandoned babies were left in their care every day of the year. He added that most of those babies died within days, and he casually offered the latest newcomers into Sue's care. Dumbfounded at the doctor's casual disregard, they quickly ran to the street outside and bought small hand towels to wrap the naked babies in.

Looking at them on the cot, I could see that they were premature and very tiny. Their umbilical cords were tied off with old pieces of cloth and it was obvious, at a glance, that the babies should be in an intensive care facility. Within days, two of them had died, but thankfully the other two survived the rigors of their entry into the world and grew strong.

That day Sue and Mani experienced a microcosm of life in Calcutta. Babies were born and died by the thousands, for no reason other than the circumstances of their births. Life became cruel and heartless when too many people populated too small an area.

IMH had been created specifically to help in those circumstances. We would take the poorest and most vulnerable and try our best to give them a chance. We couldn't begin to even scratch the surface of India's problems, but one by one we would take each life we could and make it better. We offered our love to all the thousands of babies that came through our doors, and in return, they gave me the purpose in life I had been seeking.

The mission grew, and we worked with children whom we found in the jails of Calcutta. These children had committed no crime. They were simply put into the jails, sometimes as toddlers, because there was no room for them in the government orphanages. Because they had no skills to even exist outside the jail, many were picked up by the police as lost children and were destined to spend their life in prison.

We released hundreds of those children, and for those who were too old for adoption we arranged marriages in India.

212

Our Intensive Care Nursery was to become one of the finest in the Third World. Doctors came from all over to train at IMH, and hundreds of lives were saved each year. We also started a school for the mentally handicapped, adult education classes, unmarried mothers' programs, and a dispensary that served the medical needs of thousands of Calcutta's poorest.

To accomplish anything worthwhile requires the help of others. We were joined in our work by Dick and Sue Wisner, who adopted three beautiful children from us. We had the help in America of hundreds of volunteers who made our work possible with their donations and their loving support of our work.

My life had changed dramatically—from Indiana to Vietnam, and then finally on to India. The common thread behind the thousands of miles of traveling was that I was helping abandoned and orphaned babies and children. I believed I had truly found my purpose in life, and finally I had a sense of belonging.

My personal life had undergone a series of dramatic changes as well. In October 1978 I gave birth to Shoshauna Anjali, a darling daughter, and a token of the love that had grown between Sunil and me. My children did well in India and attended school. They came to love the people and the culture.

In 1982, I gave birth to another beautiful girl, Preyanka Jayanti, my tenth child. Sunil and I felt our family was complete. But even as I loved my daughters and carried on working with the poor and abandoned in India, one small part of my heart was forever in Vietnam. I would have given anything to somehow learn what had happened to our friends after we left. I hoped that one day, somehow, I would answer those questions.

Return to Vietnam

Book Three

*C*heryl Markson, my old friend and confidante, telephoned me in India in the summer of 1988 with the news that FCVN had been contacted by the Vietnam representatives to the Mission of the United Nations in New York.

Vietnam was opening its doors to the world, and they wanted to invite child welfare organizations, with experience of working in Vietnam before 1975, to visit the country and offer help to their young.

Cheryl was excited. She told me that the FCVN Board of Directors had agreed to send some representatives to Vietnam, and she cordially invited Sunil and me to join them on the trip.

The prospect of returning to Vietnam seemed so alien to me that I initially declined Cheryl's invitation. I couldn't imagine returning to the country again.

Cheryl stayed in touch throughout the summer of 1988 and kept me posted on their progress in obtaining Vietnamese visas. Finally in September she called and told me that the dates were set; they would be in Vietnam during the first week of October. During that conversation something snapped inside me and I said that I wanted to go with them. I knew I would be safe in Vietnam with Sunil, Cheryl, Mick, and Ted and Connie Ning— other FCVN volunteers I'd known for years.

We discussed how we could join the party at the last moment. I told Cheryl that Sunil and I could pick up visas from the Vietnamese Embassy in Bangkok, Thailand, if she could obtain the necessary permissions from the Vietnamese in New York.

Sunil had heard so much about Vietnam over the past twelve years, he seemed almost as excited as me about the trip to Vietnam.

We hurriedly made arrangements for the staff and doctors to run the IMH program during our two-week absence, and we flew to Thailand. We met everyone in Bangkok, and on the third of October we flew, by Air Vietnam, into Hanoi's Noi Bai airport.

❦

As the old Russian Tupolev aircraft bounced in the turbulent air, I looked through the windows towards the ground; all I could see was bank after bank of wet, gray clouds and rainwater streaking across the small, scratched windows. Seatbelt fastened securely, I tensed up as we approached to land. Suddenly I was consumed by doubts and fears. I wondered what it would be like on the ground. I had heard that the people from northern Vietnam were cold, brusque and formal, whereas I had been used to dealing with the ever-smiling southerners.

What of my old friends and colleagues? Virtually everyone had heard of the Boat People who had fled the country; more then a million people had died attempting to escape, and we had heard of the reeducation camps. The movie *The Killing Fields,* released in 1984, depicting the atrocities that the Khmer Rouge had inflicted on their fellow Cambodians, had been watched with revulsion by many people throughout the world. I fervently hoped that my Vietnamese friends had not suffered too much.

It was still raining as we approached the airport and the old plane bumped along the runway. A battered, ancient bus collected us from the plane and took us to the terminal building, where we were greeted by Vu Khac Nhu, a government official. Mr. Nhu was a rising star in the Vietnamese party and would later become the first Secretary of the Vietnamese Embassy in Washington, D.C., after normal diplomatic relationships were reestablished in 1995. He spoke to us in English and smiled warmly. Suddenly my fears evaporated and the range of emotions I'd felt on the plane receded. I knew I could cope.

After we cleared immigration, we were collected by a Foreign Ministry van and set off for the hour-long drive into Hanoi center.

We all watched the passing countryside with great interest, noting farmers in black pajamas with their conical straw hats, working in rice fields despite the drizzling rain. The roads were nearly deserted, with very few cars or trucks to impede our progress; we didn't see any buses along the route. The few people we did see moving about were riding old-fashioned bicycles.

As we neared the city, we were surprised to see that all the people in the streets seemed to be wearing the same clothing: drab green military-style jackets and matching trousers, and most of the men wore dark green helmets.

The city streets were quiet but immaculately clean. Lots of large red banners painted with Vietnamese slogans were strung across the streets, and flags hung from many of the larger buildings. It was eerie to think that we were probably the largest group of Americans in the country.

The government office buildings were all painted a mustard yellow color over traditional French colonial-style architecture; the buildings seemed reminiscent of Parisian street scenes. We saw wide tree-lined boulevards with small, neat parks and squares.

The Foreign Ministry guesthouse we were taken to was three stories high, tucked behind the opulent Foreign Ministry Reception Hall, where delegations and diplomats from other countries were entertained. Although this guesthouse was used to house visiting foreign diplomats and heads of state, the accommodations were basic in the extreme. Inside the pea green building there was no elevator, no telephones in our room, no televisions or other normal hotel amenities. The beds were very basic straw-filled pallets covered with rough cotton sheeting—not the sort of bedding that anybody would want to get used to.

I felt distant and unconnected. This drab, austere Hanoi was nothing like the vibrant, bustling streets of Saigon that had always represented Vietnam to me. I felt like a first-time visitor rather than an adopted daughter returning home.

After unpacking our bags we met again with Mr. Nhu, who escorted us across town to the Foreign Ministry, housed in a palatial building across the street from the dark granite Ho Chi Minh mausoleum.

Inside the Ministry we were escorted up the red carpeted staircase to the second floor, where we met with Dang Nhiem Bai, a senior official in the Foreign Ministry. We all sat down and took tea with him—some things never change, and it seemed that no meeting could ever be started in Vietnam without the offer of a drink of tea.

Mr. Bai was in his sixties, short, with large ears and a perpetual smile. His English was good and he took delight in recounting to us stories of his role in the Paris Peace Talks. The meeting lasted for more than an hour and whatever topics we talked about, he always managed to turn the conversation back to the subject of American servicemen "missing in action."

Mr. Bai told us that we could visit any orphanages or handicapped centers we wished, and that he would be responsible for our welfare while we remained in Hanoi. He had appointed Mr. Nhu as our interpreter and guide during our stay in Hanoi; he would accompany us whenever we visited any of the prescribed locations.

The next morning we were awakened abruptly at dawn by loudspeakers blaring the Vietnamese national anthem into the streets. Following the anthem we were regaled with lengthy speeches and newscasts in Vietnamese, guaranteed to shake even the sleepiest from their beds.

Looking out our window towards the park opposite, I was surprised to see lots of people taking their morning exercise, despite the chill, damp air. Young and old mixed together, walking, exercising, playing badminton, and some even practicing tai chi. The place was alive with people, and the sun was shining. Hanoi was looking a great deal better.

Sunil and I quickly dressed and joined the others in the dining room. Breakfast was a plain, dull affair; half-boiled eggs were placed in front of us by a rather apathetic staff dressed in white shirts, grayed with age, and stained black pants. There was no menu, and nobody asked us what we would like to eat—breakfast was either eggs or eggs.

As we picked over our plates, Mr. Nhu bounded into the room, smiling and cheerful. He proudly announced that he had organized a full five-day schedule for us, including trips to handicapped centers, a school for the blind, an orphanage, a women and children's hospital, and a round of meetings with government officials. The events were due to begin immediately after breakfast, which gave us a good excuse to leave the eggs and go out to start the day.

Mr. Nhu took us to the Thuy An Handicapped Center. The center was a two-hour drive from the city, set in a sea of endless rice paddies. The weather had cleared up, and the sun shone brightly for the first time since our arrival. We drove out of the city, seeing for the first time the splendor of the land. Rice fields stretched for miles, tended by groups of farm workers who toiled, bent-backed, in water up to their knees. We saw ancient irrigation systems being worked by hand. There was no evidence of modern farming; electric pumps, tractors and farming implements had never reached that part of the country, and all the work was done manually. Nothing had changed in thousands of years.

The Thuy An center was very poor, lacking basic facilities but it was immaculately clean and the children looked well cared for. The director had to some extent overcome the lack of equipment by innovation. A physical therapy room had been set up, with small concrete blocks passing as weights and ingenious pulley systems employed for the children's exercises. All the children seemed happy, pleased to see us, and smiled continually.

We were in the heart of communist Vietnam. The northern regions of the country had long embraced communism. There were only two private restaurants, which were spartan, with no menus or selection, but the food was excellent. The only other restaurants were within the two or three hotels in the city, and the food was terrible.

There was little evidence of free enterprise—no advertising, and almost everything we bought was from the government Friendship Shops that accepted only dollars from foreigners. They stocked everything from a sparse selection of ceramic souvenirs to heavy, imported Russian appliances. The capitalist South had been defeated, and now the whole country was united as one communist state. Victors they may have been, but there was no air of prosperity in Hanoi.

The local currency was dong, and the exchange rate was 350 dong per dollar. The largest bill was 2,000 dong. Sunil jokingly said that they were probably spending more money printing the dong then what it was worth. The hotels were all operated by the government and could officially change money, and there was a State Bank where you could take twenty dollars and come out with a bag full of dong. We quickly learned from the cyclo drivers, who were the prime mode of transportation when we were not in the government vans, that the dollar rate on the street was four thousand dong to the dollar.

In 1986 the Vietnam government had been powerless as the country's economy crashed. The U.S. trade embargo meant that there were virtually no foreign exports, and hard currency was almost nonexistent. The only friends the Vietnamese had at that time were other communist bloc countries.

Desperate to remove the suffocating trade embargoes, and to feed their people, the Vietnamese opened their doors to aid organizations, including organizations like ours. They were keen to put on a good show and proudly demonstrated their best.

When we visited hospitals, we were appalled at the need we saw. There were no antibiotics for the sick and little medical care of any kind. Sunil and

I had just traveled from one of the poorer areas of Calcutta and were used to seeing grinding poverty, but facilities in India were still years apart from the absolutely bleak despair and lack of basic necessities that we saw during our trip to Hanoi. We felt a great compassion for the stoic patients who endured the lack of help without complaint.

Perhaps no place touched me as deeply as the Women and Children's Hospital in Hanoi. We were led through old rooms of what had once been a French convent, which were now being used to house patients. We saw three mothers with three infants sharing one bed, and my heart broke as we met the twenty-five-year-old father of a young son, as he sat holding the hand of his dying wife.

We sat down in the guesthouse and discussed our overall impressions. We were all dismayed by the lack of equipment in every place we visited. But we were impressed by the cleanliness, the attentive staff, and the smiling faces of the children that followed us throughout our visit. We knew that if the centers could receive medicines and equipment, the standards of care for the children would greatly improve. The only thing lacking was a way to get them the equipment they needed.

On the eighth of October, my forty-third birthday, Mr. Nhu escorted us to the airport, where we caught the only flight of the day to Saigon at six in the morning. After five days of intense preprogrammed activity we had seen enough and were ready to move on. We took our formal leave of Mr Nhu, who remained in Hanoi. We were sad to leave this newfound friend, who had done his best to make our stay in Hanoi as comfortable and friendly as he could.

We flew on a very old and decrepit Tupolev Air Vietnam plane down to Tan Son Nhut airport—the same airport from which I had been evacuated thirteen years before. My departure from Saigon and Vietnam had been forced, hurried and frightening as we escaped just before the country fell. I had thought then that I would never return to Vietnam, and even during the first five days of my stay in Hanoi I hadn't really felt like I was back in Vietnam. Now it was uncanny that I was a guest of the communist government and being flown into the very same place I'd escaped from.

When we landed at Tan Son Nhut, the first thing that struck me was the sameness of the place. The airport looked exactly like it had over a decade before. The terminal, the graffiti-covered hangars, the peace symbols were just as I had remembered them.

I was quick to point out the airplane hangers where we had sat in the burning sun caring for babies. The fire station looked the same; the terminal was familiar as we walked to get our luggage.

We were met by Mrs. Hoa, another Foreign Ministry official, who waited on the tarmac . In formal English she welcomed us to Ho Chi Minh City, the new name given to Saigon by its communist victors. Mrs. Hoa was middle-aged, spoke good English in a commanding and lordly manner, and from the outset made it clear that she was in charge of us for the duration of our stay in Saigon. The contrast between her and Mr. Nhu was remarkable.

She herded us through the airport and into a waiting government van. Passing through the terminal, I smelled the same Saigon that I'd known and loved before. As we drove out of the airport, one major change struck me. Tan Son Nhut Airport had been a major strategic base for the military, and security had always been very tight. Soldiers, airmen, jeeps and trucks had been thick on the ground, but now there wasn't a soldier or a jeep in sight. Cyclos and bicycles peddled by, and there was no military presence at all.

On the main road, we looked over towards the old FCVN Center on Bui Thi Xuan. The street was familiar except that the big blue FCVN sign that had been clearly visible from the base exit had disappeared. Everything was the same and everything was different at the same time; it was a strange feeling.

On the drive to our allocated Foreign Ministry guesthouse we all watched the activity in the streets. The place was warmer and much livelier than Hanoi. We immediately noticed that the green uniform-type garb favored by the northerners hadn't caught on in Ho Chi Minh City; its more flamboyant residents preferred bright, colorful clothing. That alone made the whole city seem more alive and happier.

Mrs. Hoa had planned a tight schedule. Barely an hour after setting foot on the tarmac, we were in a meeting with a group of officials, headed by the Director of Social Welfare, Mr. Nguyen Van Chi. We were taken aback when we saw the women wearing *ao dai*, the traditional Vietnamese dress.

Mrs. Hoa translated as Mr. Chi warmly welcomed us to Ho Chi Minh City, and personally welcomed me back. He was obviously well briefed and knew a lot about us. We talked at length about FCVN's work before we left in 1975. I inquired about various people and places I'd known previously. He answered all my questions with a smile, and told me that I could visit anywhere I wanted in the city, and meet up with my old friends.

As we sat in the second-floor office, sounds of the street drifted in through the large, open doors. People shouting as they went about their business, horns blaring, music, and the familiarity of the language, all came together and for the first time I really felt I was back in Vietnam.

Sitting quietly, I tried to listen to Mrs. Hoa's translations as Mr. Chi talked on about our visit, but it was too much for me. I felt tears well into my eyes. Sunil gripped my hand and told me that the meeting was almost over. "Just hang on," he said. I could not. I stood up from my seat and, as everyone turned to look at me, walked to the balcony, hoping not to disturb them. It was as if all of the sorrow and the sadness of leaving Vietnam suddenly came to me at once. I wept with all the tears that had been stored inside of me for this lost land that I loved so much. I could not hold back. I was so happy to see the bright streets and the familiar trees and flowers, and so sad that I had missed it for so long. I was back in Vietnam, in the familiar, though renamed, city that I knew so well and loved so much.

Mr. Chi and the two lady officials came out to me. I felt embarrassed and tried to gain control, but the situation became hopeless. Mr. Chi patted me on my back, and both women put their arms around me; gradually they too had tears running down their faces. Madame Hoa joined us to translate for Mr. Chi. He spoke softly, his voice broken as he searched for words. He told me they all understood and that it had been a hard time for everyone who had lived through those days—we had all lost so much. Comforting me, he said that if I wanted, Vietnam could now be my home forever. At that moment a friendship was forged that would last for years to come.

The rest of our time in Vietnam passed too quickly as I revisited the places I'd known more than a decade before. For me one of the most wonderful reunions was when we found Hong, our nurse. She was happily married and had a son. We met briefly in the shadow of the huge Cathedral in downtown Saigon. The Vietnamese were not yet comfortable enough to meet a foreigner in a public place, and it was forbidden for us to go to their homes.

We also made the trip to the Delta and passed through the cities where I had worked. The absence of the military was striking. The bridges looked deserted without all of the artillery. This was a land at peace. Our ultimate destination was Can Tho as we crossed the same old ferries of long-ago days.

More tears were yet to come when I was reunited with Sister Eugenia. Many of the other Providence sisters that we had worked with were also there. There had been no slaughter. They were poor but living in the familiar place where we had said good-bye so long ago. My joy at seeing Sister Eugenia was reminiscent of coming home to visit a loved one whom you had feared you would never see again. With the same familiar laugh I remembered so well, she told me that she had been positively certain that I would return someday and that she had been waiting. This was certainly something that *I* had doubted! She told everyone that I was the last American she saw and the first to come back.

During the few days that we were in Vietnam, we visited the FCVN Centers, where so many babies had survived and gone on with their lives. The memories of the ones who died, many who were so very dear, brought more tears. Walking down the lane to our house on Tran Ky Xuong, I wondered how we had ever made it through the thousands who had packed the alley during those tense final days. The Center had now been converted to a school, and we were able to go inside the classrooms.

At first I would often lapse and refer to the city as Saigon, then quickly stutter to say Ho Chi Minh City. After a few days I realized that every Vietnamese I met called the city Saigon in spoken language.

Everyone wanted to know what I felt had changed the most about Saigon since my return. Most obvious was the absence of the vehicles of war, the lack of concertina wire strung across the streets, the missing sandbag bunkers on most of the corners and around the offices. Names of streets had changed, and many were now one-way.

But for me the greatest change was the silence outside at night. For me Saigon had always been a city that came alive at night with explosions and gunfire. It was at last so peaceful.

On the last day of our visit, Cheryl and I went to a center for handicapped children and the elderly. After wandering around for a time, I realized that we were at Phu My Center, where Rosemary Taylor had begun her work. We went to visit the children, and among the handicapped and mentally retarded, Cheryl found a little girl named Nga. As she held her we realized that she was a bright little two-year-old suffering from a heart disease. Her little lips were blue, and we wished that we could do something to help her.

At that moment we could never have dreamed that Nga would be the first of several thousand babies that International Mission of Hope would bring to America for medical treatment, adoption and the love of a family. She was to become the first child adopted from Vietnam to an American family since 1975.

How different our lives would be if we could lead them as our passion dictates, in the immediate present, without fear of the future or regrets of the past. How fortunate we are that sometimes life gives us a second chance. This trip to Vietnam was a crossroads in my life.

Again, I boarded an airplane that would take me away from Vietnam. But there were no tears as I left; I knew I would return.

The Clark Family in Colorado
June of 1975.
On tree:(back) Ron, Dan;
(lower branch)Nam, Beth;
(Standing) Tom with Joanna and
Brian, Cherie with Jenny and hold-
ing Thanh.

Bernie Mantey

Clark family in 1990
(back, from the left) Joanna, Brad
(Jenny's husband with their son Kai)
Ron, Dan, Brian; (middle) Preya,
Shauna, Thai (Beth's husband),
Nam, Jenny;
Beth holding Maya, Thanh.

Douglas S. James

Mother Teresa and Cherie meet for the first time in Calcutta, September 1975.

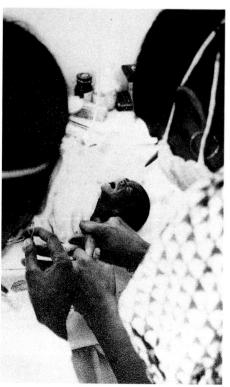

A very painful death Calcutta, 1981.

Calcutta bus.

Return to Vietnam. Cherie meeting with Foreign Minister Nguyen Co Thach.

Noel Neuberger

Dawn prayer at Hoan Kiem Lake, Hanoi.

Paul J. Miller

Cherie meeting in Da Nang with Sister Angela and other sisters in 1989.

Vietnam Veterans Restoration Project (VVRP) led by Fredy Champagne went to Viet Nam to build a clinic in Vung Tau in 1989. IMH contributed to this project.

Amerasian children in Saigon processing center in 1989.

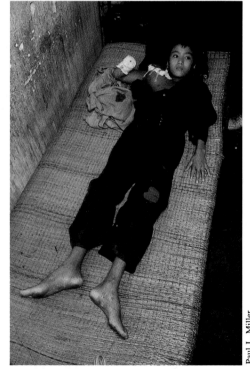

Constuction of a surgical ward in Vinh, one of the most heavily bombed cities in the world. The conditions when IMH began this project in 1989 were desperate. IMH fully funded the project as well as paying for volunteers of the VVRP to come to work in Vinh.

This little boy was in his family field in Vinh working when an unexploded bomb went off and he lost his right arm in 1989.

Paul J. Miller

Beth Clark with children at the polio center in Ho Chi Minh City, Vietnam 1990.

Cherie in 1990 at the dedication of the Rural Health Care facility in My Lai at the site of the massacre. The funding for this program and the need for help continues.

Paul J. Miller

Cherie talking with one of the survivors of the My Lai massacre. Nearly 600 civilians mainly women and children were killed by U.S. soldiers.

District Court Judge Paul Markson (Mick) and Cheryl Livingston Markson, Executive Director of FCVN.

Le Thi Bach Thuy (second from left) with her son, Chau, and his daughter; son-in-law and Kiki who has a baby daughter and just graduated from medical college.

LeAnn Thieman is the author of a book on the Babylift "This Must Be My Brother" with husband Mike, and her children Angela, Mitch and Christie.

teven Johnson with his sons Christopher and
Anthony. Steven is Director of Planning at
Northern Illinois University.

Christopher and Anthony in Saigon, 1974.

Ross Meader, now an attorney in California, with his wife Michelle and daughters Amy and Leah.

Ethan is the son of Jeff and Rachelle, the daughter of Jeremy.

Shawn is the son of Ron Clark and lives in Colorado.

Jason, Jeff and Jeremy.

Jeremy (Nhan), Jeff (Thanh), and Jason (Tho) with unidentified soldier in St. Paul's Orphanage, Qui Nhon.

Ron with his wife Huong, They were married in January 2000 in Hanoi, where Ron works for IMH.

Dan with his daughter Katria who is half-Thai. Dan works for IMH and lived in Thailand for 12 years.

Nam graduated from the University of Colorado, Boulder and now lives in Washington, D.C..

Joanna lives and works in Colorado.

Jenny (right) lives in Colorado with her husband Brad and their son Kai.

Brian lives and works in Hanoi for IMH.

Beth and her husband, Thai, with their children Maya, Mia and Jason.
They live in Saigon and work for IMH.

Andrew (Minh) Pettis was brought into the FCVN center as one of the first children in 1974. He married Cherie's daughter, Shoshauna Anjali, and they have a daughter, Khazana. Andrew and Shauna reside in Hanoi and work for IMH.

Cherie's youngest daughter and tenth child
Preyanka Jayanti
graduated from the United Nations School
in Hanoi, Vietnam in
June 2000.

Thanh and his wife, Kamala, who was adopted
through IMH India, with their children, Sunil
nd Sunita. Thanh has been in the U.S. Navy for
seven years.

A reunion of the adopted children from Operation Babylift was sponsored by Holt International and Tressler Lutheran Services in Washington, D.C., on the 25th anniversary of the airlift. The adoptees visited the Vietnam Memorial. Guests of honor included adults who took part in the care of the children and the evacuations, as well as Mr. Nghiem Xuan Tue of the Ministry of Labor, Invalids and Social Welfare, in Hanoi. We are grateful to Holt International for allowing us to use the photographs.

Appendix

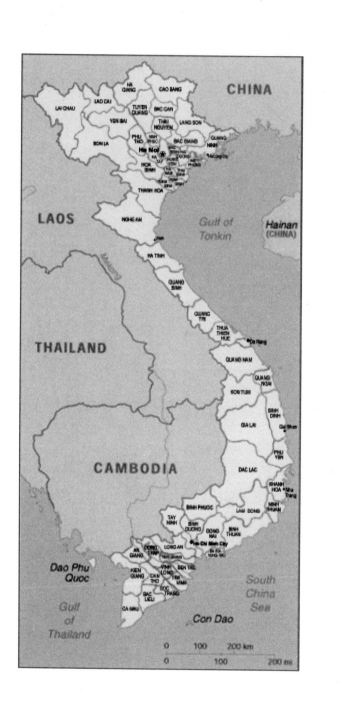

Glossary

ARVN: Army of the Republic of Viet Nam—the regular South Vietnamese National Armed Forces

DAO: Defense Attache Office, an agency that was part of the U.S. Mission sent to South Viet Nam following the January 1973 Paris Accords that ended the American war. A replacement for MACV, DAO administered the U.S. Military Assistance program to the GVN, 1973-1975.

DMZ: Demilitarized Zone, the area separating the country into North and South Viet Nam

FCVN: Friends of Children of Viet Nam

FFAC: Friends for All Children

Frequent Wind: The code name of the U.S. evacuation of Saigon in April 1975

GVN: Government of Viet Nam

IRC: International Rescue Committee

MACV: Military Assistance Command, Vietnam

Mission Warden Police: Attached to the U.S. Mission Vietnam

MIA: Missing in Action

NVA: North Vietnamese Army

POW: Prisoner of War

PRG: Peoples Revolutionary Government/South Vietnam (Viet Cong)

RVN: Republic of South Vietnam

Tet: The Vietnamese lunar new year and the most important holiday

USAID: United States Agency for International Development

International Mission of Hope

was founded on the principle that
children are the future of mankind
and that it is the undeniable right of each
child to be nurtured, loved, and protected, ideally
by his or her own family.

If for some reason, this is impossible,
because of poverty, sickness, death, or lack of
concern, then the child must be cared for
by the human family.

We are dedicated to the philosophy
that every child who enters the world
should be the recipient of the gift that was
promised from the moment of birth—

the gift of Life.

Cherie Clark
1977

Department Of State
Agency for International Development
Washington, D.C. 20523

22 October, 1975

Mrs. Cheryl Markson
Executive Director
Friends of Children of Viet Nam
600 Gilpin
Denver, Colorado 80218

Dear Mrs. Markson:

The Agency for International Development heartily commends you and all of the members of your staff for the outstanding humanitarian services rendered by Friends of Children of Viet Nam in the conduct of Operation Babylift. We would appreciate your conveying our thanks to those staff members who labored long and hard receiving, caring for, and delivering the evacuated orphans to their adoptive parents in the United States.

It has been a singular privilege and a pleasure for all of us at A.I.D. to have been associated with FCVN in the successful evacuation of the orphans to safe haven countries. We hope that the hardships attending this effort will never be experienced again; but we are confident that FCVN and its staff of dedicated men and women would again meet the challenge and perform in the same exemplary fashion.

We hope that there will be opportunities for collaborating with you in the care of disadvantaged children in other less developed countries.

Sincerely Yours,
(Signed)
Michael H. B. Adler
Bureau for East Asia
Printed with the permission of FCVN

UNITED STATES IMMIGRATION AFFIDAVIT
SUBMITTED BY Cherie Clark

All of the children placed by FCVN who had no paperwork were assigned this document, which was prepared and presented to Immigration and Naturalization authorities who accepted it in lieu of paperwork for the children.

AFFIDAVIT

State of Colorado

County of Denver

      Cherie Clark, Overseas Director of Adoption for Friends of Children of Viet Nam, being first duly sworn upon her oath, deposes and states the following:

THE INFORMATION BELOW IS AS IT PERTAINS TO EACH SPECIFIC CHILD:

Child:
AKA:
Sex:
Adoptive Parents:
Adoptive Address:

In order to facilitate the investigation being conducted by the United States Immigration and Naturalization Service and to further clarify the status of the infants brought to the United States by Friends of Children of Viet Nam, I state the following:

The above-identified child is an infant who traveled to the United States during April of 1975, under the auspices of Friends of Children of Viet Nam. Friends of Children of Viet Nam was a charitable organization which engaged in Vietnamese adoptions by contract with the Republic of Viet Nam, and is a licensed child placement agency in the State of Colorado.

Friends of Children of Viet Nam's primary role was that of life support. As a secondary program, we facilitated the adoption of hopelessly and undeniably abandoned children. Children assisted by Friends of Children of Viet Nam were, to a large degree, malnourished new-born infants abandoned at maternity hospitals and orphanages. These infants were entrusted to the custody of orphanages with out identity, usually in a very marginal state of health.

The normal procedure that occurred in the adoption process, as followed by our agency, was directly related to the philosophy of our organization which was to assist the child most in need, i.e. the premature, the malnourished, the debilitated, the handicapped, or by other definition, the high risk child.

As part of our routine, we would travel to the Mekong Delta once a week to visit orphanages provided that the circumstances of war did not prohibit travel. The purpose of these trips were – first to deliver desperately needed food, medical supplies and contributions to the orphanages; second, to evacuate children, mostly infants who were in dire need of medical care which was unavailable. Due to the ever-increasing rate of abandonment, the orphanages accepted increasing numbers of babies into their care. This increase of abandoned children greatly taxed and overwhelmed them.

We would return to Saigon from these weekly trips to the orphanages with fifteen to twenty critically ill infants, often losing a child on the way. These infants had no identity – they were abandoned as newborns with background information simply "unknown child, born of unknown parents, and abandoned." A death certificate for such an infant would read "anonymous." At our center, our medical staff would admit these abandoned infants with a complete medical examination and at this time they would be assigned a "nursery name." To us, the giving of this name symbolized for the *first time* the individuality of this child.

It was at this time our struggle for the infant's life began – a struggle too often lost. Lost because at times, even in Saigon, there was a shortage of medical equipment and supplies. Lost because of the times we were turned away at the hospital's door with a critically ill infant in our arms. Lost because of lack of medicines, when we had tons of supplies hopelessly tied up in Customs. Lost because of Pnuemocystis Carini, a disease rarely seen in the United States but a prime killer of the babies Viet Nam bore. Lost because in 1975, even though we had the medical knowledge, we were forced to use 1945 medical techniques. Lost because of poverty so severe that the new-born child was critically underweight and lacking almost any natural immunity. Lost because American-conquered diseases such as measles were killers of epidemic proportion in Viet Nam. Perhaps saddest of all were those children who were lost because they simply did not have the will to live.

An epidemic of measles ravaged the Friends of Children of Viet Nam Nursery in October and November of 1974, claiming the lives of forty of our babies, one–third of our nursery. The psychological impact of this loss was severe for our Vietnamese and American staff, yet we knew that in spite of this tragic loss, our babies faced a better chance of survival in our Center than in the orphanages where the infant mortality rate was often as high as eighty percent.

If our initial struggle for life was won, the infant would be placed in the care of one of our Vietnamese foster mothers, thus isolating the baby from massive exposure to communicable diseases, which were ever present in our nursery.

A referral photo and information sheet was prepared for each infant and sent to our agency in the United States. The information transmitted presented the infant by "nursery name," approximate age, general health, racial background, sex, and included any information pertinent to the infant. The infant was then offered to a family approved by our agency. When the infant was accepted by the family, the family's dossier was forwarded to the staff in Viet Nam.

During the interim, the Delta orphanages would give us birth certificates they had secured for groups of infants that they had entrusted to our custody. The method used to obtain these birth certificates was for the orphanage to randomly select names for a group of infants who were born at approximately the same time; in some instances, fictitious mothers' names were also furnished. This information was then filed with the Provincial Court by the orphanages and after varying lengths of time certificates would be issued. We would then bring these birth certificates to our office in Saigon.

In the case of abandoned infants entrusted to our care and custody in the Saigon region, the method of obtaining birth data was for us to fill out an application for a Birth Judgment (substitute for a birth certificate). The information listed would coincide with the number, sex, and approximate age of the group of children whom we had been given. This application was then signed by the director of the orphanage and submitted to the court in Gia Dinh. In six to eight weeks, the paper known as a Birth Judgment was issued. It stated a name, sex, month and year of birth, and read "parents unknown." These papers were then given to us.

The difficulties in obtaining these types of birth papers varied throughout Viet Nam. In some areas, it took but a few days; in others it took precious months for issuance.

Upon receipt of a family's acceptance of a child, a birth certificate or birth judgment was then selected for the child from the birth papers provided to us by orphanages. An orphanage release was then prepared by us listing the name and address of the adopting family, and the name, age and sex of the child to be adopted. Once the release was prepared, it was taken to the orphanage where it was signed by the Director or Directress and legalized. The legalized release was then added to the child's dossier, which was necessary to begin the proxy adoption and emigration process.

After a period of three months of continual effort and frustration, a Vietnamese passport would be issued. This passport was necessary to obtain the entry visa from the U.S. Embassy, which the adopting parents had initiated.

At times during this process, our struggle for a child's life was lost. When this occurred, another infant was selected and sent to the adoptive parents using these completed papers. Since these papers had arbitrarily been assigned, had made it through the system, and had often contributed to a child's death (due to the length and involvement of the process), they were used to provide a future for another human being.

In March of 1975, Friends of Children of Viet Nam had in its care and custody approximately one hundred infants residing in our Vietnamese foster homes and approximately thirty infants in the intensive care unit at the Friends of Children of Viet Nam Center in Gia Dinh. As the war escalated, we continued to receive custody of abandoned infants from orphanages with whom we had worked closely in the past.

Throughout the entire time of our association with these orphanages we never had any reason to question or distrust them in their relinquishment of children to our agency for the purpose of adoption. Never did a mother or a relative contact our agency seeking the return of a child relinquished to us by one of these orphanages. Further, we were never aware of a single incident in which a mother or a relative appeared at one of the orphanages to reclaim a relinquished child.

The orphanages continuously exhibited their ability to us to distinguish between adoptable and unadoptable children, i.e. the abandoned or irrevocably released child versus the child placed in the orphanage by its family for custodial care. The directors of these orphanages were very reluctant to release any older children for adoption, even though these children had lived there for many years and had not had family contact.

During March and April, 1975, the routine adoption procedures were completely disrupted due to the escalation of the war. There were circumstances present prior to the final evacuation of our children which prevented us from obtaining orphanage releases for them. These obstacles included our inability to return to the North as provinces fell; conditions of war prohibited our travel to the Delta; orphanage directors refused to sign papers for they feared that this act would endanger their lives; and officials were reluctant to authenticate documents.

Based upon the basic arbitrariness of assigning identity to infants who had been abandoned at birth, the costly delays in paperwork processed through the Vietnamese government and the worsening wartime conditions, the orphanage release paper seemed of little importance since the infant had already been entrusted to our care and custody for the purposes of adoption and emigration.

Both the Vietnamese and U.S. government representatives stated to me that children within our agency's care and custody would be eligible for evacuation.

When we received notification of the pending evacuation to the United States (for the first time, on the very day of the first flight), we inquired of the Ministry of Social Welfare as to procedures to be followed. We were instructed to prepare a list of names of our children. Our inquiry as to what to do concerning some of our infants, not yet placed, who had only "nursery names," was answered by the instruction to "choose Vietnamese names." We did this to coincide with the number of unnamed infants in our custody. The prepared list was then turned over to the proper Ministry of Social Welfare authorities, where it was approved, signed, and sealed. A copy of this list was then used to prepare arm bands in duplicate, listing the name and our agency identification. The sole purpose of these arm bands was to identify the infants as belonging to our agency, for we had no time for further identification.

In just forty-eight hours we had to physically bring one hundred infants from foster homes scattered throughout Saigon to our center, with travel constantly impeded by hordes of panicked people. We were working under a limited timetable and were further handicapped by an imposed curfew. We, with our child care and nursing staff, accustomed to caring for thirty infants, were now inundated with the care of one hundred and eighty children during a two-day period. We also had to prepare for the impending flight. This meant we had to gather medical supplies necessary to sustain the lives of the critically ill infants, and to prepare gallons of formula as well as vast amounts of clothing and diapers.

Once these infants arrived in the United States and were placed with approved adoptive families, we provided them with a paper. Papers were assigned to provide the infant with an identity; this was thus done as it had been done in the past. The papers assigned were the very papers which we would have used for this class of infants had we remained in Viet Nam. These infants and papers came into our care and custody through one of the following eight orphanages licensed in the Republic of Viet Nam:

1. Providence Orphanage, Can Tho
2. Providence Orphanage, Soc Trang
3. Vung Tau Christian Children's Home, Vung Tau
4. Sancta Maria Orphanage, Gia Dinh
5. Saint Paul's Orphanage, Vinh Long
6. Good Shepherd Orphanage, Vinh Long
7. Rose De Lima Orphanage, Hoc Mon
8. Le Pension de la Notre Dame, Gia Dinh

Over three-fourths of the infants brought by Friends of Children of Viet Nam on the orphan airlift came from Providence orphanage located in Can Tho, or Providence Orphanage located in Soc Trang, or Sancta Maria Orphanage located in Gia Dinh, or Vung Tau Christian Children's Home located in Vung Tau.

The statements and facts presented in this affidavit relate to a particular class of orphans: namely, infants abandoned at birth and relinquished to our custody. These infants were a part of the total number of children evacuated under the auspices of Friends of Children of Viet Nam. The above-named child is a member of this class of orphans.

The statements made in this affidavit pertain to Friends of Children of Viet Nam, their staff, and their actions alone.

Sworn affidavit of CHERIE CLARK, 1975

Letter to the Federal District Court

This is a letter which was submitted to the court after the class action lawsuit was filed in the name of our social worker's relatives. The case was dismissed, after costing hundreds of thousands of dollars, on February 13, 1976. The intent was to return all of the evacuated children to Viet Nam with the claim that the children had been kidnapped from their biological families. In the class action suit, six members of the extended family of the children in question filed affidavits in the court to confirm that the children had left Viet Nam with the full knowledge and consent of their parents to be placed for adoption in America. FCVN intervened in the case as "Friends of the Court." This was a politically motivated case without merit, brought by individuals who did not have the slightest comprehension of what was going on in Viet Nam at the time of the airlift.

The letter was dated September 17, 1976:

Judge Spenser Williams
Federal District Court
450 Golden Gate Avenue
San Francisco,
California

Dear Sir,

The purpose of this letter is to explain my position in the case of the Vietnamese children, Nguyen da Yen, Nguyen da Vuong, and Nguyen da Tuyen.

In April 1975, while working as a volunteer at the Presidio, the above named children appealed to me to help them find their family. As a mother, I had strong feelings for these children. I could imagine how distressed I would be if my children were lost in another country and no one helped unite the family. I expressed these feelings to people working in the Babylift operation, as well as to others outside, in an attempt to clarify the identification and disposition of these children. Everyone was very busy and things were somewhat chaotic.

A few days later, I was approached by the lawyers currently handling the lawsuit. They appealed to me to be the guardian *ad litem* on behalf of Nguyen da Yen, Nguyen da Vuong and Nguyen da Tuyen, to reunite them with their family. I was very reluctant to become involved in a legal action as I knew nothing about legal matters. However, since I was the only one who had talked to the children, I agreed to participate in the lawsuit.

For the past sixteen months, I have been going along with the position of the lawyers, even though in some instances I did not understand or agree with what was being done. Generally, I felt that the interests of the children and their family were being lost in the ambiguities of legal matters. I continued with the case because it seemed the only way to reunite the children with their family. I never imagined that this task could become so complex and drawn out.

It is now my desire to withdraw from any further participation in this case. The letter sent to the family in Viet Nam is the reason for my decision.

I had approved a draft of the letter. That version was altered, translated into Vietnamese, and sent before I saw it. The entire tone and content of the letter sent was not the same as the draft I approved. If a letter is sent in my name, it should contain only what I want it to contain.

That is why I refused to sign a new compromise letter. I deny that the signature on the letter sent to Viet Nam was mine and I wish to disassociate myself with the letter and its contents.

I do not wish any further involvement with people who seem to be using me and my feelings as a mother to further their political ambitions. Therefore, I will appreciate your official dismissal of me as guardian *ad litem* of Nguyen da Yen, Nguyen da Vuong, and Nguyen da Tuyen.

Sincerely,

(Signed)
Muoi McConnell

International Mission of Hope

was founded in 1977 by Cherie Clark.

The work in Vietnam and India continues.

Donations are welcome to help
with the ongoing projects that IMH supports.

Please visit our web site at
IMH-VN.org
Email IMH at imh@imh-vn.org

Tax-deductible donations can be sent to:

IMH-VN
Box 735
Fort Collins, Colorado 80522-0735

If you would like to specify a donation for a specific project in India
or Viet Nam, please let us know, and we will be happy to direct the
donation to where it is designated, or to send it to wherever it is
needed most. The children are there; they still need our help.

For information on the newest books please contact
www.cherieclark.com

Book Two: **Before They Had a Name**
Book Three: **Return to Vietn.am**

LTPubl@aol.com

In loving memory of Carol Westlake

Carol with her adopted daughter Thuy in Saigon, 1974

Carol Westlake was an intergal part of FCVN for many years, facilitating the adoptions of hundreds of orphans and abandoned children from Vietnam, as well as being a close personal friend. Carol died in 1976 at the age of thirty-seven, leaving behind seven children.